Antitrust and the

Triumph of Economics

MARC ALLEN EISNER

Antitrust

and the Triumph of Economics

Institutions, Expertise, and Policy Change

© 1991 The University of North Carolina Press

Manufactured in the United States of America

The paper in this book meets the guidelines for permanence and
durability of the Committee on Production Guidelines for Book
Longevity of the Council on Library Resources.

95 94 93 92 91   5 4 3 2 1

Library of Congress Cataloging-in-Publication Data

Eisner, Marc Allen.
Antitrust and the triumph of economics : institutions, expertise, and
policy change / by Marc Allen Eisner.
p.   cm.
Includes bibliographical references and index.
ISBN 0-8078-1955-7
1. Antitrust law—Economic aspects—United States.   2. Trusts,
Industrial—Government policy—United States.   3. Trade regulation—
United States.   4. United States. Federal Trade
Commission.   5. United States. Dept. of Justice. Antitrust
Division.   6. Government economists—United States.   7. Chicago
school of economics.   8. United States—Politics and government—
1981–1989.   I. Title.
HD3616.U47E43   1991
338.8′0973—dc20   90–46785
CIP

To Patricia

CONTENTS

TABLES & FIGURES

Tables

Figures

ACKNOWLEDGMENTS

I conducted most of the research and wrote most of the manuscript while at the University of Wisconsin-Madison, completing the book at Wesleyan University. The University of Wisconsin supported my work with a modest grant that covered some of the costs incurred in conducting interviews and archival research in Washington, D.C. More important, the University of Wisconsin and its Department of Political Science provided a unique and supportive environment for intellectual pursuits. Wesleyan University, my new professional home, has provided a similar environment. A number of professors, friends, and colleagues at Wisconsin and Wesleyan have made direct and indirect contributions to the arguments in this book.

In particular, I benefited greatly from the guidance and critical comments of five individuals. Professor Leon Lindberg read numerous drafts and spent much time discussing the nature of the American political economy and the role of economic ideas in the policy process. His broad theoretical and comparative interests and his infectious passion for scholarship continue to be an inspiration. My approach to political economic questions reflects, in many ways, his influence. Professor Ken Meier weathered many lengthy discussions of antitrust. His impressive knowledge of public policy saved me from a number of empirical errors. Professor Booth Fowler, with his critical eye and warm heart, continually reminded me that the most important questions are not questions of economics or administration. Each of these individuals provided something unique to the book—and something lasting to me as an individual. In addition, two anonymous readers reviewed the manuscript and forced me to clarify my argument in some very important ways. If I had been more responsive to the suggestions of all those involved, this might have been a better book. However, it would have been a much different book.

While I was in Washington, numerous officials, staff attorneys, and economists at the Federal Trade Commission and the Justice Department met with me to discuss with some candor the events of the 1970s and 1980s. Former officials corresponded when meetings were impossible. These individuals contributed a wealth of historical and practical insights. They revealed a keen

Acknowledgments

interest in the problems of professionalization, the history of their agencies, and the evolution of antitrust policy. They provided access to valuable documents and information that would have been otherwise unavailable. This book would have been impossible without their kind assistance.

On a more personal level, I would like to thank my family for encouragement and support. My parents, Dale and Sharon Eisner, have always promoted hard work, commitment, and respect for the truth. The lessons they taught and the examples they set have permanently shaped the way I understand the world and my place in it. My first son, Jonathan, spent much of his first two years sitting next to the computer as I worked on the manuscript. My second son, Benjamin, was spared a similar fate because his birth coincided with the completion of the book. They both continue to prove that life consists of more than research. The greatest thanks, however, are reserved for my wife, friend, and partner, Patricia. She read drafts of the manuscript, endured many lonely evenings, and bore more than a fair share of our domestic responsibilities. And yet, she persevered with grace. This book—and so much more—is dedicated to her.

Antitrust and the

Triumph of Economics

CHAPTER ONE

Antitrust and the Redefinition

of Public Authority

The latter half of the nineteenth century was a time of monumental economic and social transformation. The rise of the modern corporation and trust allowed businesses to plan expansion, manage competition, and realize greater efficiencies. Nonetheless, the revolution in business organization proved to be a source of political unrest because it forced the integration of local economies and created opportunities for corporate abuse. The trusts provided a convenient target of political discontent. The dramatic changes of the period were also a source of great ambivalence insofar as they were difficult to reconcile with competing tenets of American liberalism. The fear of the concentrated economic power of the modern corporation was difficult to justify in light of the ideological legitimacy of market activity. The demands for relief questioned the inviolability of private property. Moreover, a decision to address the trust problem through direct regulation would tax the administrative capacities of the national government while raising the specter of concentrated public authority. Policymakers had to discover some means of governing a burgeoning corporate economy while maintaining allegiance to liberal norms rooted in the eighteenth century.

Antitrust policy emerged in this context as a first attempt to force corporate accountability on an economywide scale. By casting policy as law enforcement, market competition was promoted in a manner fitting within the prevailing norms of government intervention and the practical limitations of the preadministrative state. Although this expansion of public authority was initially resisted by a host of political and corporate interests, by the middle of the twentieth century it enjoyed broad acceptance.[1] Writing from the perspective of the postwar period, Richard Hofstadter counted antitrust among the more permanent features of the American political landscape. Appealing to the strong if dormant support for the policy, he noted that "once the United States had an antitrust movement without antitrust prosecutions; in our time there have been antitrust prosecutions without an antitrust movement."[2] Indeed, the place of antitrust seemed so well established that it was often understood as much a national tradition as an economywide microeconomic policy. Noting the almost irrational devotion to antitrust, Andrew Shonfield went as far as to describe antitrust as nothing less than an American religion.[3]

The secure position of antitrust largely derived from its close ties with the central concerns of American liberalism. The legislative debates and subsequent court decisions explicitly associated antitrust with a complex of economic, political, and social goals. By maintaining open markets and a deconcentration of economic power, antitrust could promote individual economic opportunities that might otherwise be foreclosed, preserve small business and local ownership, and protect individual property rights. As an expression of these goals, antitrust was often referred to as a constitution for the American economy, implying a system of legal restraints placed on the exercise of power. The courts, for example, presented antitrust as "the Magna Carta of free enterprise," a "Bill of Rights" central to the preservation of economic freedoms.[4] Walter Adams placed the policy within the distinctively American political-economic tradition, when he stated that the antitrust laws "are founded on a theory of hostility to the concentration of power in private hands so great that even a government of the people can be trusted to have it only in exceptional circumstances."[5] From the perspective of the 1980s, such reflections seemed strikingly nostalgic. The vision that motivated antitrust at its birth was lost as the policy approached its centennial.

A Reagan Revolution in Antitrust?

The broad bipartisan consensus that protected antitrust for much of its history disintegrated by the 1980s. During the Reagan presidency, antitrust policy was defined in the terms presented by the Chicago school, a body of microeconomic theory that depicts markets as self-sufficient and at all times efficiency promoting. Given the benefits of market governance, the role of public authority in governing the economy is highly constricted. The efficiency of the market is contrasted with the wastefulness and corruption of the state. Government cannot provide a cure for monopoly because it is all too often its source and its patron. Based on this understanding of the political economy, the Chicago school presents limited circumstances under which corporate autonomy should be challenged. The Reagan administration's Chicago school interpretation of antitrust deemphasized and in many cases rejected the political and social goals of policy. The only objective that could be correctly derived from the history of antitrust was the promotion of business efficiency—a goal often best realized through systematic deference to the market. The Chicago-based redefinition of policy was in keeping with the Reagan agenda, which questioned the legitimacy of state "intervention" in a number of policy areas. It troubled many antitrust scholars, who saw the redefinition of antitrust as an explicitly political act justified through an appeal to economic theory. As one antitrust scholar noted: "The selection of efficiency as the only appropriate touchstone of policy is not indicated by either the statutory language, which is ambiguous, or the legislative history, which is multivalued. . . . The isolation of efficiency as the sole goal of antitrust requires a conscious rejection of equally dominant values that underlie the antitrust statutes."[6]

Most critics—academic and political—saw the Reagan antitrust policy as a significant departure from past administrations. They characterized it as a policy revolution: the fundamental goals of policy were reconceptualized to promote the very forms of corporate behavior and organization that antitrust was designed to prevent. Senator Howard Metzenbaum, a leading proponent of antitrust in Congress, seemed genuinely perplexed by the Reagan administration's position. "The Administration bellows on supporting free enterprise. . . . If you are for free enterprise, then you must be for antitrust. You just can't be for one and against the other—that is, unless you are the Reagan Administration."[7] While the congressional response was often sharply negative, the Reagan antitrust philosophy did not encounter the bureaucratic resistance one might expect with dramatic shifts in policy. Indeed, the administration's proclamations were quickly translated into policy, as revealed by the agency caseloads, which reflected distinct Chicago school priorities. The majority of cases were brought against minor cartel-like price-fixing agreements, many of which were characterized by their large number of participants and local effects. This was a direct expression of the Chicago doctrines that identify horizontal restraints as one of the few areas where antitrust enforcement could yield economic benefits. Other violations either were never prosecuted or were positively affirmed in public addresses and new agency guidelines.[8]

This book explores the origins of the recent changes in antitrust policy. In a span of less than two decades, antitrust was redefined in such a manner as to strip away a host of well-established social and political goals. Once policy was recast in Chicago terms, the traditional objectives and enforcement activities were seen as lacking in technical justification. How did the Chicago redefinition of policy take place? A convenient and popular explanation focuses solely on the events of the Reagan administration. The Reagan administration came to Washington with the mission of reducing the government's presence in the domestic sphere by limiting expenditures in social welfare and removing the regulatory burden. Conservative lawyers and economists were appointed to the antitrust agencies, where they exercised discretion over the caseload and refused to enforce the laws when not in accordance with the dictates of Chicago microeconomics. Indeed, they sanctioned many forms of corporate activity that were subject to prosecution under existing case law.[9]

While this may be an adequate if overly brief description of the events of the Reagan administration, it is not an explanation of policy change—even in the most limited sense. An examination of the enforcement record and history of the antitrust agencies reveals that the new policy priorities found an expression well before the advent of the Reagan presidency. From the early 1970s onward, the agencies began generating a Chicago-based enforcement agenda, despite the policy declarations of political elites and the demands of a Congress seeking more vigorous enforcement and contemplating significant expansions of the antitrust laws. The Reagan "revolution" in antitrust was but an extension of well-established trends within the two antitrust agencies. It is, perhaps, no overstatement to say that while the Reagan administration may have accelerated the pace of change, it was not decisive. The changes would have taken place in its absence. The redefinition of the caseload was not politically directed. If we are to understand the antitrust policy of the 1980s, it is necessary to explore changes in organization and process at the two agencies which predated the elections of 1980 and made the redefinition of policy inevitable.

The changes in antitrust policy are interesting when taken by themselves. Antitrust policy structures the activities of a majority of firms in the U.S. economy. Accordingly, any policy change which dramatically redefines the terms of business activity is worthy of attention. However, as I shall argue below, the changes in antitrust are important for another reason. The factors that forced policy change over the resistance of elected officials and their appointed surrogates are not exclusive to the antitrust policy subsystem. Indeed, the shifts in policy are symptomatic of broader institutional problems that fashion the form and content of public policies and place constraints on the capacity of public officials to define the terms of policy change. The unanticipated and undirected changes in antitrust may find parallels in any number of policy areas where expertise provides a fundamental role in the definition and implementation of policy.

Institutions, Expertise, and Policy Change

The critical role of specialized expertise in the definition of public policy can be understood only when placed in the broader institutional context. In the United States, public policy is formulated and implemented within a system characterized by the institutional fragmentation of political power along horizontal and vertical dimensions. What Richard Neustadt describes as "a government of separated institutions sharing powers" is combined with a federal system that divides implementation powers among national, state, and local authorities.[10] Hypothetically, political parties could successfully link actors in multiple institutions, providing their activities with a greater sense of coherence. However, weak electorally based political parties and frequent elections invest local interests with national significance.[11] To make public policy and bridge the system of separate institutions sharing powers, it is necessary to combine multiple constituencies and form interest coalitions. This arrangement, in turn, often requires the kinds of compromises that are possible only by casting policy at a relatively high level of abstraction and thereby delegating authority to bureaucrats who will bear the responsibility for giving substantive content to the statement of legislative intent. The most important problems are unaddressed, left to be resolved by administrators. Delegating authority to bureaucrats also allows legislators to appear responsive to constituent demands while simultaneously vesting the ultimate responsibility—and blame—for policy in an administrative agency. While delegation is often a product of symbolic politics in which the legislators have no intention of seeing broad legislative mandates transformed into policies,[12] delegation is also a child of necessity: the uncertainty associated with a new policy may lead legislators to eschew responsibility for the final product.[13]

While the logic of coalition formation undoubtedly comes into play, the lack of congressional resources combined with the increasing demands placed on the institution suggest that delegation is an unavoidable element of modern public policy-making, particularly in areas characterized by high levels of complexity.[14] As the frontiers of state regulation have expanded, elected officials have accepted the responsibility for making policy in a host of highly complex issue areas. Legislators lack the expertise necessary to make reasoned and technically competent judgments regarding the details of policy, nor can they anticipate the problems that may emerge during implementation. Increasing complexity entails increasing unpredictability. Lacking the knowledge and resources to analyze complex problems and address the details of public policy, legislators devolve authority onto the bureaucracy. This delegation of authority entails a recognition both of bureaucratic competence and the need for a measure of flexibility in the ultimate transformation of political will into public policy.

It would be comforting but erroneous to believe that all legislators make an unprejudiced appeal to expertise whenever the demands of policy exceed their own technical proficiency. Legislators are at all times subject to the electoral sanction. They must create sufficient public support and nurture constituents if they are to secure reelection. David Mayhew's observation regarding the electoral incentive has almost become an axiom of American political studies.[15] Legislators may possess multiple goals. But the proximate goal is—and must be—reelection, for it is upon electoral success that all else rests. In policy areas characterized by high levels of complexity and saliency, the latter will exert the greatest influence: one can expect the technical content of policy alternatives to be of secondary importance. Often, policies will be selected to appeal to special constituencies. Politicians will seek to employ ideas in the fashion described by so many public choice theorists—as a means of justifying policies that are designed explicitly to secure the endorsement of special interests. Impartiality may only veil instrumentality; ideas may be attractive on political grounds to serve as a means to a politically defined end.

Growing bureaucratic power and administrative capacity has reinforced and is in large part stimulated by the routine and systematic delegation of authority. The sources of bureaucratic expertise are quite obvious. Bureaucracies are designed to complete difficult feats via a division of labor and authority based in task specification and technical competence. Moreover, bureaucratic expertise is derived from accumulated experience with a given body of policies and policy problems. Organizations learn by doing; this practical knowledge is subsequently embedded in bureaucratic routines and accommodated by organizational change. Increasingly, however, bureaucratic expertise reflects the skills of professionals within bureaucratic agencies.[16] As policy problems have grown increasingly complex and the delegation of authority has become almost unremarkable, the need for specialized expertise within the bureaucracy has become indisputable.[17]

Professional expertise is an important source of bureaucratic power. It reinforces the delegation of authority and limits the willingness and ability of political officials to intervene in bureaucratic affairs. This is particularly the case with respect to professionalized agencies (e.g., those agencies staffed by members of the so-called learned professions). Francis Rourke notes that the "combination of obscurity of means and clarity of results" enhances the influence both of professionals within an agency and professionalized bureaucracies in the broader political environment.[18] Experts that employ highly specialized knowledge to accomplish tasks of central importance to the policy process are in many ways insulated from political forces. Their mastery of esoteric subject matter and norms of self-regulation are used to justify autonomy. Moreover, the well-established, if spurious, distinction between politics and administration that fueled the Progressives' drive to professionalize the bureaucracy continues to exercise influence today—much to the benefit of professionals. They commonly expect and enjoy great independence in their activities. Autonomy is deemed necessary to protect the integrity of expertise and professional judgment.

Movements toward greater professionalization are constantly taking place across the American bureaucracy as experts and expertise are granted a greater role in defining policy and process. While political executives might justify an appeal to expertise on the basis of potential managerial benefits, the drive toward professionalization is not primarily endogenous or internally directed. Rather, it is interwoven with political-institutional conflicts throughout the system of separate institutions sharing powers and is a common component of strategies designed to divert political opposition and insulate public policies from future assaults.[19] At first glance, this interconnection may seem counter-intuitive, given the acknowledged norms of professional autonomy that insulate professionals from partisan politics. However, the promise of autonomy may provide politicians with reasons for promoting professionalization. Members of Congress may support professionalization to address problems of bureaucratic behavior that cannot be resolved through casework. A greater reliance on expertise can facilitate planning and evaluation, thus enhancing agency performance. Moreover, these activities can encourage administrative efficiency, thus creating at least the impression that bureaucratic waste is being checked. However, professionalization is most creatively promoted in attempts to limit the vulnerability of policy to future political conflicts. Because professionals demand great independence, vesting policy-making authority in a professionalized agency is commonly seen as a means of dissociating established policies from future political disputes and preserving the policy status quo.

A similar set of incentives can be attributed to interest groups, which are often active advocates of professionalization. Once an interest coalition has been successful in transforming its demands into policy, it is faced with the prospect that any victories could be ephemeral, subject to future revision. While attempts may be made to secure political victories through the passage of detailed legislation (e.g., the Clean Air Act amendments of 1970, the Federal Water Pollution Control Act amendments of 1972), this strategy is of limited utility for a number of reasons. First, legislation remains susceptible to future political reversals. Detailed legislative mandates may limit bureaucratic discretion and prevent policy from being subverted at the administrative stage. But it fails to govern the future activities of political officials. Second, knowledge problems become most acute in complex issue areas, limiting the capacity of elected officials to design technically competent policies. Finally, detailed legislation promotes rigidity. It limits the bureaucratic discretion that is often necessary to address complicated policy problems. Detailed legislative mandates may dictate unrealistic policies that in turn create problems of implementation. Precise and exhaustive legislation may protect policy, but only at an exceptionally high cost. Thus, legislative specificity is a distinct second-best alternative.

The best alternative is to vest authority in a professionalized agency or to promote the professionalization of the agency responsible for implementation. Professionalization and the autonomy it entails can be seen as a means of protecting policies from future revisions at the hands of less sympathetic officials and limiting the range of future conflicts. In a study of the National Labor Relations Board, Terry Moe shows that business and labor were supportive of agency professionalization because professional autonomy shaped NLRB politics while limiting the scope of policy change. He notes:

> Professionalism and political control are more usefully understood as integral parts of the same institutional system. Professionalism is valued by business and labor because it protects their mutual interests in stability, clarity, and expert judgment. They also value it as a vehicle for the orderly exercise of political control: the choice of professionals with known ideologies—the choice of types—guarantees the groups a measure of control over the agency without the necessity of exercising any direct influence. Thus, the NLRB is highly autonomous, run by professionals according to their own best judgment without interference from politicians or groups. At the same time, it is firmly under political control and very sensitive to the shifting political winds.[20]

When politically defined policies are recast as matters of administration, they are partially depoliticized, in the sense that variations in policy must remain within the discretionary field associated with a given set of professional norms.

Professionalization may also be coerced through networks of resource dependency. Agencies may be compelled to comply with the demands of other institutions if they are to maintain access to financial and political resources. Examples are not difficult to find. An executive order requiring that all new policies be justified on the basis of cost-benefit criteria can force an agency to provide economists with an enhanced role in the policy process and agency management. To do otherwise would incur the wrath of the Office of Management and Budget and risk a reduction in resources. Similarly, an executive order may require that all new regulations be accompanied by an environmental-impact statement, thus placing a premium on scientific risk assessment. In both cases, professionalization may be a necessity, even though not the explicit intention of the executive orders. Likewise, court decisions may begin to acknowledge the contributions of one or more professions, requiring—albeit implicitly—that new values and extrajudicial theories be brought to bear in justifying regulations or framing prosecutions. Victory before the courts may be contingent on compliance with even the most subtle of judicial mandates. Once again, professionalization (or, at the very least, an elevation of experts in agency affairs) is an unintended consequence of decisions made within a different institution.

Whatever the circumstances surrounding professionalization, there is little dispute that an organization's administrative capacities can be expanded by granting a greater role to experts in the definition and administration of public policy. Once given an organizational presence, experts can provide clarity and a certain objectivity to otherwise complex and politically muddled policy problems. They can analyze a given societal condition to identify complex chains of causality that are critical to designing an adequate policy response. By bringing their training to bear on a given problem, they can introduce specialized knowledge into administrative choice, allowing for policies that are both politically practicable and technically feasible. Moreover, expertise can simplify complex policy problems. Analysis can be condensed into decision rules and criteria that can be applied by nonexperts in the administration of policy. Individual bureaucrats can employ administrative guidelines to address a complex reality in an economical fashion. Finally, access to expertise may provide agency officials with a greater capacity to plan policy actions, anticipate future contingencies, and evaluate the impact of past activities through reference to technically informed criteria. As a result, the agency may be able to move from a reactive posture in the policy process, gaining a greater degree of autonomy and effectiveness.

There is no question that professionalization carries great potential benefits. However, its disruptive effects may be quite consequential. The introduction of professionals into an agency may result in heightened conflicts. The vertical and horizontal divisions of authority and function that characterize bureaucratic organizations complicate control and coordination. Internal cleavages and conflicts have long been recognized by students of bureaucratic politics. Political executives and career bureaucrats may possess incompatible understandings of policy that ultimately lead to resistance and latent contests. The relationships between line and staff administrators may be burdened by irreconcilable role perceptions. These traditional tensions are only exacerbated by new conflicts as professionals defy administrators and members of one profession challenge members of another. Given sufficient and reinforcing external pressures, the new professional staffs may redefine the organizational mission so as to force a new distribution of authority within the bureau and the establishment of specialized criteria in planning and the selection of enforcement actions. Conversely, experts may be marginalized, exiled to planning or evaluation offices, where their impact on process and policy is often minimized. In either event, bureaucratic roles and relationships come to reflect the internal configuration of forces, albeit often after a period of conflict and adjustment. However, a positive outcome cannot be taken for granted. Conflicts and tensions may endure, impeding the effectiveness of the agency.[21]

An additional source of tension derives from the common functions served by bureaucratic organizations and professions. Robert Bell explains: "Professions and organizations are alternative ways of institutionalizing values. Professions socialize workers to become committed to major social values. . . . Organizations coordinate activities on behalf of socially approved goals. Professions and organizations are also alternative ways of institutionalizing expertise. Professions inculcate expertise in individual workers, and organizations expertly coordinate work."[22] When professionals are introduced into a bureaucratic context, they are expected to observe professionally defined values in the pursuit of politically defined goals, to employ their expertise within the policy process. When the two roles come into conflict—as they commonly do—professionals demand greater autonomy to follow disciplinary imperatives exempt from the detailed interference of career administrators and political executives. To do otherwise would be to subordinate expertise to politics and recast knowledge as advocacy. This tension can give rise to a clash of professional and bureaucratic values sufficient to subvert the policy process. Thus, Bell continues, "A major challenge for modern organizations is to maintain the integrity of organizational purposes while utilizing professional expertise and integrating professional values."[23]

Most analyses of professionals working within bureaucratic agencies focus on the strength of professional norms and standards and the organizational biases they create.[24] Professionals are cast as individuals observing rigid standards inculcated through professional socialization. Thus, an attorney will value procedural propriety and will observe court precedent and rules of evidence. Economists will value efficiency; their activities will reveal a concern with opportunity costs and the interplay of costs and benefits. All things being equal, we should expect economists to place a greater emphasis on efficiency than other professionals do. Moreover, we should expect their professional norms to shape their orientation toward their work. The predictability of professional activity may minimize the effects of the lack of effective political control and reduce the likelihood of opportunistic behavior. This aspect of professionalization is widely acknowledged. Because professional norms are rigid, much of the research on professionalization has been animated by the potential conflicts between norms, bureaucratic rule systems, and organizational mission.[25] Even if it is convenient to depict the professional as an individual acting within the confines of a set of specialized norms, it remains a limited vision of the professional—one that minimizes the potential impact of professionalization on public policy.

Separating out the question of professional standards, it is important to stress that the professions cannot be addressed as a monolithic grouping. Important distinctions can be identified along a variety of dimensions. For present purposes, the most important distinction is the differential orientation toward external communities. Expert-administrators drawn from the sciences and social sciences are simultaneously members of a profession and members of a larger scholarly community. The community provides standards which regulate their professional activities. However, it also provides means of assessing the intellectual quality of professional endeavors. Peer recognition— or at least the realization that work is being conducted within the confines of acknowledged analytical parameters—is an essential part of community membership.[26]

The differences between external orientations can be clarified with an example. Attorneys operate according to distinct professional norms. However, they are among the least academic of experts working within the federal bureaucracy. Legal training, while having a significant scholarly component, is largely vocational in nature. Attorneys are technicians, much as engineers are technicians. They are trained to carry out legal activities, gather evidence, frame cases, and litigate in accordance with a given set of standards. Perhaps nowhere else is it easier and more appropriate to associate a profession with a given set of procedural standards. The contrast is clear when one compares attorneys with scientific and social scientific experts. The latter combine the professionalism of an attorney with a concern over advances and shifting orthodoxies within their disciplines. They seek to abide by procedural standards while simultaneously keeping abreast of new research and advances within their scholarly community.

Attorneys work within a set of procedural norms derived from their professional training. The substantive content of the law, however, is determined within the political system by the courts. Although jurists are responsive to changing fashions in legal studies, the point remains the same. The imperatives that inform the attorney's activities also shape the implementation of public policy. This factor, in part, makes attorneys the administrators of choice, given the legalistic nature of government regulations and the central role of the courts in defining the authority of government institutions.[27] With respect to other professions, however, dependency on the courts is replaced by a dependency on, and participation in, a discipline or specialized academic community. The substantive content of economics as a social science, for example, is determined by the discipline of economics. Because the economists' constituency is found outside of the political system, the compatibility of intellectual innovations and public policy is at all times indeterminate.

This distinction is of critical importance. The procedural standards that define acceptable activity within a given profession are relatively stable. Socialization processes ensure that the standards are reproduced in successive generations of professionals. However, the consensus within the disciplines that defines the scientific or social scientific orthodoxy is in a constant state of flux. Scientific and social scientific knowledge is at all times tentative, contingent on recognized advances within existing research programs. As the dominant understanding of acceptable modes of inquiry and verification evolves and underlying assumptions are reformulated, the content of knowledge changes. Accepted wisdom is discredited, revised, or replaced as a result of intellectual innovations or new discoveries. New paradigms emerge to replace old paradigms; heterodox theories become the basis for a new orthodoxy. As a result, reliance on expertise necessarily entails a certain ambiguity. While one can expect scientific and social scientific experts to abide by certain professional and methodological norms of inquiry, one should not expect stability in the relationships and assumptions underlying their analyses.[28]

The indeterminate nature of scientific and social scientific knowledge might not be a source of intense concern if there were reason to believe that the orthodoxy in a given academic community simply reflected the results of a dispassionate and ongoing pursuit of truth. However, as scholars working in the sociology of knowledge suggest, scientific and social scientific activities are best understood as collective in nature.[29] As reflected in the structure of academic disciplines, the organization of these collective endeavors plays a central role in conveying "scientific status" on particular ideas or doctrines. Richard Whitley provides an insightful definition of the scientific or social scientific disciplines as "public sciences." He notes that they "constitute a distinct type of work organization and context in which research is oriented to collective goals and purposes through the pursuit of public scientific reputations among a group of colleague-competitors. In such reputational work organizations, the need to acquire positive reputations from a particular group of practitioners is the main means of controlling what tasks are carried out, how they are carried out, and how performance is evaluated."[30] At any given time, an academic community will determine which individuals, ideas, and modes of analysis will be presented as "authoritative" to internal and external audiences. When those deemed authoritative by the profession "negotiate meaning and truth and collectively decide what are facts and what are fictions," the universe of ideas available and the scope of research becomes highly constrained.[31]

Autonomy is the price of professionalization. While professional autonomy may be a necessary condition of detached competence, it is politically costly—particularly if expert-administrators are charged with defining the substantive content of policy—for it entails a significant but subtle loss of political control. The slippage between political expectations and public policy as implemented may be great. In part, this is a practical difficulty associated with preserving the principal-agent relationship in complex policy areas. The complicated aspects of many policy problems that force legislators to delegate policy-making authority to the bureaucracy simultaneously limit the determination of whether bureaucratic decisions conform with the original aims of the legislation. As a result, legislators and political executives are often forced to defer to the expertise of professional staffs. While the predictable nature of professional activity—the adherence to strict norms—may appear to limit the significance of delegation, the acute orientation to shifts in external academic and professional communities makes delegation all the more consequential. While political officials could engage in the active selection of knowledge to force conformity with policy goals, it would prove highly problematic on normative grounds and would ultimately undermine the goals associated with bringing expertise to bear on policy. The chain of delegation is thus lengthened: from the legislature to the bureau, from the bureau to the expert-administrators, and ultimately, to the external community of specialists that provides the norms of professional endeavor and determines the truth content of competing theoretical frameworks. While the organizational adoption of policy-relevant expertise may result in an expansion of administrative capacities, it creates a vulnerability that may ultimately undermine an agency's mission.

The Argument in Brief

The book begins with a simple premise: to understand changes in antitrust, it is essential to examine the way in which the institutions of antitrust have evolved. More to the point, it is imperative to trace the changing status and organizational presence of economic expertise in the antitrust agencies. The critical period with respect to organizational change was 1960–80 at the Justice Department's Antitrust Division, and 1970–80 at the Federal Trade Commission (FTC). However, the events of this period cannot be understood in isolation: we must first explore the institutional relationships and organizational dynamics that emerged during the decades preceding the 1960s. The agencies did not act independently but were part of a broader political-institutional network, fully integrated into the system of separate institutions and subject to the tensions associated with making and implementing public policy in this system.

Federal antitrust policy was initiated in 1890 with the passage of the Sherman Act. The legislative mandate was remarkably vague, reflecting the needs of coalition building, unresolved questions regarding the nature and significance of the trust problem, and a lack of a strong regulatory tradition to draw upon. Policy-making authority was delegated to those responsible for enforcement. However, the delegation was problematic because the Justice Department lacked the administrative capacity necessary to define and administer policy. As the single institution most directly involved in the definition of property rights, the Supreme Court quickly intervened to fill the vacuum and give the act substantive content. Judicial power was only occasionally balanced by executive activism. However, Congress was regularly involved in the definition of public policy and agency authority. While Congress and the Court shared in the definition of antitrust, the conflicts between the two institutions were minimal. Indeed, the judicial support for market liberalism was complemented by Congress's electoral vulnerability and responsiveness to the mobilization of business interests. Both had the same end result: an unwillingness to condone active intervention on questions of corporate organization and management. Both Congress and the Court actively guarded against excessive agency authority and routinely deferred to business, leaving complex questions to be resolved in the market. Paradoxically, the same institutions that successfully limited the authority of the agencies and the scope of antitrust were critical in promoting agency reforms—including economic professionalization—and the expansion of agency authority in a later period.

The context of agency professionalization was not determined solely through the interplay of political institutions. Their organizational legacies combined with the constraints imposed by external institutional actors gave rise to distinct internal dynamics that shaped policy. Antitrust was cast as law enforcement. Thus, the Justice Department and FTC evolved as litigating agencies dominated by attorneys. Because both agencies were dependent on the courts, they were predisposed to support those cases that rested on firm points of law and were easily litigated to a successful conclusion. As one might expect, the cases that were easiest to prosecute (e.g., naked price-fixing, minor horizontal and vertical restraints) were also the cases that tended to have limited economywide significance. The potential political reaction to agency activism—the mobilization of business interests—created reinforcing pressures supporting the prosecution of trivial violations and cases that could go largely unnoticed.

In large part, the economic impact of enforcement was left unaddressed. Antitrust was understood as law enforcement. Policy consisted of the aggregate of cases selected on an individual basis. Neither agency had the capacity to plan, monitor, or evaluate enforcement efforts. Both the FTC and the Antitrust Division had economic staffs that could potentially assist in the administration of antitrust. However, they were marginalized. In the case of the FTC, economists occupied a separate bureau—at times, located in a separate building, miles away. Economic analysis was rarely integrated into agency affairs. Economists in the Antitrust Division were members of a support staff; economic analysis was subordinated to a legalistic culture and a strong prosecutorial dynamic. In both instances, the decision to prosecute was understood as a legal decision best left to attorneys with knowledge of court precedent and the demands of litigation.

During the decade of the 1960s, the debates in the antitrust policy community increasingly addressed antitrust in economic terms. Drawing on industrial organization economics, participants in the policy debates were critical of existing court doctrines and agency enforcement efforts. The shifts in the policy debates found an expression in the courts, as judicial decision making increasingly employed economic decision rules to address complex industrial structural problems. Partially in response to judicial decision making, partially in response to the growing consensus that an economically sound antitrust necessitated a qualitatively different form of administration, political executives at the two agencies sought to enhance administrative capacities by providing economic expertise with a central role in policy planning, evaluation, and case selection. Through professionalization projects, highly qualified economists were brought into the two agencies. However, the organizational status of economists and economic analysis complicated professionalization efforts. Agency officials were forced to search for a means of integrating economics into agency affairs while countering a well-established organizational legacy. A series of organizational and procedural changes gradually provided economists and economic criteria a presence at each stage of the policy process. Economic analysis was seen as performing at least two critical functions. First, economic analysis could bring a greater coherence to a body of policy directed by court precedent by providing simple decision rules. Rather than selecting cases solely on the basis of court doctrine, cases could be chosen with an eye to their effects on industrial organization. It is important to stress that Court doctrine was evolving in a similar direction. Second, because economic analysis could allow for an objective assessment of competing enforcement actions, it could facilitate planning and allow for the efficient use of the fixed resources available for prosecution.

Largely as a result of their contributions to the policy process and the growing dominance of economic analysis in judicial decision making, economists were promoted from members of a support staff to central actors in the definition of policy. The economists' professional values and evaluative criteria became central to defining the caseload. Initially, this economic translation of policy was relatively unproblematic. The dominant school of industrial organization economics was compatible with the multiple goals of policy; it linked the economic, social, and political goals in a coherent fashion to an understanding of industrial organization. However, the correspondence of the policy goals and the dictates of economic theory was fleeting. Professionalization provided an institutional transmission belt connecting the antitrust agencies with the larger intellectual community. Intellectual advances in industrial organization economics were transmitted into the agencies. Once economic theory was fully integrated into the agencies' policy processes, the emergence of a new orthodoxy forced a reconceptualization of business activity and the role of public authority in governing a market economy. Policy—as represented in the agency caseloads—was redefined, albeit not as an expression of executive politics but as the product of the interplay of institutional evolution, organizational change, and critical shifts in the economic expertise that informed the antitrust debates.

It is common to explain the influence of ideas in public policy by associating them with individuals who assume leadership positions within the government or an agency. The prestige of position allows for a restructuring of policy debate or the introduction of bold new initiatives. While this vision is often correct, it is nonetheless incomplete. The case of antitrust provides a context for exploring the more subtle ways in which ideas shape public policy, without the advocacy of elected officials or their appointed surrogates. It is my contention that ideas can force policy change once they have an institutional presence and are integrated into the policy process. To the extent that elected officials are incapable of controlling the content or policy implications of emerging bodies of knowledge, political values may be defined and redefined over time through the historical interplay of ideas and institutions. The principal-agent linkages that are expected to force a measure of accountability and responsiveness fail to serve this function once the content of policy is determined by experts. Given the growing complexity of policy issues and the almost routine delegation of policy-making authority to expert-administrators, the implications of the argument may extend well beyond the confines of antitrust. Indeed, one may question whether the institutional vulnerabilities clearly exhibited in the case of antitrust—and the loss of control they entail—is a systemwide source of concern.

This study proceeds in the following fashion. Chapter 2 addresses the institutional context, focusing on the formal and procedural aspects of the antitrust agencies and their relationship to the Court, Congress, and the president. Chapter 3 examines the historical legacy, describing the way in which the two agencies evolved, both in terms of their external relationships and institutional vulnerabilities and as policy-making organizations. As noted above, these factors set the stage for professionalization and established the internal organizational biases that would have to be addressed as part of the professionalization process. Chapter 4 addresses the economics of antitrust and the ways in which economic theory came to structure the antitrust debates. I introduce the concept "community of expertise" as a focal point for analyzing the shift in antitrust norms and the ways in which new norms were transmitted into the agencies. Chapters 5 and 6 examine the professionalization process in the Antitrust Division and the Federal Trade Commission, noting the ways in which the agencies' relationships with the Court and Congress conditioned the introduction of economic expertise. Chapter 7 examines the events of the Reagan administration and the ways in which policy executives sought to further both the convergence of law and economics in antitrust policy and a conservative enforcement agenda. Finally, chapter 8 concludes the study with observations regarding the role of expertise in institutional development and policy change, and some comments on the future of antitrust policy.

The argument of this book essentially links the histories of institutions and ideas to explain changes in public policy. As such, there are several limitations that are best acknowledged at the beginning. First, the following study is not an exhaustive analysis of antitrust case law. Many fine texts on this subject exist. Major cases in the history of antitrust are examined only when they directly conditioned agency authority, shaped public policy, or redefined in some manner the status of economics in the policy process. In addition, this is not a comprehensive history of the antitrust agencies.[32] While a case-study format is used, there is no attempt to review the events of each presidential administration or address each aspect of organizational change. The histories presented here are highly selective in nature: they address only the aspects of agency evolution that contributed to the expansion of administrative capacities, conditioned the organizational integration of expertise in the policy process, or concretely affected the agency's relationship with other institutional actors. Finally, this is not strictly a critique of the Reagan administration and its policies. While the Reagan presidency constitutes an important chapter in the history of the two agencies, it is but a chapter. The most significant changes in organization and policy took place in an earlier period. An exclusive focus on the Reagan antitrust policy fails to illuminate the causes of policy change and may lead one to place undue stress on the role played by personalities and situational factors. Thus, it is critical to locate the events of the 1980s within the broader history, showing the ways in which the Reagan administration's successes were contingent on earlier shifts within the organizations and policy debates.

CHAPTER TWO

The Institutions of Antitrust

The argument presented in chapter 1 was quite straightforward. To understand the changes in antitrust, we must focus on the historical interplay of institutions and ideas. More to the point, we must analyze the ways in which the antitrust agencies evolved to provide economic expertise with an organizational presence and economic norms a central role in defining the enforcement agenda. Professionalization and the adoption of objective, technical criteria for the administration of policy can be promoted on their own merits; they are commonly justified out of a concern for management. However, they often emerge as a result of political contests, or as part of attempts to shape or limit the scope of future conflicts. In the case of antitrust, the drive to professionalize and base enforcement decisions on economic analysis was a product of institutional conflicts involving the antitrust agencies, the courts, Congress, and to a lesser extent, presidents. In this chapter, I briefly examine the institutions of antitrust, which will serve as a preface to the case studies. After discussing the legislative foundations of policy, I provide an overview of the structural and procedural features of the Antitrust Division and the Federal Trade Commission. The focus then expands to address the other institutions (i.e., the courts, Congress, and the executive) and the formal relationships linking these agencies in the policy subsystem. The interplay of these institutions defined in broad terms the content of policy and the limitations of agency authority, especially during the early history of antitrust, when the agencies were organizationally underdeveloped and the Court had yet to acknowledge the authority of other agencies to define property rights. Subsequently, it provided the context of agency professionalization and policy change.

The Legislative Foundations

Antitrust finds its basis in the Sherman Act of 1890, the Clayton and Federal Trade Commission acts of 1914, and a number of major amendments. Section

1 of the Sherman Act states, "Every contract, combination in the form of trust or otherwise, or conspiracy, in restraint of trade or commerce among the several States, or with foreign nations, is hereby declared to be illegal." According to section 2, "Every person who shall monopolize, or attempt to monopolize, or combine or conspire with any other person or persons, to monopolize in any part of the trade or commerce among the several States, or with foreign nations, shall be deemed guilty of a misdemeanor." The Sherman Act established that violations would be punished by a maximum fine of $5,000, and/or by imprisonment not exceeding one year. Section 7 of the Sherman Act made available treble damages to private parties. In 1955, the maximum fine was increased to $50,000; in 1974, the fines for antitrust violations were increased again to a maximum of $1 million for corporations and $100,000 for individuals. Violations of the Sherman Act were upgraded from a misdemeanor to a felony, carrying a maximum prison term of three years.

As chapter 3 will reveal, the immediate impact of the Sherman Act was quite limited. As a piece of legislation, it was remarkably ambiguous. The courts quickly intervened to give the law substantive content and much-needed precision. However, they did so largely by narrowing the scope of the act. The Court assumed the responsibility of determining when restraints of trade were reasonable and thus beyond the reach of the new legislation. By the early years of the new century, it was clear to most observers that the Sherman Act provided a blunt instrument for economic regulation. It could be used to address the most striking forms of corporate abuse, but it could not address the complexities of a rapidly changing economy. What was needed was not an extension of nineteenth-century legal doctrines but a fundamental transformation of the relationship between the state and corporations. Although the debates surrounding the potential shape of a new regulatory regime addressed the possibility of a corporatist departure from the antitrust tradition, the end result was an extension of antitrust with the Clayton Act of 1914.

The Clayton Act brought greater specificity to antitrust by enumerating the forms of corporate activity that were subject to prosecution. The act supplemented the vague prohibitions of the Sherman Act by declaring illegal the use of discriminatory prices in the sale of "commodities of like grade and quality" (sec. 2), exclusive dealing and tying contracts (sec. 3), the acquisition of "the stock or other share capital of another corporation" (sec. 7), and corporate interlocks (sec. 8) to be illegal where the effects "may be to substantially lessen competition or tend to create a monopoly in any line of commerce." Section 4 of the Clayton Act allowed for the recovery of treble damages and legal fees in private antitrust suits. In the same year Congress passed the Federal Trade Commission Act, creating a new antitrust agency to serve an advisory and regulatory function. The FTC Act provided the commission with a broad grant of authority with respect to antitrust. Section 5 of the act, as amended by the Wheeler-Lea Act of 1938, established a catchall prohibition of "unfair methods of competition in commerce and unfair or deceptive acts or practices in commerce." The commission was empowered to bring civil proceedings against business practices not explicitly declared illegal by the Sherman and Clayton acts.

The Clayton Act has been amended on a number of occasions, strengthening the prohibitions and expanding the authority of the antitrust agencies. The Clayton Act prohibition on price discrimination (sec. 2) was amended and altered substantially with the passage of the Robinson-Patman Act in 1936. The act addressed the concern that small, locally owned businesses were being displaced by large national chain stores. The purpose of the act was clear: to protect small businesses by preventing large buyers from securing unwarranted cost advantages when dealing with suppliers. It prohibited the provision and acceptance of price discounts when unjustified by related cost differentials. Even when justified, however, cost differences were considered illegal if they undermined competition or contributed to the creation of monopoly. The act granted the FTC the authority to establish criteria for determining the reasonableness of quantity discounts and to establish price ceilings.

The Clayton Act prohibition of certain corporation acquisitions (sec. 7) was strengthened and amended by the Celler-Kefauver Act of 1950 and the Antitrust Improvements Act of 1976. The original legislation prohibited the acquisition of "the whole or any part of the stock or other share capital or another corporation engaged also in commerce" if the acquisition restrained commerce or tended to create a monopoly. This section was originally referred to as the holding-company section of the act because it prohibited the kinds of acquisitions that could be used to create trusts. The courts adopted a restrictive interpretation of this prohibition, arguing that it did not apply to the acquisition of physical assets (i.e., mergers). Congress responded with the Celler-Kefauver Act, which reconstituted section 7 to state that "no corporation subject to the jurisdiction of the Federal Trade Commission shall acquire the whole or any part of the assets of another corporation engaged also in commerce, where . . . the effect of such acquisition may be substantially to lessen competition, or to tend to create a monopoly." The Celler-Kefauver Act was designed to address monopoly in its incipiency, before it would be necessary to seek relief under the Sherman Act. After its passage, the prosecution of merger cases became a central activity of the antitrust agencies. The Antitrust Improvements Act of 1976 facilitated merger enforcement by creating a premerger notification program that required parties of a certain size to provide information about potential acquisitions prior to the consummation of the merger. The program allowed the agencies to gather sufficient information to judge the competitive impact and legality of mergers at an early stage. Transactions could be restructured or prevented rather than seeking divestment at a later date.[1]

The Antitrust Agencies

In a book entitled *The Folklore of Capitalism*, Thurman Arnold made an interesting observation regarding the origins of political organizations. "Where there is a conflict between an ideal and a social need recognized as legitimate, [the government] tends to create two organizations, both of which are respectable. However, the one representing the ideal will have a higher place in the hierarchy than the one ministering to the practical need."[2] This insight holds true in the case of antitrust. The Sherman Act addressed the trust problem without dramatically redefining the relationship between the state and business. Policy took the form of law enforcement: corporations were prosecuted for breaking the laws. Because regulation was cast as law enforcement and corporations were personified, this expression of regulatory authority did not directly contradict the ideal of free markets. The Justice Department's Antitrust Division emerged as the embodiment of the Sherman Act. It functioned as a law enforcement agency concerned less with managing competition than with prosecuting those who would violate the behavioral norms of a market economy. It was created to police markets without governing economic organization because such questions were believed best left to the market.

The Sherman Act was imprecise in effect, and the Justice Department was ill equipped to address the complexities of a rapidly expanding economy. As the antitrust laws were expanded in 1914, the FTC was created to apply expert knowledge and flexible procedures to regulate the economy. If the Antitrust Division was the organizational embodiment of market liberalism, the FTC embodied the ambiguity over the role of the state in a rapidly changing economy. It had the practical tools necessary for monitoring a complex economy and regulating the interaction of large corporate interests. And yet, without the support of Congress and the Court, the agency lacked the ability to fulfill its mandate.

The Antitrust Division is responsible for enforcing the Sherman Act and shares enforcement of the Clayton Act with the FTC. Despite the apparent statutory division of labor, the FTC regularly brings cases that could be prosecuted under the Sherman Act. These complaints are filed under the prohibition of "unfair methods of competition" established in section 5 of the Federal Trade Commission Act. Because the common jurisdiction is so great, there have been persistent suggestions that antitrust activities be centralized in the Antitrust Division, leaving the FTC free to concentrate on consumer protection. Jurisdictional conflicts were partially addressed when a liaison arrangement was established in 1948. Duties were allocated between the two agencies on the basis of type of violation and sector of the economy. This separation of powers was based on the experience and expertise of the two agencies, rather than objective economic or legal factors. Thus, for example, the division assumed responsibility for acquisitions in the brewing industry, while the FTC accepted jurisdiction over monopolization and price discrimination in the same industry.

The Justice Department's Antitrust Division

The Antitrust Division is under the leadership of an assistant attorney general and a number of deputy assistant attorneys general. The assistant attorney general usually relies on an economics office, an office of policy planning, and an operations office for agency management and planning activities. Although the division has been reorganized on a number of occasions in the postwar period, typically it has consisted of one or more litigation units and a number of more specialized sections dealing with patents, foreign commerce, and regulated industries.[3]

The Institutions of Antitrust

The Antitrust Division is hierarchical in organization; prosecution efforts are formally approved by the assistant attorney general, working closely with the deputy assistant attorneys general. There is regular close interaction between the legal and economic sections at the staff level, especially in case selection and investigation. Historically, the division has based most of its actions on private complaints regarding damages stemming from alleged violations of the antitrust laws. For example, a manufacturing interest may charge that dominant firms in the industry are setting prices below costs to eliminate competitors. Complaints are initially assessed on the basis of data found in business publications, private antitrust cases, filings with the Securities and Exchange Commission, premerger notifications, complaints from other government agencies, and market studies. There has been a growing tendency in recent decades to rely on economic analysis in the identification of violations. With the growing emphasis on planning, evaluation, and goal-oriented case selection, the division's economists have assumed important positions in the policy processes. Division attorneys, working with staff economists, determine whether potential cases have sufficient legal and economic merits to warrant formal investigation. All formal investigations and case filings must be approved by the assistant attorney general.

The Antitrust Division has great investigative powers. If there appears to be grounds for filing a case after the preliminary inquiry, the division will initiate a formal investigation. In civil cases, the division can issue civil investigative demands (CIDs), the equivalent of administrative subpoenas. The CIDs may be directed to a corporation, corporate officials, or third parties when there is reason to believe that the party possesses necessary information or relevant documentary material. Division CIDs may be enforced by the courts, should the recipients fail to comply. Criminal investigations are commonly conducted through the grand jury system. Subpoenas may be issued to force the disclosure of corporate records for inspection. Grand jury investigations constitute a significant threat to corporations because the scope of inquiry is unlimited: previously unrecognized violations may be revealed through discovery. Moreover, documentary evidence derived from grand jury subpoenas may be acquired by private parties and used as a basis for treble-damage suits.

On the basis of its investigation, the division has the option of filing a criminal complaint, seeking civil action, or bringing concurrent criminal and civil proceedings. Criminal proceedings are usually filed in response to activities which are per se illegal, such as price-fixing. Under the Antitrust Procedures and Penalties Act, violation of the Sherman Act is a felony, punishable with fines of up to $1 million and/or prison sentences of up to three years. Once criminal charges are filed, the accused often enters a plea of nolo contendere rather than preparing a defense. This strategy is sensible because it minimizes the costs of a lengthy and expensive trial. Moreover, because a plea of nolo contendere is not an admission of guilt, it cannot be entered as evidence in private antitrust cases.

Civil proceedings are often filed to achieve regulatory remedies (e.g., court injunctions placing restrictions on the future behavior of the firms in question). Civil proceedings are rarely brought in response to criminal violations because an injunction would only restate what was already fixed in law. Civil cases may be settled out of court through the negotiation of a consent decree with the division. Consent decrees allow for relief without the expense, delays, and disclosures associated with a trial. In addition, a consent decree is inadmissible as prima facie evidence of an antitrust violation in private suits. For these reasons, both parties are often quite willing to negotiate consent decrees rather than allowing cases to be settled in the courts. Once a consent decree has been negotiated, it must be published in the *Federal Register* along with a statement of competitive impact sixty days before going into effect. This statement sets forth both the facts of the case and the effects of the proposed decree. The district court must confirm that the decree is in the public interest before it becomes binding. The majority of civil cases are resolved through negotiated settlement.

In recent years, the Antitrust Division has supplemented its prosecutorial function with an advisory function. It regularly informs businesses as to the legality of proposed activities in the hope of preventing prosecutions. When firms question the legality of a proposed arrangement, they may request a business review letter, a statement of division enforcement intentions in a specific case. Review requests must be accompanied by all relevant documents and information and are honored at the discretion of the division. The review is made public along with a press release describing the transaction; thirty days later, all related documents are released. While the business review provides a statement of division policy, it is fully relevant only to the party requesting the review, is never binding on the division, and will be disregarded if the firm failed to disclose all of the relevant facts.[4]

The advisory function of the division was standardized in the late 1960s and again in the 1980s, when the Antitrust Division released its merger guidelines. The guidelines provided a statement of enforcement policy with respect to Clayton Act section 7 cases. The detailed guidelines informed businesses of the circumstances in which the division might intervene to enjoin a merger. The guidelines were designed to prevent mergers that might otherwise become the object of division proceedings. Similar guidelines were released in 1985 to clarify division policy with respect to vertical restraints.

With the passage of the Hart-Scott-Rodino Antitrust Improvements Act of 1976, the Antitrust Division assumed the added responsibility of premerger screening. All firms planning to engage in a merger with combined assets of $110 million or over were required to provide information to the Antitrust Division and the FTC. The agencies have sixty to ninety days (depending on the kind of transaction in question) to rule on the merger. The vast majority of mergers pose no competitive problems and are quickly approved. However, if it appears that the merger may have a substantial anticompetitive effect, the agencies may request additional information, thus extending the waiting period. The agencies notify the firms if the transaction will create competitive problems. Although the division may seek injunctions to prevent a merger before its consummation, a statement of agency intentions usually makes injunctive relief unnecessary. Increasingly, the division has worked with corporations to restructure mergers that raise competitive concerns. The division's "fix it first" policy facilitates a close working relationship between the division and businesses; parties work together to eliminate or minimize the anticompetitive aspects of a potential merger. The division often recommends a premerger restructuring of some portion of one or both enterprises. A firm might be required to divest of a subsidiary which, when combined with the acquired firm, could raise competitive problems. When time constraints make this action impossible, mergers may be allowed, subject to the terms of a consent decree requiring subsequent divestiture.

Since the 1970s, the Antitrust Division has devoted a substantial portion of its resources to non-enforcement-related activities. It has frequently filed amicus briefs in private cases which could affect important precedents or have a significant competitive impact. In addition, the division has engaged in regulatory intervention at the national and subnational levels. The division has appeared periodically before a number of regulatory agencies, oftentimes to present analyses of the competitive impact of mergers between two firms in a regulated industry or to comment on changes in rates or regulations. The division typically argues on the side of market competition, seeking to minimize regulation. In recent years, division personnel have appeared before a number of congressional committees and a host of regulatory agencies, including the Interstate Commerce Commission, the Federal Maritime Commission, the Federal Reserve Board, the Federal Energy Regulatory Commission, the Nuclear Regulatory Commission, the Securities and Exchange Commission, and the Department of Transportation.

The Federal Trade Commission

The Federal Trade Commission derives its power and authority from the Federal Trade Commission Act of 1914. Section 5 of the FTC Act provides the agency with the power to bring proceedings against "unfair methods of competition in commerce." A 1938 amendment extended section 5 to deceptive acts or practices. This broad grant of authority has provided the FTC with a considerable source of power, allowing it to file cases that could not be brought under the prohibitions of the Sherman or Clayton acts. The FTC is headed by a five-member commission with a chair. The commissioners are presidential appointees serving staggered seven-year terms. The FTC is bipartisan in composition: only three commissioners may be of the same political party. The agency has been reorganized on a number of occasions. Alternately, the FTC's bureaus have been organized along functional lines (e.g., with investigative and litigative bureaus) and program lines (e.g., with an antitrust bureau and a consumer protection bureau). At present, it is organized along program lines, with a Bureau of Competition and a Bureau of Consumer Protection. The Bureau of Economics has been relatively untouched by the series of reorganizations. Historically, one of its major functions—compiling information and reports on American industry—has been largely disconnected from the antitrust and consumer protection functions. In addition to these three bureaus, there are a host of offices to facilitate agency management and coordination.[5]

Throughout its history, the Federal Trade Commission has been characterized by cleavages separating the commissioners from the bureaus and the bureaus from one another. Commissioners have found it difficult to monitor and manage the affairs of the bureaus and direct agency activities toward predefined ends. Rigid divisions separating the bureaus have resulted in problems of internal coordination, although some significant attempts have been made to integrate the economic and legal bureaus in recent decades.[6] The vertical and horizontal cleavages have found their expression in intraorganizational conflicts, which, in turn, have affected agency performance. During the 1970s and 1980s, efforts were made to enhance coordination and management. Recent efforts to transform the commission are the subject of chapter 6.

The Federal Trade Commission Act provided the FTC with unprecedented investigative powers to gather evidence for enforcement proceedings, to determine whether existing regulations and legislation are adequate, and to compile economic reports. According to section 6 (a) of the Federal Trade Commission Act, the FTC has the power "to gather and compile information concerning, and investigate from time to time, the organization, business conduct, practices and management of any corporation engaged in commerce, excepting banks and common carriers . . . and its relationship to other corporations and to individuals, associations and partnerships." To this end, section 6 (b) provided the FTC with the power to demand of corporations "reports or answers in writing to specific questions, furnishing the Commission such information as it may require as to the organization, bureau conduct, practices, management, and relation to other corporations, partnerships, and individuals of the respective corporations filing such reports or answers in writing." The act also allows for physical access to documentary evidence—a power that is rarely used. Exercise of the investigative powers is not contingent on evidence of illegal activity. The commission can demand information "merely on suspicion that the law is being violated, or even just because it wants assurance that it is not." Despite early court challenges, this power has been used on a regular basis, particularly when the commission has been engaged in studies of entire sectors of the economy.

The information-gathering capacity of the FTC was greatly enhanced in the 1970s with the creation of a short-lived Line of Business program. Under this program the commission required selected firms to provide annual figures on a host of corporate activities, including production, sales, costs, and outlays for research and development. The Line of Business program provided the FTC with the most extensive set of figures on American industry ever collected. The program was discontinued during the Reagan administration. With the Hart-Scott-Rodino Antitrust Improvements Act of 1976, the FTC gained an additional source of economic information. As noted above, the act required that firms planning a merger notify the antitrust agencies in advance and provide extensive information on the firms in question. Access to this information increased the ability of the agency to detect harmful mergers in advance and prevent their consummation.

As with the Antitrust Division, cases may originate from a number of sources, including industry complaints, referrals from the other antitrust agency, business publications, Hart-Scott-Rodino filings, and economic market studies. Although the FTC has access to considerable economic expertise and sources of information, historically a majority of cases originated from industry complaints. In recent years, the commission has developed a greater capacity to generate cases through economic analysis, thus decreasing its dependency on complaints. Prior to initiating formal "seven-digit" investigations, potential antitrust cases are assessed in merger screening and evaluation committees. These committees are centralized in the Bureau of Competition; economists form part of the evaluation team and serve to apprise the legal staff as to the economic merits of enforcement.

When the Bureau of Competition staff believes that a corporation has violated the law, it requests that the commission file a formal complaint. The commission's decision with respect to section 5 cases is generally based on two criteria. First, there must be sufficient evidence to prove that an unfair method of competition has been employed. Second, the commission is bound by its organic act to determine whether filing the complaint would be "to the interest of the public." Since all decisions are made by majority vote, the Bureau of Competition must present its evidence to persuade a majority of the commissioners as to the merits of the case. Memoranda from the Bureau of Economics assessing the economic aspects of proposed cases are commonly provided to the commissioners and serve, along with the legal recommendations, to inform their decision.

Once a complaint is issued, attorneys from the Bureau of Competition work with staff economists to compile evidence and prepare a case. Attorneys representing the bureau and the accused appear before an administrative law judge, who defines the limits of discovery, approves depositions, and hears the case. After considering the case, the judge prepares findings of fact, findings of law, and a written decision. The initial decision must be filed within ninety days after the hearing. If the commission does not act on a decision and it is not appealed within thirty days, it automatically becomes the decision of the commission. Decisions are frequently appealed before the commission. It has the power to accept, reject, or modify decisions. The commission usually issues a cease-and-desist order (the administrative equivalent of an injunction) on the basis of the adjudicative decision. While the accused has the option of appealing the FTC's decision to a U.S. court of appeals, the findings of fact are normally accepted by the courts. Accordingly, if a commission decision is overturned, it will usually be on the basis of findings of law. Violation of a cease-and-desist order may result in a fine of $10,000 per day, insofar as each day is defined as a separate violation.

As with the Antitrust Division, few cases are actually litigated to a conclusion. A majority are settled by the negotiation of consent orders. After a complaint has been issued, the accused is provided the opportunity to negotiate a settlement with the commission, thus putting an end to litigation. The consent order is often constructed at the same time that the complaint is filed, reflecting the common appeal to this form of settlement. The consent order has all of the advantages of the division's consent decree: litigation is costly and time consuming, and facts that are revealed in the process may provide a basis for subsequent treble-damage suits.

The FTC is primarily a regulatory agency and regularly provides industry guidance to specify the forms of business activity prone to prosecution under the broad prohibitions presented in section 5 of the Federal Trade Commission Act. To this end, the FTC publishes industry guides and regulatory rules. The industry guides provide administrative interpretations of the law as they apply to firms operating in specific sectors of the economy. Between 1950 and 1980, thirty guides were released. The regulatory rules, in contrast, are more formal and carry the force of law. The rules may address specific industries or specific forms of business activity with applicability over a number of sectors. Complaints may be issued in response to violations of these rules. In 1975, Congress expanded the commission's rule-making authority and authorized the FTC to bring civil proceedings in district court, obtaining injunctive relief and civil damages when commission rules have been violated. The greater power of commission rules and the expanded rule-making authority have limited the importance of guidelines. As a result, rule making has—until recently—increased; existing guidelines have not been revised to reflect changes in commission policy.[7]

Corporations may request that the commission issue an advisory opinion, the FTC's version of a business review letter. Advisory opinions are issued at the agency's discretion, and only if the course of action in question has not yet been adopted and is not presently under investigation. Unless rescinded, advisory opinions are generally binding. However, the advisory opinion will be discarded if the party fails to disclose all of the facts or fails to comply with the commission's advice. Commission opinions have declined in importance in recent years because of the long periods of time that commonly separate the requests and the final opinions. Between 1978 and 1987, over one-half of all opinions were issued over nine months after they were requested, with some opinions being issued only after several years had elapsed. Between 1983 and 1989, only one advisory opinion was released.[8] As a result, businesses have increasingly sought informal advisory opinions from the Bureau of Competition staff. While these opinions are neither approved by nor binding on the FTC, they are issued with less delay and allow firms to keep their business affairs out of the public record. Firms may also rely on business reviews from the Antitrust Division to avoid the delays associated with requests made to the commission.

The Political-Institutional Network

The Antitrust Division and the Federal Trade Commission are responsible for setting policy priorities and selecting cases best suited for their pursuit. While the goals and performance of the two agencies can be tied to a number of organizational factors, their discretionary fields are not boundless but defined through their interaction with the courts, Congress, and executive branch agencies. This combination of forces influences the evolution of policy and agency development. As the case studies will reveal, the history of antitrust policy was shaped largely through the interplay of organizationally specific factors and institutional actors. During the first several decades of antitrust, the content of policy was in many ways determined by other institutional actors who imposed priorities and defined the limits of agency authority. Even the appeal to economics that would shape the policy of the postwar period was partially coerced by the demands of the Court, Congress, and the president, although the relationships were far more reciprocal and coincided with the growing recognition in the policy community that economics could provide an indispensable foundation for policy and administration.

The Antitrust Division and Federal Trade Commission are characterized by different organizational structures and policy processes that have created vulnerabilities to the demands of different institutions. During the postwar period, however, there have been distinct tendencies toward convergence with respect to policy and administration. This has been less the product of institutional coercion than the product of ideas, of understandings of policy and administration that have evolved within the policy community. Since the policy community and the ongoing debates over the foundations of policy are the subject of chapter 4, a few words here must suffice. While the antitrust community does not include the various agencies, it does include a host of actors who have held or hold official positions. The community consists of present and former policymakers from the FTC, the Antitrust Division and other government agencies, prominent members of the antitrust bar, and industrial organization economists. Through their ongoing intellectual interaction they structure the way in which policy and administration are understood, problems analyzed, and solutions constructed. While Congress, the courts, and various executive branch actors have a direct impact on agency activities by virtue of their control over political and administrative resources, their demands and the priorities they promote often express the orthodoxies established within the antitrust community. Court decisions, presidential programs, and topics of oversight often reflect the concerns central to the debates in the antitrust community. During the 1950s and 1960s, there was a growing recognition that economics could provide a central role in guiding enforcement and bringing a new and much-needed coherence to antitrust. As economics was adopted to structure policy discourse, it found an expression in the activities of community members. However, as chapter 4 will reveal, the content of the economic knowledge was not stable. As antitrust became subject to economic norms, it simultaneously became subject to shifting orthodoxies within the body of relevant economic expertise.[9]

The Courts

The courts in general, and the Supreme Court in particular, deserve special attention when analyzing antitrust. Court doctrine determines the limits of agency discretion and, in doing so, structures the state-economy interface. Moreover, the courts actively define property rights, thus conditioning forms of corporate organization and market and nonmarket relationships between firms. It would be no overstatement to describe the market itself as the product of the law as interpreted by the courts. Let us address these points individually.

The authority that Congress vested in the Department of Justice and the Federal Trade Commission can be exercised only within the discretionary field established by the courts. Their capacity to enforce the antitrust laws is contingent on court doctrine. The Antitrust Division is, in essence, a law enforcement agency. If it is to enforce the antitrust laws, it must file cases in district court. It must possess the evidence and resources necessary to litigate each case to a successful conclusion. The final outcome of cases may be decided in a court of appeals or in the Supreme Court. Although the majority of division cases are resolved through negotiated agreement and are thus removed from the courts, this insulation is largely superficial because of the courts' role in structuring the environment of implementation.

The division's ability to enforce the laws through administrative means rests on three factors. First, precedent must provide the division with the authority to bring a particular kind of case. Although the division may seek to test the limits of the law, such adventurous activities are rare in an environment of resource scarcity. Second, the accused must have reason to believe that the costs of a judicial decision would be equal to or greater than those associated with a negotiated settlement. This will be determined through an examination of past judicial behavior in similar cases. Without question, other factors (such as the potential cost of litigation) may weigh in the decision and provide incentives for settling a case through administrative means. However, judicial behavior in past cases is a critical decision variable for firms facing prosecution. Third, since all consent decrees are subject to court approval, the division must possess the administrative capacity to collect the necessary data and conduct the analyses to design and justify the desired relief. In short, division policy must be reconciled with the policies of the Court.

In two respects, the Federal Trade Commission's vulnerability to the courts is somewhat less direct. First, reflecting the FTC's expertise and broad adjudicatory powers, the courts may hear an appeal based on question of law but rarely will accept an appeal based on questions of fact. Second, because the Supreme Court has recognized the broad prosecutorial authority vested in the commission under section 5 of the Federal Trade Commission Act, it may be granted greater latitude. In other areas, however, the FTC's dependence on the courts is equal to that of the Antitrust Division. The accused will rarely consent to a negotiated settlement if there is reason to believe that a commission decision can be overturned on appeal. Past court decisions place limits both on the willingness of the parties to arrive at agreements prior to adjudication and on the willingness of the commission to file a formal complaint. As in the case of the Antitrust Division, negotiated settlements may be rejected by the courts.

Given the processes described above, one might assume that the agencies could shape court doctrine through the careful selection (or exclusion) of cases. This, however, would be an incorrect assumption. The antitrust laws provide the promise of treble damages in private suits, thus creating great incentives to file complaints against competitors. As a result, the number of private cases is far greater than that initiated through the combined efforts of the antitrust agencies. Most private antitrust actions are routine, with little significance for the development of the law. Many are contractual disputes that are framed as antitrust violations in the hope of recovering treble damages. However, private cases have often provided a context for significant shifts in judicial policy. The agencies may file amicus briefs in cases which they believe will affect precedent or have a negative economic consequence. But the courts are under no compulsion to consider the agency positions in deciding a case. The agencies remain subject to policy developments over which they exercise little control.

John R. Commons once described the Supreme Court as "the first authoritative faculty of political economy."[10] This characterization is quite appropriate. The courts have actively engaged in the definition of property rights throughout U.S. history, defining the content of laws covering contracts, liability, and corporate organization. Markets emerged as an expression of laws structuring individual transactions and ongoing economic relationships. Court doctrine also conditioned the relationship between the state and economy by forcing agencies to meet criteria of just compensation, public purpose, and reasonableness when attempting to regulate the use or value of private property. By making all public-private transactions subject to court review, the courts have been able to define acceptable modes of intervention.[11] As a generalization, the courts have proven unwilling to sanction significant departures from market governance except during periods of crisis. Nonetheless, there has been a general growth of the state's regulatory authority, largely as a result of changing court doctrine. As will become clear in future chapters, the discretionary authority of the antitrust agencies has undergone a similar expansion.[12]

Although courts make policy on a case-by-case basis, court doctrine is characterized by a certain logic and coherence because of the reliance on precedent and the relative insulation of the courts from electoral pressures. Public authority is seldom expanded in a haphazard fashion. Robert Solo argues that the Court's capacity to make coherent policy reflects institutional factors that are quite singular, especially when compared with Congress and executive branch agencies. He characterizes Congress and the executive as "composite" decision-making systems by virtue of their electoral vulnerability and procedural norms that guarantee access to competing organized interests. Policies made within these institutions will tend to be an expression of the interaction of multiple interests. As Solo notes: "Composite choice, emerging out of a diversity of interests and pressures, is without a specific point of reference save in the weight of counterbalancing forces. . . . The process of composite choice cannot be the expression of a unitary purpose, a reasoning mind and an integral ideology."[13] As a result, the policies promoted by these institutions often work at cross purposes, resulting in inconsistencies across broadly defined policy arenas. Alternatively, the need to compromise and forge coalitions may force policymakers to pitch policies at such a high level of abstraction that their substantive content is unclear. In contrast, Solo presents the courts as authoritative decision-making systems. They are relatively insulated from pluralist pressures. This fact, combined with their preeminent role in defining property rights, provides the opportunity and capacity to express and enforce a coherent ideology. According to Solo: "The authority of the judiciary, given its form of decision, constitutes necessarily a bastion of ideology (just as the system of choice associated with Congress and the other American agencies of accountability give the greater weight to interests in the processes of composite choice). For that reason . . . the American Supreme Court has spearheaded the search for and formulation of an idea of what is and ought to be, that is, for an ideology appropriate to this age."[14]

Throughout the history of the antitrust agencies, the courts have delineated the sphere of legitimate state activity. Initially the courts were hostile to antitrust and supportive of pure market governance. With a few notable exceptions, questions of corporate organization and conduct were left to the discretion of market actors. The courts challenged the constitutionality of antitrust and adopted a constrained definition of governmental authority. Once the legitimacy of antitrust was acknowledged, court decisions continued to determine the circumstances under which state authority could be exercised. Early on, the courts recognized the validity of cases brought against violations such as price-fixing. They were considered per se illegal regardless of effect. In contrast, the courts retained final authority in determining whether a host of activities and modes of organization would be subject to prosecution. Under the rule of reason, the court claimed the authority to decide on a case-by-case basis whether certain restraints were reasonable, given the effects of the restraints and the particular demands of producing in a given industry. The rule of reason—particularly in the decades prior to the New Deal—promoted a systematic deference to business and a bias against the direct public administration of private interests.

The evolution of court doctrine had an undeniable impact on development of the antitrust agencies, particularly during the postwar period. Since the 1940s, court decisions have conceded the authority of the antitrust agencies to address questions of business organization and conduct. Through a series of decisions, the courts recognized the role that economic analysis could play in interpreting the competitive significance of various forms of industrial organization and modes of activity. Contemporary economic theory could help in determining the reasonableness of intercorporate relationships, strategies, and forms of conduct. These questions did not have to be surrendered to the market; they could be resolved by policymakers. As economics increasingly served as a technical cornerstone of judicial decision making, officials at the antitrust agencies sought to accommodate the changes by providing economic expertise with a more central role in the policy process. As the antitrust agencies relied on economics as a basis for prosecutions, the courts increasingly resolved legal problems through an appeal to economics. The relationship, in many ways, has been reciprocal. Nonetheless, the changing foundations of judicial doctrine had a formidable influence on the evolution of the agencies and the policy-making process.

Accepting Solo's position that the courts are relatively well insulated from pluralist pressures, one must not overlook their vulnerability to changes in the antitrust community. The courts' tendency to appeal to economic analysis when addressing difficult legal questions has reflected the changes in the structure of policy discourse identifying economics as the single form of expertise most applicable to antitrust. In this instance, the courts are another channel of transmission linking the policy community and the antitrust agencies. Because of a number of formal relationships between the courts and the antitrust agencies, the convergence of law and economics in judicial decision making has had a substantial effect on agency activities and policies.

Congress and the Executive

As elective institutions, Congress and the presidency are sensitive to shifts in public opinion and interest-group demands. The need to nurture broad electoral coalitions forces elected officials to respond to the interests expressed by organized and unorganized constituents. In general, public opinion has been supportive of antitrust. There have seldom been calls for its elimination. Indeed, the major political parties have regularly expressed their allegiance to antitrust and their support for continued enforcement.[15] The close link between the policy goals and the central concerns of American liberalism has undoubtedly contributed to the perceived legitimacy of policy. In addition, for much of its history antitrust served little more than a symbolic function. The small number of prosecutions and the meaningless sanctions did little to mobilize opposition. Since antitrust enforcement claimed few resources (political or financial), support for the policy carried few costs.

The support granted to antitrust has not eliminated its political dimensions. When considering this aspect of antitrust, it is useful to separate the politics of policy initiation and ongoing interest-group activity. Elizabeth Sanders has analyzed the politics of policy initiation by examining the changing political-economic coalitions underlying the extension of the antitrust laws.[16] After examining the congressional voting record, Sanders argues that support for antitrust legislation has reflected the conflicts between competing regional economies, a domestic economic core, and the periphery. The Sherman, Clayton, and Federal Trade Commission acts found support among legislators representing the regional-economic periphery. The agricultural and small-business interests of the South and West promoted antitrust as a means of protecting themselves against the abuses of big business centralized in the northeastern core. By the 1970s, shifts in the national economy had reversed the economic power and political agendas of the various regions. The northern industrial cities, now in decline, supported the expansion of regulation, hoping to slow the transformation of the economy. The Scott-Hart-Rodino Antitrust Improvements Act of 1976 was but one of the initiatives that received the political support of the old industrial core while engendering the resistance of the Sun Belt. According to Sanders, the politics of antitrust—and, indeed, the policy itself—reflect the conflicting interests of regional economies during periods of rapid economic change and industrial adjustment.

While the initiation and legislative extension of antitrust has been highly politicized, the administration of antitrust has not given rise to much in the way of ongoing interest-group activity. Antitrust has not been the direct object of interest-group politics, although over three-quarters of the nation's firms fall under the jurisdiction of the antitrust laws. Of course, this is what one would expect, given the logic of interest formation and activity. Antitrust is characterized by a diffusion of benefits and a concentration of costs.[17] Assuming that antitrust enforcement creates self-policing markets and minimizes various forms of collusionary and exclusionary activity, the economic benefits are enjoyed by all through an increase in economic opportunities, the maintenance of a competitive industrial structure, a greater selection of products, and lower prices. Because the benefits are diffuse, one would not expect to find strong advocacy groups forming around the antitrust agencies. Although consumer groups and small-business associations are supportive of antitrust, it remains of secondary interest when compared with policies that have a more immediate impact on their constituencies. Since the costs are highly concentrated among those prosecuted for antitrust violations, there is once again an insufficient basis for the formation of stable interest organizations devoted to limiting the scope of antitrust. Nevertheless, there have been noteworthy incidents of interest mobilization in reaction to episodes of FTC activism.

Leaving the questions of policy initiation and the rare occasions when interests have been mobilized in opposition to antitrust, we must address the ongoing relationships between the antitrust agencies, Congress, and the executive. To what extent are the policy priorities of the antitrust agencies dictated by these institutions? Because the agencies have few organized constituents lobbying Congress, interest-group politics are not of central importance in explaining agency policies. From the perspective of the antitrust agencies, this is a mixed blessing: the low level of interest-group politics creates a distinct weakness in that few interests call for dramatic increases in agency authority or resources. Moreover, when the antitrust agencies have fallen from grace, they have not been able to rely on the support of broad and committed interest coalitions. As noted above, the support of consumer groups and small-business associations has been, at best, episodic because antitrust policy is seldom central to their agendas. Business associations occasionally have sought to redirect antitrust enforcement activities. Because the costs of antitrust are so concentrated, firms have typically appealed to Congress for individual or sectoral exclusions rather than seeking to affect policy on a case-by-case basis. Congress has been quite responsive. It has granted full or partial exclusions for meat-packers, the insurance industry, common carriers, agricultural cooperatives, labor unions, and business research partnerships. The demands should only increase as U.S. corporations seek to tie poor performance in the international economy to the antitrust prohibitions.[18] At other times, Congress has placed restrictions on investigations that could have provided a basis for major enforcement efforts. Individual corporations have, on occasion, sought to convince Congress or presidents to influence the outcome of individual cases. However, there is no evidence that these efforts have been successful in more than a handful of cases.[19]

Presidents may seek to manipulate the enforcement priorities of the antitrust agencies through the power of appointment. The attorney general, assistant attorney general for antitrust, and other officials in the Antitrust Division are political appointees serving at the pleasure of the president. As executive branch officials, it is expected that division executives will represent presidential policy goals. While there is little evidence that great care has been taken in the selection of assistant attorneys general, they have been removed on occasion for failing to promote the administration's program or for endangering its relationship with the business community. However, more discrete means exist for promoting a particular agenda. If an assistant attorney general attempts to bring cases that clash with an administration's policies, presidents may intervene through their attorneys general. Since the early 1940s, all potential cases and policy statements have required the clearance of the attorney general, thus enhancing political control over the caseload and the division's declared policies.

Presidents also appoint new commissioners to the FTC when vacancies arise. However, the status of the FTC as an independent regulatory agency places limits on the presidential authority.[20] The commission must remain bipartisan, with no more than a simple majority representing the president's party. Unlike assistant attorneys general, commissioners do not serve fully at the pleasure of the president. Presidential control is further limited by the inability to remove commissioners over questions of policy. To preserve the FTC's independence, the president can replace an appointee only as a result of "inefficiency, neglect of duty or malfeasance in office."[21] Nevertheless, the chairman is a presidential appointee expected to advocate the president's agenda. This political mandate is combined with the formal authority to direct the allocation of financial and administrative resources, and thus the power to influence agency enforcement priorities. Control over the chairmanship has been, at times, a source of substantial power. President Nixon used this power to bring about significant and long-term changes in the FTC when he appointed Casper Weinberger and Miles Kirkpatrick as successive chairmen. Likewise, Ronald Reagan's appointment of James Miller to the chairmanship was a clear sign of agency reorientation.

The Senate has the opportunity to influence the selection of presidential appointees through its power of confirmation. However, senatorial deference to presidents over questions of appointment has been the norm in antitrust, as in other policy areas. Nonetheless, the opportunities and incentives to evaluate potential appointees have been far greater with respect to the FTC. Because the FTC is an independent regulatory commission, Congress feels greater responsibility for its activities, particularly when compared with the Antitrust Division, which is clearly part of the executive branch. Accordingly, Congress has proven less willing to review the presidential choices on purely technical grounds. Objections have been raised on policy grounds, particularly when the president has attempted to appoint sympathetic independents or members of the opposition party who share the president's policy positions. The fact that chairmen Paul Rand Dixon and Michael Pertschuk held top staff positions in important Senate subcommittees at the time of their selection is suggestive of the Senate's power in this area. In addition, congressional control is enhanced by the fact that the FTC has a multiheaded executive. While commissioners are appointed for seven-year terms, they rarely complete their terms of office, thus creating frequent opportunities for the consideration of commission appointments.

Presidents could potentially set antitrust enforcement priorities through the budgetary process.[22] As part of this process, the Office of Management and Budget reviews the requests of the two agencies, making whatever alterations it believes necessary. The final figures become part of the executive budget. For several reasons, however, the OMB has not exerted much influence over agency priorities. First, since antitrust has been rather uncontroversial in the postwar period, there has been little incentive to alter agency priorities. Second, since the budgets of the two agencies are relatively small and increase at a relatively slow pace, they have not attracted much attention from the OMB staff. Third, to the extent that presidential appointees to the two agencies screen their budget requests prior to the submission to the OMB, any policy-related alterations have already taken place. Finally, it is doubtful that dramatic budgetary reductions would be sustained by Congress. In the 1980s, for example, the magnitude of the OMB-recommended budget cuts was substantially reduced by Congress, often over the objections of political appointees.

House and Senate appropriations subcommittees also review the agencies' budget requests to determine whether increases in appropriations are justified. Although the subcommittee members often express their dissatisfaction with certain aspects of the agencies' activities, substantial revisions of budget requests are rare. Indeed, it is not uncommon for members of the House subcommittee to state with some pride that they have always supported antitrust and met the needs of the agencies. Members have usually supported the agencies, regardless of party and agency performance. As was the case with the OMB, the attention focused on these agencies' requests has been minimal. Their budgets and requested increases are relatively small when compared with those of the other agencies scrutinized by the relevant appropriations subcommittees. For these reasons, the antitrust agencies have not received the critical consideration one might expect, given the dramatic contrast between the broad mandate and economywide jurisdiction, on the one hand, and the relatively small number of prosecutions and the common fixation with trivial cases, on the other. The congressional portion of the budgetary process appears to be of little importance as a forum for shaping the priorities of the antitrust agencies.

Congressional oversight, while necessary to maintain the political accountability of the bureaucracy, is seldom a congressional priority. In part, this fact is a product of congressional incentives: when compared with legislation and constituent service, oversight provides few benefits for individual members of

Congress.[23] The problems are only compounded in complex policy areas where members may lack the expertise necessary to assess agency performance. In the case of antitrust, oversight rarely addresses central policy questions. During the antitrust oversight hearings, members do not engage in detailed analyses of policy. What oversight exists focuses on crude indicators of bureaucratic activity while providing little meaningful evidence of agency performance. Typically, members question the agency representatives as to the number of investigations, the number of cases filed, the number of cases won, and the severity of penalties. These figures are often assessed through a comparison with the previous year's enforcement record, or some year in the distant past in which the figures were abnormally high. Members periodically question officials about staff morale and turnover rates, long-standing problems at both agencies. At times, the subcommittee members will inquire as to agency efforts in specific industries or the status of certain cases, particularly if the activities in question have some impact on the members' districts or have been identified through constituent complaints. While the performance of agency officials may be challenged if the level of activity is deemed inadequate, they are rarely forced to justify the priorities established in the caseload. Indeed, policy priorities are seldom discerned or discussed.

On occasion, however, House and Senate subcommittee oversight has focused on major problems in particular sectors of the economy and the economy as a whole and has attempted to assess the agencies' efforts to address the problems under consideration. The Senate Judiciary Committee has been the primary actor involved in the oversight of the Antitrust Division; the Senate Commerce Committee has been most active in overseeing the activities of the Federal Trade Commission. While senators have often expressed dissatisfaction with the number of prosecutions in a given year, the relationship has been quite friendly, especially with respect to the Antitrust Division. Senators regularly defer to division officials during questioning, accepting their word that it would be inappropriate to discuss certain subjects, cases, and investigations. While Congress has been generally supportive of the FTC, on occasion the relationship has been quite prone to conflict. The reasons are many. First, by virtue of its status as an independent regulatory commission, the FTC is closely connected with Congress and at least marginally insulated from the executive branch. Second, unlike the Antitrust Division, the FTC has a dual existence as an antitrust agency and a consumer protection agency. Even when its role as an antitrust agency has not raised congressional concern, its consumer protection activities have stimulated business resistance. With its industrywide rule-making authority, each decision creates its own constituency. Third, given the flexible administrative procedures, the broad grant of discretionary authority under section 5 of its organic act, and its consumer protection duties, the FTC has not had the luxury of being seen primarily as a law enforcement agency. It has been cast as a regulatory agency. The problematic status of regulation in the American context has undoubtedly contributed to the commission's exposure to Congress.[24]

At times corporate pressure has been great enough to force Congress to redefine the FTC's authority, restrict its investigations, or reduce its resources, reflecting Congress's own vulnerability as an elective institution. The sensitivity of Congress to the concerns of organized interests and corporate actors has provided the basis for a dynamic that has found expression throughout much of the Federal Trade Commission's history. Congress supports and protects the FTC as long as it remains in a state of relative inactivity. As agency activism increases, the coalition of corporate interests increases in size, as does the pressure to place restraints on the FTC. As will be shown in chapter 6, the Federal Trade Commission Improvements Act of 1980 was an explicit expression of this dynamic. In response to a high level of activism and experimentation in antitrust and consumer protection during the latter half of the 1970s, agricultural cooperatives, cereal producers, oil companies, lawyers, doctors, car salesmen, and funeral directors were mobilized against the FTC. Congressional veto power over commission rules was established, and a number of existing investigations were undermined.[25]

The network of relationships that connect the antitrust agencies with other institutional actors within the policy process structures their evolution and, in doing so, shapes policy as well. While the antitrust agencies have much in common, there are significant differences that are worthy of emphasis. The Antitrust Division is relatively well insulated from political pressures with respect to its relationships with other institutional and group actors. It has no clientele relationships, nor is it subject to intensive interest-group politics. Its enforcement activities concentrate costs in such a manner as to militate against interest mobilization. As part of the executive branch, it is relatively immune from congressional pressures, an insulation that is enhanced by the lack of priority attached to oversight. Nevertheless, the division has remained at all times subject to court doctrine. If any external agency can be identified as being central to the definition of division authority and policy, it is the Court. Relative to the division, the Federal Trade Commission is more vulnerable to political and institutional pressures. In addition to sharing the division's dependency on the courts, it has close ties to Congress. As an independent regulatory agency, it is a creature of Congress. While this relationship may shield it from executive-led assaults, this protection is gained only at a considerable cost. The commission is indirectly subject to the localism and electoral pressures that plague Congress. On occasion, the combination of its consumer protection activities, industrywide rule-making authority, and broad investigative authority have promoted interest-group activity in opposition to the FTC. Agency activism has stimulated interest formation and mobilization, which in turn has fueled intense institutional conflict.

CHAPTER THREE

The Historical Legacy:

Institutional Conflict, Organizational

Impotence, and the Definition of Antitrust

Public policy is more than an expression of legislative will—and often quite less. For reasons explored in chapter 1, legislation is often nothing more than a vague statement of intention; the authority to define the substantive content of public policy is devolved upon the bureaucracy and the courts. The organic legislation remains important insofar as it places broad limits on bureaucratic and judicial discretion. But policy analysts must be concerned with the pattern of actions that constitute public policy as implemented.

In this chapter, I examine briefly the two antitrust agencies from the time of their creation through the 1950s. As will become quite clear, the enforcement priorities of the two agencies were not simply products of political choice. Rather, the interplay of organizational dynamics and institutional forces created biases that found a distinct expression in the evolution of policy. During this period, antitrust was, with a few notable exceptions, a policy in search of a purpose. When the agencies actively sought to enforce the laws, they were forced to act within the discretionary arena defined by the president, Congress, and the Supreme Court. The Court was of critical importance in its hesitancy to sanction a significant extension of administrative authority over the market system. Because the agencies failed to develop the capacity to make policy in a coherent fashion, the Court filled an important void. The agencies lacked mechanisms for planning and selecting cases according to any standardized criteria. Thus, authority over the definition of the caseload was devolved upon the staff. This combination of internal and external forces resulted in a preoccupation with trivial cases that could be won with relative ease and would not arouse the hostility of other institutional actors. The noble sentiments embedded in the organic antitrust legislation found a most ignoble expression in the enforcement actions of the two agencies.

The Political and Normative Foundations of Antitrust

Antitrust was designed to preserve open, competitive markets. However, this principle was not seen as a means to a single, economic end. Market exchange seemed best suited to promote individual liberty and preserve economic opportunities while keeping government at arm's length. It was argued that competitive markets and the forced accountability of large corporations would promote economic justice and political freedom, at least as they were understood in the last decades of the nineteenth century.[1] Because antitrust was cast to preserve the idyllic market system of an earlier era, it assumed a symbolic importance which greatly outpaced its practical impact. While markets continued to serve a symbolic function, they increasingly ceased to promote the desired values in a positive sense. They were incapable of adapting to the major economic structural changes of the era. The latter half of the nineteenth century witnessed chronic recession, the effects of which were most severe in the rural regions, where low prices for agricultural goods resulted in major economic dislocations. The nation was simultaneously undergoing a revolution in economic organization with the emergence of the modern corporation and the consolidation of formerly separate regional economies and locally owned businesses.[2] In the 1870s and 1880s, voluntary cartels were replaced by formal trust arrangements: corporate owners vested control in trustees who operated multiple facilities to exercise monopoly power. While the real impact of the trusts may have been limited, they became a focal point of dissent and the source of great political unrest. The trusts, many argued, exploited their control and realized excess profits by artificially raising prices and limiting production. The rejection of the new corporate order found a partial expression in the populist movement. The populists demanded state legislation regulating railroads and placing restrictions on the trusts. By the end of the 1880s, seventeen states had passed antitrust legislation and attention turned to national legislation.

The congressional debates of the late 1880s revealed a concern over the economic, political, and social impact of the trusts. Senator George aptly summarized the economic critique: The trusts "increase beyond reason the costs of the necessaries of life and business and they decrease the cost of the raw material, the farm products of this country. They regulate prices at their will, depress the prices of what they buy and increase the price of what they sell. They aggregate to themselves great, enormous wealth by extortion which make the people poor."[3] The legislators argued that competitive markets could be preserved or reestablished through the elimination or regulation of large economic aggregates and a diffusion of market power. The congressional debates also revealed a general concern over questions of justice. The trusts were charged with stripping individuals of the rightful fruits of their labor. Senator James Jones described the monopolists as having one goal: "to plunder the public." He called for immediate relief. "The iron hand of the law must be laid heavily upon this system, or the boasted liberty of the citizen is a myth. If the proceeds of the labor of our men and women are not to be their own we have no liberty and our Government is a farce and a fraud."[4] The trusts were exploiting their monopoly positions, foreclosing opportunities, and forcing individuals to accept less than fair compensation for their labor.

The trusts had an undeniable political dimension. They were charged with exercising their power in an abusive manner. There was no countervailing public or private power to force accountability. Antitrust was presented as a means of restraining the exercise of economic power, as the Constitution checked the limitless exercise of political power. Senator Sherman made this point with passion and clarity. "If the concentrated powers of this combination are entrusted to a single man, it is a kingly prerogative, inconsistent with our form of government, and should be subject to the strong resistance of the State and national authorities. If anything is wrong this is wrong. If we will not endure a king as a political power we should not endure a king over the production, transportation, and sale of any of the necessaries of life. If we would not submit to an emperor we should not submit to an autocrat of trade, with power to prevent competition and to fix the price of any commodity."[5] The legislative response expressed the liberal concern with concentrated power, whether public or private. It reflected the conviction that such power—if it is to exist at all—must be exercised within the boundaries established by representative institutions. It should not be used to define the economic options available to the citizenry. Grover Cleveland emphasized this very point in a message to Congress when he declared that corporations were becoming "the peoples' masters" and citizens were being "trampled to death beneath an iron heel." Corporations had to be held accountable and made "the carefully restrained creatures of the law and the servants of the people."[6]

While the multiple dimensions of the trust problem were apparent, they were not linked in a coherent fashion within the congressional debates. Because the trust problem was not clearly delineated, a reasoned response was difficult to formulate. Over a two-year period, legislators sought to find the least intrusive, constitutionally based means of addressing the trusts. The debates reflected a sense of urgency, reflecting the growing popular dissatisfaction. Moreover, the body of state-level regulations was growing steadily, creating problems for economic activity in what was quickly becoming a national market. The Sherman Act addressed the trust problem by placing legal prohibitions on unreasonable restraints of trade, a response that was attractive for ideological and practical reasons. In a minimalist Lockean state, officials had little justification for direct intervention in corporate affairs. Law enforcement was least intrusive and thus most compatible with existing political norms. Of course, few practical options existed. With the uninspired exception of state-level regulation, there was little experience with direct regulation. Once policy was cast as law enforcement, officials could rely on strands of common law and the judiciary as the implementing agent. Moreover, antitrust held the promise of creating self-policing markets—a most desirable and efficient alternative, given the limitations of a preadministrative state.[7]

Early Sherman Act Enforcement

Congress passed the Sherman Act in 1890 without allocating funds for its enforcement. While this fact reflected some legislators' lack of commitment, others were convinced that government enforcement would be unnecessary because of the promise of treble damages in private antitrust suits. However, the act was sufficiently vague as to limit the willingness of private parties to engage in antitrust litigation. The law remained unexplored and undefined. The lack of resources proved critical insofar as it placed material limits on the vigor of enforcement. In 1890, the department employed eighty persons, eighteen of whom were attorneys. There had been no increases in resources over the past decade, despite a dramatic increase in the demands placed on the legal system. By 1890, the department's ten Washington attorneys were responsible for thirteen thousand claims pending against the government. Moreover, there were few U.S. marshals available for conducting investigations in the field. A number of major violations of the Sherman Act went unaddressed because of resource constraints. In some instances cases went ahead only because the U.S. attorney was willing personally to absorb the expenses of hiring special counsel.[8] The resource problems were exacerbated by internal administrative problems. Attorneys in the field (including district attorneys) received a small stipend but collected most of their salary through the fee system: they were paid a percentage of the fines levied in the cases that they initiated and litigated. This system created a bias favoring cases that could be brought to a rapid and successful conclusion. There were no incentives to test the limits of a new and undefined body of law like antitrust. This state of affairs was only reinforced by the paucity of administrative sanctions at the disposal of the attorney general: field attorneys were neither easily dismissed nor replaced. With few incentives and sanctions at hand, attorneys general could not direct the department toward more vigorous antitrust enforcement.

By the Fifty-Seventh Congress, it was clear that the department would be unable to enforce antitrust unless provided with greater administrative and financial resources. In 1903, Congress authorized the hiring of a special assistant to the attorney general for antitrust and the creation of a specialized antitrust staff with five attorneys and four stenographers. Moreover, the legal staff was fully salaried, thus eliminating the fee system and its inherent biases. Relaxation of civil service regulations provided attorneys general with greater discretion in the appointment and employment of the staff.[9] Congress also complied with President Roosevelt's request for funding by providing a separate resource base of $500,000 for antitrust activities, to be spent over the course of five years. While the budget continued to grow (from roughly $100,000 per year for the period 1903–5 to $300,000 per year by the 1930s), appropriations and staffing levels remained insufficient. Indeed, by the 1920s the professional antitrust staff had only grown to twenty-five, a figure which would remain relatively constant into the next decade.[10]

While the limited resources available for antitrust posed a problem, efforts to enforce the Sherman Act were also undercut by the indifference and, in some cases, open hostility of presidents and their attorneys general. The figures for the years 1890 to 1930 reveal that the antitrust laws were enforced infrequently and the penalties were trivial. The average number of cases filed increased from 1.5 per year during the first decade of enforcement to 12.1 cases per year by the 1920s. While the department was often successful before the courts, the victories were hollow. Significant penalties were infrequent. While over three hundred cases were filed during this forty-year period, the total fines equaled a mere $2.17 million. Excluding suspended sentences, only twelve prison sentences were imposed, accounting for a total of five years, twenty days, and eight hours of imprisonment; three-quarters of the prison terms were handed down in cases against labor. Corporate officials had little reason to observe the Sherman Act or seek a negotiated settlement when the courts made violating the law an inexpensive venture.[11]

Initially, it appeared that the antitrust experiment would be short lived. In *United States v. E. C. Knight Co.* (1895), the Supreme Court adopted a narrow definition of commerce that almost brought an end to antitrust.[12] The sugar trust's control of 98 percent of the industry qualified it as a monopolist. However, the case focused on the manufacturing or refining activities that necessarily took place within state borders. Since the case did not focus on "interstate commerce" as defined by the Court, the government did not have the authority to intervene. Within two years the Court modified its position and acknowledged federal jurisdiction.[13] Although the definition of "commerce" was expanded, the courts retained their control over the evolution of policy.

The courts separated antitrust violations into two separate categories. The first and most clear-cut was that of per se offenses, activities that were illegal regardless of their effect. In a series of cases including *United States v. Addyston Pipe and Steel Co.* (1899) and *United States v. Trenton Potteries Co.* (1927), agreements between competitors to fix prices and output levels or to divide up markets were considered per se illegal.[14] As Justice Stone commented in *Trenton Potteries*: "The power to fix prices, whether reasonably exercised or not, involves the power to control the market and to fix arbitrary and unreasonable prices. . . . Agreements which create such potential power may well be held to be themselves unreasonable or unlawful restraints, without the necessity of minute inquiry whether a particular price is reasonable or unreasonable."[15] The Court also established the illegality of some agreements to share information because they could promote price-fixing. In *American*

Column and Lumber Co. v. United States (1921), the Court condemned the "open competition" plan of a manufacturing association.[16] The plan required that members compile and exchange detailed information on daily production, sales, and deliveries; prices and stocks were adjusted to maintain profitability and prevent overproduction. However, in a subsequent case, *Maple Flooring Manufacturers' Association v. United States* (1925), the Court found a similar arrangement to be legal because the data gathered and distributed were more general (e.g., average costs), and there was no evidence of price-fixing.[17]

A second, more complex, and ultimately most troublesome category was that of cases subject to the rule of reason. In *Northern Securities Co. v. United States* (1904), the Supreme Court dissolved a holding company which combined two separate and competitive railroads.[18] The Court viewed the positive drive toward the creation of market power sufficient proof of monopolization and thus declared the trust to be in violation of the Sherman Act. Within less than a decade, however, the Court's position had been revised. In *Standard Oil Co. of New Jersey v. United States* (1911) and *United States v. American Tobacco Co.* (1911), the Supreme Court clarified the means by which it would approach Sherman Act cases.[19] Section 1 of the Sherman Act declares illegal "every combination in the form of trust or otherwise or conspiracy in restraint of trade or commerce." Since all contracts and agreements restrain trade to a greater or lesser extent, the legality of an arrangement rested on the question of whether a restraint was reasonable. This question, in turn, forced the Court to address the nature and competitive effects of the restraint. In the *Standard Oil* case, the government argued that the company controlled 90 percent of the market and could, as a result, dictate prices. However, the Court found that the existence of market power was not prima facie evidence that the Sherman Act had been violated. As Justice McKenna stated in a later case, "The law does not make mere size an offense or the existence of unexerted power an offense." Size could easily reflect superior performance, efficiency, and normal methods of industrial development. Market power had to be combined with a purpose or intent usually exhibited through aggressive behavior; "the existence of unexerted power" was not in itself illegal.[20]

The establishment of per se rules empowered the department. While it had to prove the existence of a violation, the burden of proof was limited because it did not have to show evidence of intent or weigh competitive harm against other factors. In contrast, the rule of reason forced an expansion of judicial discretion. However, this is not to say that the Court claimed unbridled authority. As Robert Bork correctly notes, "The rule of reason . . . was entirely a mode of analysis, a system for directing investigations and decisions."[21] Under the rule of reason, the Court weighed the positive and negative effects of a given restraint before ruling on its legality. This balance was clearly a necessity, given the complexities of economic organization and the lack of precise legislative prohibitions. To resolve the question of legality, the Court examined the means by which market power was established and determined whether the "intent and purpose" of a company was to gain a position from which various noncompetitive strategies could be used to eliminate its rivals.[22] The department's burden of proof was far greater in these cases. As the rule of reason evolved, it came to cover a variety of vertical and horizontal relations, including patent pooling, exclusive dealing, various forms of price discrimination, and alleged abuses of monopoly power.[23]

The early history of antitrust was in some ways predictable. While the constitutionality of the Sherman Act was recognized, the Court was unwilling to provide the Justice Department with more than a limited grant of authority. In keeping with its historical position as the institution most clearly involved in the definition of property rights, the Court retained the authority to determine the legality of corporate arrangements on a case-by-case basis. This position reflected the Court's recognition both that the organization and activities of the modern corporation were inherently complex and that when in doubt, such matters were best left to the market. However, the courts cannot bear the full burden for the performance of antitrust. Congress revealed a genuine ambivalence when designing a public policy restricting corporate autonomy. The congressional response to the trust problem was shaped by liberal norms and a weak regulatory tradition, combined with the conflicting demands of regional economic coalitions.[24] Its irresolution found a dual expression. First, the legislative mandate was vague. While Congress debated alternative policies that would have entailed a sophisticated use of tariffs, taxes, or direct regulation, the Sherman Act provided little more than imprecise prohibitions. The ambiguity of the act forced the Court to serve as the primary policymaker. A second expression of congressional ambivalence came in its support for policy. Even when attorneys general promoted enforcement—a rare event in itself—the resource constraints placed severe limits on the size of the caseload.

This is not to say that enforcement efforts were to no avail. There were some impressive early victories that magnified antitrust's symbolic importance and political support: the railroad trust was dissolved; Standard Oil was broken into thirty-three separate companies; the tobacco trust was similarly split into three firms. The Court had established that a monopolist could be distinguished by the combination of market dominance and predatory practices designed to eliminate competition. It had also revealed that industries could be restructured under the provisions of the Sherman Act. These factors may have positively affected corporate behavior.

However, it appears more likely that antitrust actually contributed to the problems it was designed to address; the greatest impact of antitrust was unanticipated and in direct opposition to the goals of policy. As a result of the Court's apparent rejection of the Sherman Act in *E. C. Knight Co.*, the nation entered into a great merger wave. Almost three thousand mergers between 1897 and 1904 contributed to the creation of monopolies and highly concentrated market structures in more than seventy industries. With the breakup of the railroad trust in *Northern Securities*, this merger wave came to a close. Firms sought to avoid the "positive drive" to create market power that the Court had associated with monopolization. A subsequent revision of the Court's position partially stimulated a new merger wave from 1916 to 1929. During this period, well over five thousand firms merged, creating a number of oligopolistic industries. A policy designed to promote market competition was contributing to its extinction. At the same time, however, the threat of antitrust prosecution drove corporations to seek horizontal and vertical integration rather than cartelization as a means of managing overcapacity—arguably a decision that was key to the success of American industry in the twentieth century. In the end, it was not antitrust but the Great Depression that halted the consolidation wave of the first quarter of the century.[25]

The Need for New Legislation
and New Modes of Administration

The Sherman Act appeared fatally flawed in the wake of *Standard Oil*. This rule of reason was quickly denounced by a business community that feared that the courts would decide cases on an ad hoc basis and provide nothing more than inconsistent court doctrines to guide their endeavors. Demanding certitude, business wanted consistent standards that would define with precision the limits of legality. Proponents of antitrust interpreted the rule of reason as the Court's means of limiting the scope of the law. Congress shared in the criticism, fearing that the rule of reason was but an attempt to usurp the powers of the legislature and undermine congressional intent. While the rule of reason implied a distinct approach to adjudicating cases and thus could not be equated with unrestrained judicial activism, the debate it inspired reflected deeper concerns over whether the Sherman Act—a vague expression of common law—could serve as an adequate tool for regulating the emerging corporate economy. Morton Keller notes, "Both branches of government were engaged in a larger, common effort to adjust the regulatory system to an increasingly complex economy . . . it was clear that the rise of large enterprise in America went hand in hand with the rise of a complex system of government regulation."[26] While the Sherman Act could address the most blatant forms of corporate abuse, it was ill suited for governing a diverse and rapidly changing economy. Moreover, the Sherman Act was useful in addressing monopolies but of limited value in preventing the activities that gave rise to monopoly power.

The shape of a new regulatory order was at the heart of the Roosevelt-Wilson debates during the presidential campaign of 1912. Both agreed that the transformation of the American economy was inevitable. One important question remained unanswered: what role would the national government play in this transformation? Although Roosevelt had the reputation of being a "trust-buster," he was critical of the Sherman Act: it was created "to restore business to the competitive conditions of the middle of the last century." This was not the best of goals. As Roosevelt noted, "Those who would seek to restore the days of unlimited and uncontrolled competition . . . are attempting not only the impossible, but what, if possible, would be undesirable."[27] Roosevelt argued that the great corporations were able to draw on considerable expertise when planning production. Their administrative rationality and scale of production provided opportunities for realizing ever-greater efficiencies, thus contributing to national wealth. Because this power could be used in a destructive fashion, the state was compelled to assume a supervisory function. To this end, he called for the creation of a commission to direct consolidation and oversee corporate activity. It would regulate corporate securities to prevent overcapitalization and publicize corporate records and abuses. Building on the idea of the Interstate Commerce Commission, the proposed commission would also set prices and production levels. It would serve as an intermediary in industrial relations to regulate the hours, wages, and conditions under which the corporations employed workers.

Wilson rejected this vision, arguing that the preservation of competition was preferable to the regulation of monopoly. Reflecting the concerns of his adviser Louis Brandeis, Wilson believed that Roosevelt's vision rested on a spurious distinction between good and bad trusts. "A trust is an arrangement to get rid of competition, and a big business is a business that has survived competition by conquering in the field of intelligence and economy. A trust does not bring efficiency to the aid of business; it brings efficiency out of business."[28] The close supervision of corporate consolidation, he argued, would have serious consequences for the future of the economy and democratic governance. It would place the government at the mercy of large corporations. "If the government is to tell big business men how to run their business, then don't you see that big business men have to get closer to the government even than they are now? Don't you see that they must capture the government, in order not to be restrained too much by it?"[29] Under competitive market conditions individual opportunities were limitless; one automatically enjoyed the fruits of one's labor. By vesting power in the state and big business, Roosevelt's system would also place the population in a position of dependency. As presented by Wilson's "New Freedom," the choice was between benevolence and justice, paternalism and freedom.

Wilson shared Roosevelt's appreciation of the Sherman Act's limitations as a tool of economic governance. However, he believed that corrective legislation should enumerate and prohibit the practices which were commonly used to create market power. Wilson won the election without necessarily winning the debate. In the early years of his presidency, Wilson sought, and was instrumental in gaining, the rapid passage of new legislation identifying and prohibiting the specific practices that were employed in the creation of market power. The Clayton Act of 1914 supplemented the prohibitions of the Sherman Act by declaring price discrimination, exclusive dealing and tying contracts, the acquisition of competing companies, and corporate interlocks to be illegal where the effects "may be to substantially lessen competition or tend to create a monopoly in any line of commerce." Congress also passed the Federal Trade

Commission Act to create a new agency that would serve an advisory and regulatory function. The FTC was created in hopes of applying expertise and flexible procedures to the enforcement of antitrust and the regulation of competition in a rapidly changing economy. But its unclear mandate reflected a great ambivalence regarding the role of the state in the economy, an ambivalence that would be at the heart of the FTC. As an enforcement agency, it was charged with filing complaints against those who violated the antitrust laws. As an advisory agency, it was charged with investigating the economy, working closely with business and policymakers, and supervising voluntary agreements among producers. The simultaneous extension of antitrust and the creation of a regulatory commission suggests that the questions so central to the Wilson-Roosevelt debates had gone unanswered. The two models existed side by side, an uneasy partnership within the confines of a single agency. The dual functions were difficult to integrate; in the end, neither role was fulfilled.[30]

The Clayton Act of 1914 was designed to limit the discretion of the courts and remedy the shortcomings of the Sherman Act by specifying the offenses that could contribute to the creation of monopoly power. Although the act retained an arena of judicial discretion—the determination of when competition was threatened in a significant manner—the explicit prohibitions were believed sufficient.[31] The act enjoyed broad support. Business associations welcomed the act because its specificity provided greater certainty. Labor also supported the new law. Although the debates surrounding the passage of the Sherman Act revealed congressional intent that antitrust not be used to attack organized labor, the Justice Department frequently filed suit against union boycotts and strikes, with the support of the courts. The Clayton Act appeared to provide protection for labor by proclaiming, "The labor of a human being is not a commodity or article of commerce." Moreover, the act prohibited the use of injunctions in industrial disputes except "to prevent irreparable injury to property, or to a property right . . . for which injury there is no adequate remedy at law." Thus, Samuel Gompers praised the Clayton Act as the "Magna Carta" of labor.[32]

Organization, Duties, and Resources

As organized at its creation, the FTC was governed by a bipartisan commission of five, appointed for staggered seven-year terms by the president, subject to the approval of Senate. The chairmanship rotated on an annual basis. The first chairman was Joseph E. Davis, the former chief officer of the old Bureau of Corporations. The agency consisted of three separate divisions: the Administrative Division, the Legal Division, and the Economic Division. The Legal Division was composed of a separate Investigational Branch and Trial Branch: the former was charged with the task of conducting investigations and preparing the necessary evidence for cases; the latter represented the FTC in formal proceedings before the commissioners and the courts. The Economic Division had little internal organization and was charged with the task of conducting investigations at the request of Congress, the president, and the commissioners. The Administrative Division addressed questions of internal governance and provided the necessary technical support.

In large part, the FTC was an extension of the Bureau of Corporations, created under Roosevelt's direction as part of the Department of Commerce and Labor in 1903. The department's organic act charged the bureau with the task of making "diligent investigation into the organization, conduct, and management of the business of any corporation, joint stock company or corporate combinations" and "gather[ing] such information and data as will enable the President of the United States to make recommendations to Congress for legislation for the regulation of such commerce." With its investigatory and advisory functions, the bureau was much in keeping with Roosevelt's broad regulatory vision. Its reports analyzed corporate activity and used publicity as a means of limiting corporate abuses. To this end, it was staffed with a core of twenty-eight economists and support personnel conducting ongoing studies of American industry. The bureau staff provided the core of the FTC's Economic Division.[33] The FTC profited from the experience of the bureau of Corporations staff. This, however, was not its only inheritance. It also absorbed the bureau's routines and procedures, a number of its functions, and a backlog of existing investigations. Reflecting this organizational legacy, the FTC often appeared to be an agency within an agency. Throughout its history, analysts would attribute the FTC's problems to the isolation of the economists, the autonomy of litigating units, and a lack of planning and internal coordination.

From the onset, the agency was hampered by a lack of resources. The FTC's budget generally expanded on an annual basis, but the resources did not keep pace with the increasing demands for investigations. The lack of resources became quite dramatic with the onset of the world war: appropriations decreased while the responsibilities of the FTC expanded to include monitoring price and production levels. Resource scarcity was only exacerbated by high rates of personnel turnover at all levels. Moreover, disagreements among the commissioners created an instability of leadership. As one might predict, the central rift was between those who wanted to adopt an advisory posture and those who sought to emphasize enforcement. As a result, in its first five years the FTC had a total of eleven different commissioners; by 1925, only two commissioners had served full terms.[34]

The lack of clear direction from the commissioners was accompanied by distinct organizational problems. According to an early study by Gerald Henderson, the FTC was continually wasting resources and pursuing the trivial because it lacked the capacity to manage the caseload and coordinate the staff. "The attorney in charge naturally desires to make a record, and the Commission is doubtless loath to interfere with his conduct of the proceeding. The case, therefore, runs its appointed course . . . without any real control by the responsible members of the Commission. In the meantime the actual controversy may have become moot. . . . The cumbersome machinery of the Commission continues inexorably, and time and money are expended in lengthy trial and arguments, merely because the respondent does not care to admit that he has violated the law, and the Commission's attorney wants to add another victory to the record."[35] He also noted that the agency lacked any capacity to identify and eliminate trivial cases. "The Commission is handling too many cases . . . it should exercise a greater discretion in selecting those cases which involve questions of public importance."[36]

The Institutional Limits of Agency Authority

As an independent regulatory commission, the FTC is a creature of Congress and remains vulnerable to congressional will. Throughout its early history, the FTC had much closer connections with Congress than with the executive branch. Congress was largely responsible for the creation of the commission and placed great reliance on the agency's investigative work. Nevertheless, during its first decades, congressional support was mixed at best. The relationship between the FTC and Congress was conditioned by the latter's exposure to organized interests and local constituencies and the ambivalence of the FTC's mandate. The FTC's troubled relationship with Congress was best exemplified by the events of 1919. In this year, the agency completed a report on the meat-packing industry requested by President Wilson as part of an effort to study wartime prices. This investigation revealed compelling evidence of collusion and exclusionary practices. The "big five" meat-packers consciously colluded to fix the prices for livestock and finished products and to eliminate competition through a market division plan. The packers prevented new firms from entering the industry by limiting access to transportation and storage facilities. These charges were supported by documentary evidence from the records of the packers' meetings. The commission recommended that the government take control of the rolling stock, refrigerator cars, stockyards, cold-storage plants, and warehouses which were owned and controlled by the meat-packers. Under government administration, it was argued, these facilities could be made available to all existing and potential competitors at a reasonable cost. Since the meat-packers had used these facilities to maintain their monopoly power, nationalization would eliminate the opportunities to undermine competition and extract excessive profits. Even if the reasoning was flawless, the recommendations were politically naive.[37]

On the surface, the FTC's investigation appeared a success. A number of cases were filed over the vigorous opposition of the meat-packers. However, the critical report and recommendations stimulated heavy industry lobbying, thus provoking the open hostility of Congress. The congressional response was both negative and energetic. Senator Watson, a key figure controlling the FTC's appropriations, rejected the report and led an attack on the commission and its policies which spanned several months. In special congressional hearings, the commission was charged with a lack of objectivity. It was contended that the investigation was unfair and biased, conducted solely to justify nationalization. A number of FTC personnel were denounced as socialists unfit for public service and were subsequently dismissed. Budget reductions forced a major staff reduction (from 418 to 315 persons) and the abandonment of a number of future investigations. As a final expression of its discontent, Congress passed the Packers and Stockyards Act of 1921, eliminating FTC jurisdiction over the industry. Henceforth, the Department of Agriculture was responsible for the regulation of meat-packing and stockyards.[38]

Although commission reports periodically continued to serve as a basis for important legislation, the response to the meat-packing investigation was but one expression of the paradoxical relationship between the commission and Congress. Reflecting the electoral vulnerability of Congress, an inverse relationship would exist between agency activism and congressional support. Congress expected the FTC to maintain some base level of activity. However, agency activism only mobilized otherwise latent interests, as affected groups sought relief from Congress. The FTC received support only when it partially fulfilled its mission. It was rewarded for occupying the middle ground between activism and incompetence, punished for attempting to fulfill its legislative mandate.

The FTC's authority also remained subject to judicial definition. As noted above, the agency emerged, in part, out of Congress's dissatisfaction with the rule of reason. Congress desired a body that could investigate and regulate— and as a last resort, litigate. However, the courts would not readily give up the power to define the applicability of the antitrust laws. No matter how generous the organic legislation, the commission's power remained contingent on court approval. The courts would place severe restrictions on the agency's authority in both law enforcement and investigations.[39]

In the first commission case to reach the Supreme Court, *Federal Trade Commission v. Gratz* (1920), the Court severely limited the scope of the commission's authority, reasserting its position of dominance in terms that were very familiar to the opponents of the *Standard Oil* decision of 1911. The majority decision stated: "The words 'unfair methods of competition' are not defined by the statute and their exact meaning is in dispute. It is for the courts, not the Commission, ultimately to determine as a matter of law what they include. They are clearly inapplicable to practices never heretofore regarded as opposed to good morals because characterized by deception, bad faith, fraud, or oppression, or as against public policy because of their dangerous tendency to hinder competition or create monopoly. The act was certainly not intended to fetter free and fair competition as commonly understood and practiced by honorable opponents in trade."[40] The broad grant of authority provided under section 5 of the FTC Act fell victim to court interpretation. For decades following *Gratz*, the FTC would be limited to regulating or prosecuting activities explicitly prohibited by antitrust and Court precedent.

A pair of court decisions in 1926 and 1927 further limited the agency's prosecutorial powers. In *Federal Trade Commission v. Western Meat Co.*, the Court ruled that section 7 of the Clayton Act was inapplicable to the acquisition of assets through merger. The FTC could not force divestiture under the authority granted in the Clayton Act. In *Federal Trade Commission v. Eastman Kodak Co.*, the FTC attempted to reclaim jurisdiction over mergers by employing section 5 to force the divestiture of three processing plants. Following the decision handed down in *Gratz*, the Court ruled that the commission lacked the specific authority under its organic act. These decisions, when combined, constrained the FTC's antitrust authority and informed business that growth through merger was a legally acceptable strategy.[41]

An additional set of decisions placed restrictions on the commission's investigative powers. In *Claire Furnace Co. v. Federal Trade Commission* (1923), the circuit court banned a commission investigation on constitutional grounds. Reminiscent of *United States v. E. C. Knight Co.*, the decision identified manufacturing and production (the primary activities of the Claire Furnace Company) to be clear cases of *intra*state commerce. Since the agency had the authority to intervene only in cases of *inter*state commerce, the commission lacked the jurisdiction to conduct the investigation. In *Federal Trade Commission v. American Tobacco Co.* (1924), the Supreme Court restricted the commission's authority to initiate investigations when there was no initial presumption of illegality. The Supreme Court decided that a broad interpretation of the commission's investigative powers violated the Fourth Amendment prohibition of illegal search and seizure. By drawing an analogy to the limited judicial powers of investigation, the Court limited the commission's rights of access to documents that could be used as evidence.[42]

By the end of the second decade after the passage of the FTC Act, the powers of the commission had been severely restricted by the courts. The Court limited both the applicability of section 5 of the Federal Trade Commission Act and the agency's authority to initiate investigations under section 6 of the act. A contemporary observer, Thomas Blaisdell, identified the central dilemma facing the FTC with respect to the judiciary.

If the Federal Trade Commission or any other commission is to have a major influence in shaping the criteria by which business practice is to be judged, the struggle with the courts will doubtless be renewed. The judicial control of industry is so deeply ingrained in the American system of government that to give an administrative body a large part in determining vital issues affecting property rights can not be accomplished without a struggle. The existence of commissions and other administrative bodies with considerable powers is evidence that it is possible to encroach on the powers of the courts. But how far the encroachment can go it is impossible to say. . . . Any genuine control will be challenged in and by the courts.[43]

The FTC emerged as a response to the expansion of judicial discretion and the realization that the complexities of the economy could not be adequately addressed through the broad prohibitions of the Sherman Act. And yet, the FTC was dependent on the willingness of the Court to relinquish its position as the central institution engaged in the definition of property rights.

Congress and the courts created systemic constraints limiting the FTC's activities. It would indirectly fall victim to interest-group pressures if it threatened the autonomy of business. It would be subject to the Court if it sought to claim the authority to redefine property rights and the relationship between the state and corporate actors. Within this narrow discretionary field the FTC's early history was directed, in part, by presidential agendas as pursued by their appointees. The FTC's organizational underdevelopment only magnified their influence. Their policy orientations, as much as the broad structural constraints presented above, account for the activities of this period.

During World War I, the FTC deemphasized antitrust to investigate compliance with the War Industries Board guidelines and to conduct studies of wartime pricing and inflation. These experiences forged a closer relationship between the FTC and corporations and forced an emphasis on its advisory and intermediary functions rather than its prosecutorial function. The relationships with business increasingly came to resemble the corporatist vision first articulated by Roosevelt. At the close of the war Secretary of Commerce Herbert Hoover promoted associationalism, a corporatist experiment designed to manage competition and growth through state-sponsored cooperative associations and councils. Hoover's associationalist vision conditioned the government-business relations of the 1920s and provided support for the FTC's growing reliance on a nonconfrontational relationship with business.[44]

While Warren Harding's administration was rather uneventful, significant changes were evident during the presidency of Calvin Coolidge. He appointed William E. Humphrey, creating a Republican majority on the commission that would last well into the next decade. It was clear from the onset that Humphrey would not promote vigorous enforcement. He was part of the congressional opposition to the Clayton Act and had criticized the oppressive posture of the FTC. He wanted to redirect the FTC to repair its relations with Congress and enhance its ties with the business community. Accordingly, the FTC increasingly disregarded its already-neglected law enforcement duties, nurturing a close affiliation with business associations. Under Humphrey's direction, the commission placed a far greater reliance on trade-practice conferences to create standards for business conduct. By 1926, a special division had been created in the agency specifically for this purpose. Representatives of major corporations in a given sector were invited to meet with the FTC staff to discuss prevalent practices. When the participants agreed that particular practices were a source of instability or competitive problems, they were prohibited by resolutions backed by the FTC's power to issue cease-and-desist orders. The conferences provided a means by which antitrust and trade standards could be established through the voluntary interaction of interested parties. The FTC was essentially an intermediary.

The trade conferences provided a much-needed regulatory mechanism, given the sharp limitations placed on the FTC's authority and resources. A contemporary observer described the advantages of the conferences. "More adjustments through informal conferences, more sympathetic cooperation with business men, and fuller opportunity for parties investigated to be heard before any adverse public action is taken, are the features of the Commission's new policy. Under this procedure, the Commission can dispose of all except extraordinary cases, or cases of fraud, by taking from the party investigated, without publicity and without formal proceedings, an agreement to discontinue the practice complained of, and a stipulation of facts which will insure a prompt and drastic formal order, should the party later break his agreement."[45] The conferences promoted a close working relationship with business while allowing for the development of more precise standards. However, they were generally emphasized to the exclusion of antitrust enforcement, thereby vesting enforcement responsibilities fully in the Justice Department. The two models of state-economy relations existed side by side in separate agencies.

The trade-practice conferences furnished companies with a forum for making their concerns known to agency officials and for participating in the creation of standard rules of conduct. At the same time, they provided an opportunity for corporate representatives to exchange information on prices and production. By the end of the 1920s, the FTC was approving codes that endorsed price-fixing and other horizontal restraints. In 1930, the Justice Department warned the commission that its resolutions were encouraging violations of section 1 of the Sherman Act and could be subject to prosecution.[46] The judicial rejection of price-fixing through associations was well established; cases such as *American Column and Lumber* and *Trenton Potteries* provided incontrovertible evidence as to where the Court would stand in such a dispute.[47] The FTC rescinded the suspect codes and revised others without prior consultation with the affected parties. The conflict between the Justice Department and the FTC—the prosecutorial and advisory manifestations of policy—undermined business confidence in the trade-practice conferences. There were few assurances that trade-practice conferences would be meaningful and that future resolutions would be protected. Prior to 1930, the FTC had approved fifty-seven trade agreements per year. In the aftermath of this event, the FTC was able to hold only an average of ten trade-practice conferences per year.[48]

With the election of Franklin Roosevelt, attempts were made to remove Chairman Humphrey. The incentives were clearly partisan given Humphrey's stark conservatism. Roosevelt did not object to the trade conferences; they provided a model for the National Recovery Administration. Nevertheless, Roosevelt requested, then successfully demanded, the resignation of Chairman Humphrey in 1933. The decision was appealed on the basis of the commission's independence and the FTC Act, which placed definite restrictions on the president's power to remove sitting commissioners. While a commissioner could be ousted for "inefficiency, neglect of duty, or malfeasance in office," one could not be discharged over partisan disagreements. In a highly publicized decision of 1935, the Court found in favor of Humphrey, upholding the legislative limitations on the president's power of appointment and thus protecting the independence of regulatory commissions. Only Humphrey's death kept him from reclaiming his position.[49]

During the first years of the Roosevelt administration, the commission's antitrust enforcement duties were left unfulfilled, reflecting the irrelevance of antitrust during the first New Deal. The National Industrial Recovery Act of 1933 created the National Recovery Administration to draft codes for each industry that would address conduct, output, and pricing. Firms were provided with an antitrust exemption when in compliance with the codes. While the FTC played some role in the administration of the NRA programs, its role was essentially limited to filing complaints in response to code violations. However, the FTC was quickly drawn into the conflicts between Congress and the executive over the recovery program. The associationalist focus of the 1920s was replaced, albeit only briefly, with a prosecutorial posture. In 1934, Senators William E. Borah and Gerald Nye—both opponents of the NRA—initiated a congressional resolution forcing the FTC to investigate pricing policies in the steel and oil industries. The reports were highly critical of the codes' protection of price-fixing arrangements that raised the price of goods to realize excessive profits. The release of the reports was timed to coincide with the expiration of the steel code. Roosevelt extended the code but requested that the FTC and NRA initiate a joint investigation of pricing practices in the industry.[50] With the Court's rejection of the NRA in 1935,[51] many New Dealers hoped that the codes would continue on a voluntary basis. However, the FTC declared that the agreements were subject to prosecution once stripped of their legal protection. The FTC backed its declaration by filing a record number of cases against many agreements that were originated under the NRA and initiating a number of broad investigations that discovered price-fixing in over forty industries.[52]

Congress encouraged these activities by providing ever-greater resources. In 1935, the FTC's budget was $1,541,000; by 1940, the budget had increased to $2,171,000. In absolute terms, the five years after the termination of the NRA witnessed a 29.4 percent increase in the budget.[53] The FTC's growing resource base was accompanied by an expansion of statutory authority. The Robinson-Patman Act, passed in 1936, strengthened the Clayton Act prohibitions of price discrimination. It provided the FTC with the authority to pursue an entirely new category of violations and to make rules governing producer-distributor relations. In 1938, Congress once again expanded its jurisdiction with the passage of the Wheeler-Lea Act, which extended the section 5 prohibitions to unfair trade practices and made cease-and-desist orders final if not appealed within sixty days. Prior to its passage, an order would have an impact only after a party had been found to have committed the same abuse on at least three occasions. On the first occasion, the cease-and-desist order would be filed; on the second, it would be supported with a court order; on the third, the party would be found in contempt of court. Under Wheeler-Lea, violations were automatically subject to a $5,000 fine. Finally, Congress passed the Wool Products Labeling Act in 1939, authorizing the FTC to make substantive rules to govern practices in particular industries.[54]

The expanding resources and jurisdiction did not transform the commission into a vital and active agency. A number of possible reasons can be suggested. First, with the negative publicity surrounding the Humphrey affair and the FTC's role in executive-congressional conflicts, there was little guidance from the president. Roosevelt vested the responsibilities for his programs in executive agencies. In the case of antitrust, this entailed empowering the Justice Department. Second, the agency became increasingly responsive to Congress, often appearing to be little more than a repository for political favors. Budgetary increases were commonly tied to staffing decisions, with negative consequences for the quality and morale of the staff. These factors were not sufficient to render the agency impotent. Indeed, it required an episode reminiscent of the meat-packing investigation to reveal the high political costs of agency activism.[55]

Beginning in the mid-1930s, the FTC initiated a number of investigations into basing-point systems. These systems had been at the center of the price-fixing violations in the steel and oil industries and rested on the industrywide acceptance of one or more "base points" used for determining the costs for shipping goods. Combined with a common formula for calculating delivery charges, they promoted price-fixing and limited market entry. The most important case was brought against the Cement Institute, a national trade association. The Supreme Court heard the case, ultimately assessing the legality of a widely used price-stabilization scheme. More significant, the case exhibited once again the problematic relationship between the FTC and Congress.[56]

The complaint was filed in 1937; the FTC's final decision was handed down six years later.[57] The decision was based on evidence that the institute had combined a multiple basing-point system with boycotts and concerted activity to prevent the building of new cement plants. The institute distributed freight books to standardize charges and bids on private and government projects. The FTC ordered the institute to abandon the elaborate pricing system and the practices that contributed to limiting competition. The decision was over-turned on appeal, only to be reinstated by the Supreme Court in 1948. The Court found the FTC's case persuasive: the basing-point system was the centerpiece of a strategy to suppress competition.[58]

The congressional reaction to *Cement Institute* almost turned victory into defeat. In the wake of the Court's decision, cement producers began lobbying Congress for legislative relief. Because the FTC was engaged in numerous investigations in this area and had already instituted several cases, the cement producers were joined by representatives of other industries. Congress re-sponded to the mobilization of business as it had in the past: it called on the FTC to limit the scope of existing and future investigations. More important, legislation was passed to overturn *Cement Institute*. With the O'Mahoney Freight Absorption Act of June 1950, Congress sought to establish the legality of base-point pricing. President Truman successfully vetoed the legislation at the prompting of the FTC. However, the potential costs of activism were once again revealed.

Limited Capacities and Organizational Impotence

Throughout its early history, the FTC evolved within the discretionary arena defined by Congress and the courts. Two models were open to the FTC, yet neither received the clear support of the other institutional actors. There were practical problems as well: the demands placed on the agency increased, while its authority was progressively restricted. In organizational terms, the FTC remained underdeveloped: it lacked the mechanisms to promote internal co-ordination and plan policy. In this context, the events of the decades following World War II were striking. The powers of the FTC continued to expand as the result of legislation and favorable court decisions. And yet, the incapacity to manage the agency and define priorities—problems inherited from the first decades of the FTC's history—continued to shape its performance.

The congressional response to *Cement Institute* was intense but relatively short lived. Favorable legislation and court decisions removed many of the restrictions placed on the FTC in earlier decades and extended its jurisdiction to altogether new areas of economic activity. Outside the areas of antitrust, the new powers and responsibilities were significant. With the passage of the Fur Products Labeling Act of 1951, the Flammable Fabrics Act of 1953, and the Textile Fiber Products Identification Act of 1958, Congress granted the FTC the authority to make substantive rules regulating advertising and labeling practices. More significant for present purposes was the Celler-Kefauver Act, passed in the wake of an FTC report on mergers and acquisitions.[59] The act amended the Clayton Act to close the assets loophole and extend the jurisdiction of the Justice Department and the FTC to mergers. They were granted the authority to bring cases when corporate mergers were in restraint of commerce or contributed to the creation of monopoly. The commission's injunctive powers were strengthened with the Oleomargarine Act of 1950. The act was designed to prevent margarine producers from misrepresenting their product as butter. Under the direction of Senator George Aiken, the act increased the sanctions available to the FTC. The relatively small fines associated with the violation of a cease-and-desist order had been long identified as a problem which needed to be addressed. Under the new legislation, each violation of an order constituted a separate offense; each day of noncompliance was considered a separate offense subject to a separate fine.

The Court also contributed to the FTC's authority in 1950, when it essentially overturned the *American Tobacco* decision, which limited the commission's investigative powers by drawing an analogy to the judicial powers of discovery. The FTC had been restricted to requesting only documents that would be of evidential value. In *Federal Trade Commission v. Morton Salt Co.* (1948), this analogy was rejected, and the need for broad investigative powers was recognized.

> Because judicial power is reluctant if not unable to summon evidence until it is shown to be relevant to issues in litigation, it does not follow that an administrative agency charged with seeing that the laws are enforced may not have and exercise powers of original inquiry. It has a power of inquisition, if one chooses to call it that, which is not derived from the judicial function. It is more analogous to the Grand Jury, which does not depend on a case or controversy for power to get evidence, but can investigate merely on suspicion that the law is being violated, or even

just because it wants assurance that it is not. When investigations and accusatory duties are delegated by statute to an administrative body, it, too, may take steps to inform itself as to whether there is probable violation of the law.[60]

The Court conceded that the limitations of judicial inquiry did not affect the investigative powers of administrative agencies. The decision stated that requested information had to be reasonably relevant and described with enough detail as not to create an excessive burden. However, the Court identified the FTC's investigative power as a foundation upon which its other duties rested.

While the Court's new posture was welcomed, Congress limited the impact of the decision by restricting the FTC's autonomy as an investigative agency. Investigations and reports often stimulated new legislative initiatives. However, as the meat-packing and basing-point investigations exhibited, they also served as a catalyst in the mobilization of business. In an attempt to limit its own vulnerability, Congress placed constraints on the FTC's investigative activities and economic reporting by placing the following rider on its appropriation bills: "No part of the foregoing appropriation shall be expended upon any investigation hereafter provided by concurrent resolution of the Congress until funds are appropriated subsequently to the enactment of such resolution to finance the cost of such investigation."[61] Congress apparently sought to prevent the business backlash that had accompanied past investigations.

The general expansion of agency authority did not find an ultimate expression in a more coherent and comprehensive antitrust policy because of a number of organizational impediments. Although the agency was reorganized on numerous occasions, it was continually plagued by a lack of coordination and an incapacity to establish enforcement priorities. Without effective management, authority over the composition of the caseload was devolved upon the staff, resulting in a fixation on trivial Robinson-Patman and trade-restraint cases. Attempts to address major economic problems were quite rare.[62] These problems were recognized by the report of the second Hoover Commission, presented to President Truman in 1949.[63] The report focused on the inadequacy of leadership and organization. First, the chairmanship carried only minor administrative duties and lacked the power to establish broad policy objectives and direct the affairs of the agency. A second source of distress was the agency's structure: its functional organization consisting of separate investigative and litigative bureaus created problems of coordination. The report noted: "Since different bureaus of the Commission are responsible for different stages of its cases and are relatively autonomous, this creates problems of coordination between bureaus on both general programs and particular matters. . . . One bureau collects a miscellany of facts, often unrelated to any particular theory of the case, and turns the data over to the trial lawyers to be fitted into a case that will stand up in the courts. In nonroutine cases, and particularly in antimonopoly cases, there should be a close knitting of the investigation and trial aspects."[64] The separation of investigative and litigative functions blurred the relationship between investigations and the demands of litigation, resulting in wasted resources and unsuccessful prosecutions.

The lack of agency coordination was magnified by the commission's inability to plan policy and direct resources toward particular goals. The report noted, "In the selection of cases for its formal docket, the Commission has long been guilty of prosecuting trivial and technical offenses and of failing to confine these dockets to cases of public importance."[65] Modest attempts had been made to remedy this problem in 1947, through the creation of a planning council consisting of the general counsel, the bureau heads, and the division chiefs. It was supposed to define long-term policy goals, emphasize the commission's antimonopoly functions, and provide attorneys with some statement of priorities for monitoring the caseload and screening potential cases. Although the council was interpreted as a step in the correct direction, it was found insufficient. A report on antitrust enforcement released by the House Select Committee on Small Business identified the same basic problems. Even with the minor advances in the area of planning, the commission remained incapable of screening cases and governing its own activities. As the report suggested, "An indication of the failure to screen cases carefully is the fact that actions are started against firms out of business and even carried to the final stage against practices already discontinued." The report went on to speculate as to the source of the problem. "Presumably, the Commission has not had the knowledge, when the complaint was issued, that the law was no longer being violated."[66]

The reorganization of 1950 enacted some of the recommendations of the Hoover Commission. The most important aspect of the reorganization was its redefinition of the powers and authority of the chairman. Originally, the chairman had few administrative duties. The reorganization recast the chairman as a presidential appointee with the authority to select upper-level agency officials and supervise personnel. While major appointments such as bureau chiefs had to be approved by the commissioners, the power could be used to establish and pursue policy goals at the bureau level. In addition, the chairman was given extensive power over the agency, including the authority to distribute responsibilities among personnel and administrative units of the agency and control over the internal allocation of resources. This authority could be used to reinforce enforcement priorities.[67] The reorganization also erected new programmatic divisions to unite litigative and investigative duties within each program. While this aspect of the reorganization held the potential of enhancing coordination, it was short lived; the functional bureaus were resurrected four years later.

The reorganization of 1954 was based largely on the recommendations of the Heller Report on FTC management. Once again in hopes of improving coordination, it established a system which united investigative and trial attorneys as a team working under the direction of project attorneys. According to the Heller Report, the project attorneys would have "full responsibility for investigation from initial screening, through field investigation, to final deposition." They would "quarterback the work on all matters under their jurisdiction, call on others for advice and service, coordinate the activities of all interested parties, and keep on pressure for action."[68] This system facilitated coordination but failed to integrate the staffs involved in investigation and litigation. Because project attorneys were assigned without reference to past experience, they failed to gain the necessary specialization. The centralization of duties in these positions and a lack of sufficient staff support overburdened project attorneys and limited their effectiveness. Given the Heller Report's concern with agency coordination, it is surprising that it argued that the planning council's functions could be devolved upon the bureaus. Accordingly, the council was eliminated. The report recommended unsuccessfully that a special economic adviser be created to assist the commissioners in setting priorities. The only aspect of the 1950 reorganization that remained in place in the wake of the Heller Report was the reconstituted chairmanship.[69]

The efforts of the 1950s to reconstruct the FTC were ineffective: the lack of coordination and policy planning continued to plague the agency. Agency reorganization was relied upon once again by the beginning of the 1960s.

President-elect Kennedy requested that James Landis, a former FTC commissioner and business-school dean, provide a study of the regulatory agencies. Simultaneously, the Budget Bureau provided a report on the FTC. The two reports were reminiscent of past analyses. In the end, the response to the new critiques was equally familiar, equally ineffective.[70]

Both studies identified the problems of coordination and policy planning that long characterized the commission. The Landis Report focused on the need for a further expansion of the chairmanship, allowing for the president to play a more central role in defining priorities. The Budget Bureau's report was more substantial, addressing the incoherence of the FTC's enforcement activities and the lack of any mechanism by which priorities could be established and performance evaluated. It offered a solution, calling for the creation of a small program-review staff that would "(a) seek out and make use of other available staff groups in [the] FTC . . . to locate the primary trouble spots in the economy in which [the] FTC should apply its efforts, (b) evaluate competing proposals for project-type investigations, (c) determine and recommend to the Commission appropriate division of effort between antimerger, other antimonopoly, and antideceptive practices work, (d) determine and recommend to the Commission the amount of agency effort which should be devoted to 'application for complaint' investigations as opposed to project-type investigations, and (e) develop or approve standards by which such applications will be judged."[71] The recommended review staff would have consisted of an equal number of economists and attorneys charged with providing the data necessary to "weigh the priorities and determine the annual program."[72]

The Budget Bureau identified the isolation and the insufficient strength of the economics staff as one of the critical problems. It noted, "Relative to other work of the agency, economic activities have been progressively diminishing almost since the creation of the Commission."[73] Indeed, when one examines the staffing levels during the commission's history, it is clear that the economic functions had received little support. In 1928, the FTC's staff consisted of 28 economists and 86 attorneys. By 1960, the legal staff had increased to 320 persons, whereas the economic staff remained the same size. In relative terms, the economists had declined from almost 25 percent to 7 percent of the professional staff.[74] Merely expanding the economics staff was not an adequate solution, however, as long as economists were routinely excluded from the policy process and agency planning. Economists worked closely with attorneys in the complex tasks of merger analysis; elsewhere, their input was absent or subordinated to legal criteria. As the study observed, "Economic considerations do not appear to have the same easy access to the policy level of the Commission that legal questions have." To remedy this situation, the Budget Bureau report recommended that steps be taken "to assure that economic considerations are taken into account in the development of programs and policies by the Commission. A new position, Economic Advisor, should be established. The incumbent could be utilized to advise either the Chairman or the Commission as a whole. Economists should also assist the Executive Director in planning the FTC program."[75] The Budget Bureau recognized that economics could provide a key to planning and monitoring FTC efforts by identifying violations and revealing where enforcement would have the greatest impact.

On the basis of these recommendations, the Federal Trade Commission was reorganized in 1961. The powers of the chairman over the agency's personnel were expanded. A second and more significant reorganization replaced the functional divisions with a programmatic organization—an organizational framework that would survive the remainder of the decade. As reorganized, the commission consisted of six separate bureaus: the Bureau of Restraint of Trade, the Bureau of Deceptive Practices, the Bureau of Economics, the Bureau of Field Operations, the Bureau of Textiles and Furs, and the Bureau of Industry Guidance.[76] Finally, the commission sought to follow the Budget Bureau recommendations by creating an Office of Program Review to assist the chairman in the definition of appropriate policy goals. The program review officer was charged with the task of identifying relevant problems in the economy and recommending enforcement priorities which could provide remedies for these problems. However, the office failed to produce a single statement of long-term policy or reports suggestive of a broader policy agenda. Indicative of its irrelevance, when the review officer died in the late 1960s, the position was left vacant.[77]

The Evolution of the Antitrust Division

The first five decades of the FTC's history were characterized by a gradual expansion of agency authority, punctuated by congressional and judicial reactions to the expression of this authority. The contemporaneous history of the Justice Department's Antitrust Division, in contrast, is marked by the consciously directed and dramatic expansion of administrative capacities. At times, the commission's lethargy stood in stark contrast with the division's activism. The FTC's fixation on minor cases was incomparable to the attempts at the Antitrust Division to design and execute enforcement programs with industrywide objectives. Despite this contrast, the two agencies would converge by the 1950s in the pursuit of the trivial.

The New Deal and the Expansion of Capacity

The Great Depression and New Deal are often identified as major turning points in American political history. New political coalitions emerged demanding and supportive of new public policies. The role of the state was redefined through a period of experimentation and innovation. While antitrust was not a central component of the New Deal, the period was nonetheless critical in its effect on antitrust.[78] In 1933, an Antitrust Division was formally established within the Justice Department. Although there had been a separate antitrust subunit for three decades, the creation of the division symbolized the need for greater administrative specialization in an economy which was growing increasingly complex. The timing was somewhat paradoxical. The policy response to the Great Depression entailed a de facto suspension of antitrust. The philosophies of the Sherman Act and the National Industrial Recovery Act were not easily reconciled. To the proponents of antitrust, the NRA codes appeared to be little more than government-sanctioned collusion and price-fixing. What is equally astounding, then, is the fact that administration shifted emphasis from a limited form of national planning to its antithesis. When the Court overturned the central elements of the NRA, it did not mandate a return to the antitrust. And yet, Roosevelt embraced antitrust as a component of his recovery program. In part, this shift reflected the growing influence of Benjamin Cohen, Thomas Corcoran, and Felix Frankfurter, strong proponents of antitrust. In part, it reflected the need to respond to the economic problems of 1937.

Signs of an economic downturn during the early months of 1937 led Roosevelt to establish a number of study groups to examine the economy. The severity of the impending recession became clear when most economic indicators revealed sharp decline, raising the specter of a second depression in less than a decade. While government study groups and independent analysts offered a variety of explanations, a consensus formed around the theory that the recession could be partially attributed to the existence of collusive arrangements promoted by high levels of industrial concentration. The economic arguments that informed the policy debates can be conveniently referred to as economic structuralism. The central insight was that market structure was causally linked with corporate conduct and economic performance. In concentrated industries, dominant corporations worked alone or in concert to administer prices and production levels to claim high profits and limit competition. With respect to the recession, it was argued that oligopolists were extracting excess profits which they failed to reinvest. In some industries, resources simply could not be distributed efficiently because of a variety of economic rigidities. The resulting misallocations had a negative impact on demand and consumer purchasing power, thus contributing to recessionary forces.[79]

The monopoly explanation of the recession was supported by the work of some prominent economists and was popularized by a number of executive and congressional actors who had opposed the collectivism of the New Deal. Ultimately, it was accepted by Roosevelt and Congress. One product of the emerging consensus was the Temporary National Economic Committee (TNEC), established in 1938 to study the extent, causes, and effects of concentrated economic power. The TNEC united members of Congress and representatives from a number of executive agencies, including the Antitrust Division. The TNEC hearings resulted in the most detailed analyses of the American economy ever conducted. A second and related expression of this consensus was a new and unprecedented support for antitrust. The division was expanded and transformed; antitrust was given a new vitality. As the size and budget of the division increased, there was a dramatic expansion of administrative capacity.

Thurman Arnold and the Transformation of the Antitrust Division

If any figure in the history of the Antitrust Division stands out as having played a central role in its evolution, it is Thurman Arnold, a Yale law professor and social critic appointed to lead the division in 1938. Under his direction, the agency entered a period of rapid and substantial change. Contemporaries were suspicious of Arnold. In a book entitled *The Folklore of Capitalism*, Arnold presented antitrust as reinforcing myths which veiled the true nature of the economy, militated against corporate responsibility, and questioned state authority in the market. Antitrust promoted the vision of corporations as individuals in a marketplace of economic atoms. This "trick of personification" shaped the understanding of government authority. "Since the organizations were persons, they should be treated as if they had free will and moral responsibility." Given the status of the individual in American liberalism, "regulation was bureaucracy and tyranny over individuals." The autonomy of corporations qua individuals could be restricted only when they had violated the law. The symbolic significance of the Sherman Act as a criminal statute only reinforced the illusion of corporations as individuals and presented the state's role as being primarily negative and reactive.[80]

Arnold's critical analysis was often misinterpreted as a categorical rejection of antitrust. He questioned the origins of antitrust and argued that the laws reflected the conflict between national ideology and practical necessity. Antitrust was "the answer of a society which unconsciously felt the need of great organizations, and at the same time had to deny them a place in the moral and logical ideology of the social structure. They were part of the struggle of a creed of rugged individualism to adapt itself to what was becoming a highly organized society."[81] While antitrust had been successful in preventing the emergence of cartels which "raised prices immoderately without much regard for the public," it had done little to direct the growth of large corporations or promote production at full capacity. The effect was quite the opposite. "The actual result of the antitrust laws was to promote the growth of great industrial organizations by deflecting the attack on them into purely moral and ceremonial channels."[82] While antitrust "made business less ruthless and more polite," it failed to limit and regulate the exercise of market power.[83]

Arnold's interest in antitrust stemmed, in part, from his recognition of the power of large corporations and the potential for abuse. As long as corporations were personified, their existence as large complex organizations was denied. For Arnold, large industrial interests were of justifiable political concern: they acted as private governments, exercising power over society and extracting its resources without accountability. The economic bottlenecks they created distorted the allocation of resources. Nevertheless, he believed that the

Sherman and Clayton acts could potentially serve as effective instruments of economic governance. The "tradition of antitrust" could be appropriated and used constructively to resolve systemic problems.[84]

Arnold argued that "the antitrust laws have not failed. It is the organization provided for their enforcement that has failed."[85] As Arnold's division reported: "Our policy with respect to restraints of trade has never been made effective in the past because, although we have wanted a competitive economy, we have not been willing to take the necessary steps to insure its continued existence. We have treated the antitrust laws as a moral problem. We have used them to furnish precepts and maxims to business management, but not to exert an effective discipline. . . . Neither in large business nor in small business have the antitrust laws prevented the arbitrary seizure and use of economic power in private hands without public responsibility."[86] Arnold realized that a number of institutional barriers would have to fall before antitrust could be transformed from a "symbol of our traditional ideals" to an effective economic policy.[87] While the courts had played a central role in limiting the scope of antitrust, the immediate problem was one of resources. "Regardless of what judicial interpretations might have been, no adequate results could have been obtained with the limited enforcement organization available."[88] With Roosevelt's support, Arnold persuaded Congress to authorize a series of substantial budgetary increases. In 1938, the division's budget was $595,000. By 1940, the budget more than doubled, reaching $1,273,000. By 1942, the division's annual budget had increased to $1,904,000. The growth in resources allowed for an expansion of the legal staff (from 54 to 144 attorneys) within a year of Arnold's appointment. The overall staff went from 111 persons in 1938 to 583 persons by 1942. Although the resources were reduced with the onset of the war, the agency remained strong.[89]

Historically, the lack of resources placed constraints on agency officials and limited antitrust enforcement. Nevertheless, the division's problems could not be fully resolved through budgetary growth, for organizational factors contributed to the agency's poor performance. In recognition of this fact, Arnold initiated a number of organizational innovations. First, under Arnold's direction the division placed a greater emphasis on the evaluation of prospective cases, analyzing restraints at each stage of production and distribution. Because he was convinced that many enterprises provided substantial gains in consumer welfare through their efficient operations, it was imperative to focus exclusively on those corporations that used their market power to extract excessive profits and exclude competitors. Arnold explained: "It is not size in itself that we want to destroy, but the use of organized power to restrain trade unreasonably, without justification in terms of greater distribution of goods. . . . Size in itself is not an evil, but it does give power to those who control it. That power must be constantly watched by an adequate enforcement organization to see that it does not destroy a free market."[90] This philosophy of antitrust was restated by the division. "The answer to the monopoly problem . . . does not consist of destroying the efficiency of organized industry whenever that efficiency is passed on to the consumer." Rather, "the true function of an antimonopoly policy is to break down the obstacles to production created by dominant groups."[91]

"Trustbusting," Arnold argued, "is not an end in itself . . . its objective is not an attack on the efficient side but the freeing of the channels of commerce."[92] The distinction between efficiency and abuse would have significance only if some means were found to evaluate cases. Of course, planning was necessary for practical reasons as well. Although the division's budget had increased, it remained finite; cases would have to be selected carefully so as to yield the maximum economic effect. To this end, Arnold created a modest case-evaluation system. Distinct sections were also established to handle complaints, litigation, and consent decrees. Arnold created a small economics section to handle economic investigations, compile statistics, and interpret financial data for attorneys. Staffed with six economists, the section served what was basically a support function.

Whether these initiatives had any immediate effect on the division is open to question. In their study of antitrust conducted for the TNEC hearings, Walton Hamilton and Irene Till describe an agency dominated by attorneys, with a caseload that reflected their professional orientations. Staff attorneys continued to play a primary role in all aspects of division affairs. In describing the integration of the specialized sections in the division's policy process, they noted that "such units tend to be excrescences upon a structure which has made little place for them. They are not easily woven into litigation, which is the principal activity of the Division."[93] The newly created economic section in particular was not easily reconciled with the division's organizational legacy as a law enforcement agency. "The way of the law pervades the work of Antitrust. Its task could probably be best served by an amphibian who could use with equal ease the idiom of law and of economics. Yet from the first it was the need for lawyers which was manifest. . . . The first and imperative need was for men who could garner testimony, prepare cases, make them stick in court. It was only as litigation revealed the intricacies of industrial structure as treacherous realities that the need for economists was recognized. . . . [It] came as a very belated afterthought. . . . The deficit has been supplied rather by grafting some capacity at economic analysis upon a legal competence than in an open door to members of another discipline."[94] The difficulties of coordinating the activities of the specialized subunits were apparent but not quickly resolved. Indeed, the troubled union between law and economics would persist for decades, shaping policy and the success of subsequent attempts to alter organizational design.[95]

A second innovation came as Arnold made advances toward standardizing division activities and rationalizing policy. As an immediate step, new attorneys were subjected to in-house training. Senior staff members trained new recruits in methods of investigation and case building to create a greater sense of unity and a common approach to antitrust activities. However, this effort alone was insufficient: the enforcement actions and court decisions of the past had created a confused body of precedent which provided little guidance for policymakers and business. Arnold's response was simple. "Prosecution policy must be developed by precedent and on publicly stated grounds if it is to clarify the law." It was argued that "prosecution policy . . . must consider economic factors which cannot be stated in the narrow issues of a case drafted according to the necessary requirements of legal strategy.[96] To clarify division policy, Arnold began issuing public statements explaining the conditions under which the division had decided to file charges and the anticipated results of prosecution. These statements, it was hoped, would have the cumulative effect of creating a body of administrative precedents, while educating business as to the status of various forms of organization and conduct and thus preventing violations.

A third innovation came in the area of case selection. While the division lacked the capacity to rely solely on market studies and other economic evidence in the generation of cases, attempts were made under Arnold to target particular industries. Complaints and price and production data from a number of sources, including the TNEC hearings, were examined by the staff to determine the prevalence of particular anticompetitive activities and to identify the industries most vulnerable to anticompetitive forces. When there appeared to be a significant problem, a number of cases were prepared and filed on the same day, once again accompanied with press releases and great fanfare. Arnold argued that focusing efforts on the restraints on trade at multiple levels in a single industry would promote a free flow of resources through the economy. During his tenure as assistant attorney general, the division focused enforcement efforts on a number of industries, including housing construction, milk distribution, and food processing.[97]

A fourth innovation came in the area of case resolution. Rather than subjecting cases to the final determination of the courts, cases were increasingly resolved through administrative means. As noted above, judicial support could not be taken for granted. Major court decisions continued to set limits on the division's authority and undermine its objectives. Even when cases were successful in court, they commonly resulted only in minor fines or remedies that were either insignificant or simply misdirected. The legal emphasis of the courts limited the division's ability to use antitrust as a means of realizing economic objectives. Arnold was convinced that cases could be addressed more effectively and efficiently if settled by negotiated means. Although consent decrees had been in use since 1906, they were not used effectively or systematically. Under Arnold's direction, negotiated agreements were quite common. For example, 91.3 percent of the cases terminated in 1940 were settled by consent decree.[98] The division's policy was to negotiate settlements only when the relief was at least as great as that which could be obtained through the courts. Moreover, consent decrees were made available only when businesses submitted to subsequent reexamination to ensure compliance. However, the division's limited resources impinged upon its ability to monitor compliance after decrees were accepted by relevant parties.[99]

Antitrust reached one of its high points under the leadership of Arnold. The number of cases brought by the Justice Department was strikingly low prior to the Arnold years. From a low of one and a half cases per year during the first decade, to an average of thirty-one cases per year from 1910 to 1914, the two decades prior to Arnold's appointment had witnessed an average of eleven or fewer cases per year. In contrast, Arnold's division filed in excess of fifty cases per year. By the end of his tenure, he was responsible for nearly one-half of the antitrust cases filed by the Justice Department. It is tempting to attribute the new activism to the above-mentioned innovations. However, as Suzanne

Weaver suggests, other factors may have been instrumental.[100] First, the dramatic budgetary increases provided the basis for a much greater level of activity. The number of prosecutions would have increased if this had been the only change. Second, Arnold brought a sense of purpose to the division. The positive publicity surrounding the press releases and filings created a new cohesion, a sense of mission. Finally, with the prevalence of trade restraints in the immediate post-NRA period and the availability of TNEC reports, violations were readily identified. Whether or not one wishes to assign an immediate impact to Arnold's innovations, they permanently reshaped the division. These innovations were quickly institutionalized and provided the basis upon which subsequent assistant attorneys general would build.

In the end, Arnold's success and the publicity which he brought to antitrust policy made him a liability to the administration. Arnold's press releases focused public attention on antitrust and what had come to be known as the "Thurman" Act. While this publicity was largely positive, its effects were negative with respect to Roosevelt's relationship with business. The attorney general initially attempted to limit Arnold's influence by requiring that all case filings and press statements be routed through the attorney general's office for clearance. As the demands of the war increased, Roosevelt had to forge a coalition with big business and create an atmosphere more conducive to corporate activity. As the nation entered a period of wartime planning, the NRA proponents regained much of their old influence with Roosevelt, bringing with them their hostility toward antitrust. In 1943, Arnold was appointed to a federal judgeship.[101] His successors would rarely share his vision of antitrust and employ the administrative mechanisms that he had put in place.

The Prosecutorial Imperative: Policy by Default

The postwar period was one of continuity and change. The Court progressively adopted a more expansive interpretation of the antitrust laws and agency authority. Moreover, it increasingly appealed to economic structuralism when resolving complex questions of industrial organization. This reliance on structural decision rules would continue, finding its most striking expressions in the 1960s. In addition, Congress expanded the jurisdiction of the antitrust agencies with the passage of the Celler-Kefauver amendment to section 7 of the Clayton Act. As with the Court, Congress based the new legislation on the dictates of economic structuralism. There was an awareness that concentrated industrial structures contributed to monopoly by supporting various collusionary and exclusionary strategies. Before examining the Antitrust Division during this period, let us briefly explore the factors that contributed to the expansion of agency authority.

During the 1940s and into the 1950s, the Court established that two questions were of central importance to deciding whether monopoly power existed. First, did the firm in question possess a position of market dominance? Second, did the firm exercise its market power to undermine competition and drive competitors out of the market? If both questions were answered in the affirmative, there was a basis for seeking relief. In part, this was a return to the question of "intent and purpose" established in the *Standard Oil* case of 1911. However, the belief that a position of market dominance was a necessary (but not sufficient) condition of monopolization reflected the dictates of economic structuralism. These questions were at the heart of *United States v. Aluminum Co. of America* (ALCOA), decided in 1945 by the Second Circuit Court of Appeals. The question of market power was resolved through an examination of market-share data. ALCOA controlled 90 percent of the U.S. market for virgin ingot aluminum; 64 percent of the market when virgin and secondary or scrap aluminum were combined. Judge Learned Hand decided that the virgin market was the most relevant to the case. Through control over that market, ALCOA could also control the amount of scrap available for secondary markets. The definition of the relevant market was critical because, as Judge Hand argued, a 90 percent share was certainly sufficient for a monopoly, whereas the status of a 64 percent share was unclear.[102]

What was the "purpose and intent" exhibited in ALCOA's history? According to ALCOA, it was not monopolization: the prices charged and profits gained were quite reasonable. This fact was deemed irrelevant by the court: monopolization entails fixing prices and is thus covered by existing per se rules. In the end, the court resolved the question of intent by examining the history of ALCOA and the aluminum industry. The court found that early in the century, ALCOA used a variety of tactics and exclusive contracts to limit competition. Later on, it continued to expand its facilities to maintain control of the industry. This point was critical. As Judge Hand argued, "It insists that it never excluded competitors; but we can think of no more effective exclusion than progressively to embrace each new opportunity as it opened, and face every newcomer with new capacity already geared into a great organization, having the advantage of experience, trade connections and the elite of personnel."[103] A series of specific violations was not necessary to prove intent; the desire to maintain a monopoly position was made strikingly evident through an examination of company history. A monopoly position was not an unavoidable result of early patents but the product of a positive drive toward monopoly. The government won its case.

The ALCOA decision is one of the most important in the history of the Sherman Act. It rested, in part, on the belief that market position and "intent and purpose" were closely tied. Even if there was no specific proof of abuse, intent could be implied from a dominant market position and a history of purposive expansion. If the doctrine central to the *U.S. Steel* decision that "mere size is no abuse" remained the orthodoxy, it was well veiled. Indeed, under ALCOA one could question whether a firm possessing a monopoly position could ever be found innocent of monopolization. The methodology employed in the ALCOA decision was endorsed by the Supreme Court in *American Tobacco Co. v. United States* (1946) and *United States v. United Shoe Machinery Corp.* (1954).[104] The chain of reasoning linking market position and intent would inform court decisions for the next several decades. Likewise, the assumption that structure and conduct were closely linked potentially increased the power of the division by limiting the necessary evidence.

Other important decisions during this period addressed violations of the Clayton Act. In particular, the Court increasingly found in favor of the government in vertical restraint cases which foreclosed markets. In *International Salt Co. v. United States* (1947), the Court found that International Salt was using its patent on salt dispensers to require the purchase of salt. This tying contract foreclosed the market for International Salt's competitors. In *Standard Oil Co. of California v. United States* (1949), the Court found in favor of the government in an important exclusive-dealing case. Standard Oil required that its dealers purchase their gasoline only from Standard. As a result, almost 7 percent of the market had been removed from competition.[105] In other cases, however, the Court continued to present a narrow interpretation of the law. As late as 1950 (*United States v. Celanese Corp. of America*),[106] section 7 of the Clayton Act was interpreted "to prevent the secret holding of stock by one company while the captive company was held out to the public as a competitor." Since "a merger with another company . . . does not constitute an indirect acquisition of stock," the applicability of section 7 in merger cases was, at best, questionable. This interpretation forced the division to represent mergers as part of strategies to create monopoly through corporate acquisition. However, the reliance on section 2 of the Sherman Act did not limit the scope of judicial discretion, since the cases remained subject to the rule of reason.[107]

The Celler-Kefauver Act was passed as a response both to judicial decision making and to trends toward increasing levels of concentration revealed by the Federal Trade Commission. The act strengthened section 7 and expanded the division's jurisdiction by adding a prohibition on the acquisition of "the whole or any part of the assets of another corporation engaged also in commerce." With this amendment, the division was given the authority to seek injunctions on proposed mergers and to force divestiture after their consummation. Although the new Clayton Act went untested until 1955, it represented a significant expansion of agency authority.

During the early history of the division, policy reflected the personalities of those placed at the head of the agency. Because of the lack of resources and established internal processes, organizational factors were of marginal importance in the definition of policy. Arnold's tenure marked a turning point in the agency's history. Under his leadership, the division was expanded and transformed. However, the conversion was incomplete. While specialized subunits and enforcement criteria had emerged for the first time in division history, they were not easily integrated into the policy process; their impact remained contingent on the discretion of agency officials. In essence, the agency and the policy it promoted were still heavily influenced by personality. There existed no means by which officials could be compelled to engage the administrative mechanism Arnold had established. The organizational changes initiated by Arnold could be brought to their logical conclusion or simply suspended. During the decade of the 1950s, the latter path was selected.

For the decade of the 1950s, there is little evidence that the division seriously engaged in any form of policy planning or selected cases in accordance with any standard criteria. As was the case for most of the division's history, enforcement activities evolved simply from industry complaints. With no standard criteria for case selection and no broadly stated goals, agency policy reflected the interests of agency officials and, increasingly, the professional norms and orientations of the legal staff. It is critical in this context to note that during this period, the Antitrust Division came to be characterized by a new prosecutorial zeal. In 1953, Attorney General Herbert Brownell announced that the Justice Department would begin an honors program designed to enhance the quality of the legal staff. This program involved recruiting new attorneys from the top 10 percent of the graduating classes of the better law schools. Graduates were enticed by the promise of experience and competitive starting salaries. The program met with immediate success. The department in general, and the division in particular, came to be staffed with highly qualified attorneys.[108] Many of the new attorneys viewed the division as a place in which they could gain experience and a reputation before assuming a position with a private antitrust law firm. Division employment was a sort of apprenticeship that increased one's litigative skills and enhanced one's market position upon entering private practice.[109]

The new incentives had an undeniable effect both on agency stability and on policy. Attorneys seldom entered the division seeking a career in public service. Accordingly, during the decade following the initiation of the honors program, turnover peaked at 19.7 percent per year.[110] On average, new attorneys were spending but a few years at the division before leaving for private practice. More important, the new incentives had an effect on case selection. Given the incentive to gain as much experience as possible in a short period of time, the attorneys wanted to litigate, gain experience, and develop a record of victories. With this orientation, staff attorneys increasingly focused on the cases that could be brought to a conclusion in a relatively short period of time and could be argued on the basis of principles explicitly acknowledged by the courts. In the absence of mechanisms for setting and imposing priorities, this dynamic was given full expression.

There is little surprise that the Antitrust Division placed little emphasis on systematic review or evaluation during the decade of the 1950s. In this respect, the 1950s reflected continuity with the past. Any review that existed was dominated by the assistant attorneys general and their assistants. Even the otherwise uncritical Attorney General's National Committee to Study the Antitrust Laws recognized the need for intensified review. The report noted: "Making and winning a case is a normal function of a prosecutor. But making and winning a case is not always the most effective procedure for the enforcement of the Sherman Act. Careful analysis of economic and marketing problems is also required as well as an understanding review of business conduct and basic questions as to the public interest. These and related questions are best considered in an atmosphere not dominated by a zealous prosecutor bent solely on court success."[111] The committee suggested that a "detached appraisal" of cases be provided by experienced attorneys and economists without prosecutorial responsibilities on a permanent or temporary basis. The committee recommended that the review group be relied on for advice on policy questions and case selection and in designing relief and approving consent decrees. These suggestions would go largely unheeded, at least until well into the next decade.[112]

The lack of internal planning and evaluation did not translate into a lack of enforcement. Indeed, a number of important section 1 cases against electric utilities contractors resulted in fines which were unprecedented in the history of antitrust. The number of convictions in the last years of the decade were comparable to the enforcement record during Arnold's tenure.[113] Impressive as the figures might have been, the division operated without priorities. Authority was vested in the staff; the prosecutorial dynamic combined with a lack of planning and evaluation only reinforced staff autonomy. Policy was essentially an aggregate expression of professional norms and individual career incentives.

For much of their history, the authority of the antitrust agencies was challenged by the Court, their activism limited by Congress and, to a lesser extent, presidents. Within this narrow discretionary arena, antitrust policy was defined by the interplay of organizational factors and individual interests. Because the agency officials lacked the capacity to define and impose priorities, responsibility for policy was ultimately exercised by the staff. The decision to prosecute was understood as a legal decision to be based on court precedent and available evidence. Given the career incentives of the legal staff and the constraints imposed by superior institutions, enforcement actions focused on cases that proved easiest to prosecute. There was, in short, little demonstrable concern with the long-term effects of policy. Significant changes in policy and administration would be forthcoming, but they would be driven by a new understanding of antitrust. As antitrust was conceptualized as an economic policy, it became evident that past enforcement efforts were misdirected. This conclusion was imposed by members of the policy community and enforced by the institutions which, in the past, had been guilty of limiting agency authority. A new antitrust with foundations in economic theory could not be created through piecemeal reforms but required a qualitatively different form of administration. Once such an administrative apparatus was put in place, ideas gained a certain independence in the definition of antitrust.

CHAPTER FOUR

Models, Markets, and Public Authority:
The Intellectual Context of Policy Change

During the early decades of antitrust enforcement, policy seemed without a purpose or clear set of goals. The content of antitrust was not defined as much by legislative mandate as by the demands of external institutional actors and internal organizational dynamics. The period 1960 to 1980 brought dramatic changes, both in the understanding and administration of policy. Antitrust can be associated with a number of social and political goals. However, there remains one undeniable fact: it addresses economic phenomena and does so in terms that are manifestly economic. In the end, this fact proved decisive. Policymakers, practitioners, and analysts alike looked to economics to bring greater substance to a remarkably vague body of legislation. By the late 1960s, it was impossible for one to engage in meaningful policy debate without framing the contribution in economic terms. Economic concepts had become as pivotal to the definition of policy as purely legal doctrines had been to an earlier generation of antitrusters. As precedent and administrative guidelines evolved, legal concepts found new economic definitions. Members of the antitrust community used economic concepts as surrogates for legal concepts, economic values for political and social values.[1] As participants in an ongoing debate over policy and administration, policymakers were affected by the new economic interpretation of antitrust. Increasingly, policy was considered competent only if informed by economic analysis.

The shift in the understanding of policy was, in part, coerced. The courts increasingly adopted economic reasoning, relying on economic decision rules to resolve complex questions of industrial organization and conduct. The antitrust agencies and attorneys were compelled to adopt similar rules if cases were to be argued successfully before the courts. However, because policymakers, judges, attorneys, and economists were united in a common dialogue with respect to the foundations of antitrust and interacted within the confines of the policy process, causality is difficult to attribute to a single actor or set of actors. The debates and the emerging orthodoxy cut across several institutions and linked multiple agents.

The convergence of law and economics was followed by an equally significant trend. As the structure of discourse grew increasingly dependent on economic thought, fundamental changes were taking place within this body of knowledge. For many decades, the structure-conduct-performance (SCP) framework dominated industrial organization economics. Economic structuralism identified a number of relationships between the structure of industry, the behavior of constituent firms, and economic performance. It supported a broad definition of state authority in antitrust. In the 1970s, the dominance of economic structuralism was successfully challenged by Chicago school doctrines that reified free markets and presented efficiency as both the ultimate value and the product of unfettered market activity. As the economic theory changed, so changed the understanding of policy.[2]

Economic theories are frequently assessed with respect to their fit with the reality they seek to explain. While the explanatory and predictive value of competing theoretical frameworks is important, it is not the key concern of this study. Rather, the focus rests on the political force of economic ideas within the antitrust policy debates, their impact on administration, and ultimately the content of policy. Thus, competing theories are presented as alternative visions of the economy that support the pursuit of particular political values and justify (to different degrees) an active role for public policy in addressing nonmarket modes of economic activity. Because an objective assessment of the competing schools of economic thought is beyond the scope of this study, I remain agnostic on the truth value of the two doctrines. Indeed, neither may be correct—or only correct when identifying the faults of the other.

The Status of Knowledge
in the Policy Process

The increasing complexity of public policy and the new frontiers of state intervention mandate the active participation of a multitude of actors traditionally excluded from the policy process. The analytic focus of scholars studying public policy formulation has progressively expanded to include a number of actors outside of elective institutions. The shift from legislatures to policy subsystems is recognition of the importance of bureaucrats, interest groups, and policy specialists linked through a shared body of knowledge and a concern over the evolution of a specific body of policies. Attention has been directed toward issue networks and policy communities when seeking to understand the sources of policy change and the role of ideas in this process.[3]

It is overly naive to suggest that experts are disinterested analysts seeking only to interpret a complex reality and convey knowledge to policymakers. It is overly cynical, however, to present specialized knowledge as merely justifying political agendas and disguising naked self-interest. In the policy debates that link subsystem actors, expertise is wedded with advocacy. As experts, the participants bring scientific or social scientific knowledge to bear upon complex policy problems. As political actors, they may seek to further a specific agenda. Their expertise allows them access to policy discourse, structures their contributions, and legitimizes their influence. But the aspiration to reshape policy—a hope shared by most participants in most policy debates— provides the motivation to enter the debates in the first place. The two roles of expert and advocate are neither easily distinguished nor usually separate.[4]

Much of the literature on policy communities emphasizes the importance of advocacy, failing to acknowledge the critical role of specialized knowledge in shaping policy subsystems and structuring policy debate. Building on and extending the existing concepts, we can identify a set of actors within subsystems that play a primary role in defining the deficiencies of policy and administration and in encouraging a greater reliance on policy expertise. This set of actors can be conveniently labeled a *community of expertise*. The community of expertise encompasses a relatively stable set of policy specialists engaged in the ongoing examination of policy and administration, the identification of problems, and the formulation of plausible alternatives. The term, however, also refers to a common body of knowledge, the analytic tools which unify the members of the policy community. The chosen expertise plays a central role in structuring and directing policy discourse: it legitimizes certain alternatives, while excluding others from consideration. Moreover, membership in the community of expertise is often tied to one's control over the necessary analytic tools. Before discussing the community of expertise in greater detail, it may be useful to contrast it with concepts already established in the policy literature.

The Intellectual Context

In *Agendas, Alternatives, and Public Policies*, John Kingdon presents the policy community as "a community of specialists: researchers, congressional staffers, people in planning and evaluation offices, academics, [and] interest group analysts."[5] In a descriptive sense, the community of expertise is similar both to Kingdon's policy community and to what Hugh Heclo introduced as an "issue network." In Heclo's words: "An issue network is a shared-knowledge group having to do with some aspect (or, as defined by the network, some problem) of public policy. It is therefore more well-defined than a shared attention group or 'public'; those in the network are likely to have a common base of information and understanding of how one knows about policy and identifies its problems. Increasingly, it is through networks of people who regard each other as knowledgeable, or at least as needing to be answered, that public policy issues tend to be refined, evidence debated, and alternative options worked out—though rarely in any controlled, well-organized way."[6]

The actors in Heclo's issue networks and Kingdon's policy communities interact in a number of contexts, generating, examining, and refining ideas and alternative policies. Kingdon correctly adopts biological metaphors when describing this narrowing of alternatives as "a selection process in which some of the ideas survive and flourish." In the end, "the origins become less important than the process of mutation and recombination that occur as ideas continuously confront one another and are refined until they are ready to enter a serious decision stage."[7] The universe of policy options narrows as participants address questions of feasibility and value acceptability and the probability of future contingencies.

These provocative descriptions of the interaction of subsystem actors have provided for a more sophisticated understanding of the context of policy change. Although they are are of great descriptive value, one may question their usefulness when attempting to explain the origins of policy change. In the end, such accounts must rely on situational factors and pluralist politics to explain policy change. Individual political entrepreneurs and interest coalitions must mobilize—often in response to a well-publicized problem—behind particular policy initiatives or policy-relevant ideas. Certainly, Kingdon is correct when he argues that policy alternatives must fulfill certain criteria if they are to prove influential. However, this insight only displaces the problem to a different level of abstraction, while leaving the origins and influence of the chosen criteria unexplained. Since the specific criteria adopted play such a central role in the identification of problems and the formulation of appropriate responses, the question of knowledge selection cannot be left unaddressed.

The community of expertise departs from and builds upon the related concepts "issue network" and "policy community." At a descriptive level, the community of expertise does not include all of the actors within a given subsystem; only those who possess the expertise are considered qualified participants in the policy debates. As noted above, the rather small set of policy specialists is characterized by a common and highly specialized set of analytic tools. Because many of the members of the community are past or present agency officials, specialized knowledge is combined with administrative experience. While this definition of the relevant actors closely approximates that suggested by Kingdon, it is much more exclusive than Heclo's issue network.

Rather than replacing the established concepts, the community of expertise signifies a special set of subsystem actors. As the complexity of policy increases, the number of individuals capable of engaging in meaningful policy debate decreases. The highly specialized language and concepts associated with complex policies limit the number of actors qualified to participate in the debates. In essence, expertise becomes a precondition of influence and provides a highly specialized language essential for communication. As a result, communities of expertise will tend to emerge around policies characterized by high levels of complexity—for example, monetary policy, exchange rate policy, hazardous waste policy. In these subsystems, the possession of specialized knowledge and the relatively small number of influential participants provide the basis for community cohesion and are sufficient to differentiate the community from the larger set of actors. Often, the prevalence of a given set of disciplinary norms serves the additional function of insulating the core policy debates from the everyday political struggles that dominate electoral institutions.

The conditions of formation, however, are not simultaneously the conditions of influence. A critical factor when assessing community influence is the salience of the policy in question. The more salient a policy area, the greater the propensity of interest groups and elected officials to attempt to define the terms of political exchange. As one might expect, the influence of communities of expertise will be the greatest where policy is relatively unpoliticized. In such policy areas the issue network and the community of expertise may comprise a common set of actors. For comparison purposes, consider monetary policy and nuclear energy policy. While they are characterized by high levels of technical complexity, they differ with respect to salience. In monetary policy, discourse is dominated by a relatively small number of policy specialists, many of which are working within the Federal Reserve System. In contrast, the salience of nuclear energy policy translates into high levels of interest mobilization and political conflict. Specialized knowledge tends to serve an explicit advocacy function.[8] In policy areas characterized by high levels of complexity and salience, communities of expertise may continue to function. The results of community deliberation, however, will have their greatest impact only once they are popularized and used as a basis for coalition formation. The technical competence of a given alternative may, in the end, prove of secondary importance when compared with its capacity to unite multiple interests.

Communities of expertise have identifiable internal structures which condition and also reflect the relative influence of participants in defining the terms of discourse and directing policy debate. These structures include a reputational system and a closely connected system of communication and coordination. The community's internal structures fulfill a number of important functions. They simultaneously minimize community permeability and maximize stability, promoting a greater coherence and continuity of policy debate. Through the imposition and maintenance of community-defined analytic standards, the structures limit the range of alternatives and control the results of community interaction. The system of communication and coordination often takes the form of specialized journals and conferences that unite a geographically dispersed set of actors. While ideas are communicated and activities coordinated through informal channels, the more formal systems represent with greater accuracy that which is recognized as authoritative and worthy of community attention.[9]

Communities of expertise are seldom monolithic and static: there are competing groups within the community promoting different visions of policy and administration. Subsets of community actors differ with respect to their capacity to structure discourse and set the policy agenda. Disparities of influence are promoted and maintained by community structures. Certain tools of analysis, schools of thought, and disciplinary orientations are recognized as authoritative. In turn, the established orthodoxy affects the influence of competing groups within the community. In short, a community's reputational structure shapes community deliberations. It is important, in this context, to note that the reputational structure is dynamic. As the understanding of policy evolves or shifts take place within the relevant academic discipline, new sets of actors become more central to defining the terms of group interaction. The levels of analysis employed by Kingdon and Heclo do not allow for the identification of internal structures: when the universe of relevant actors encompasses the entire policy subsystem, any internal structure is obscured. The subsystem appears to be unstructured, fluid, in a constant state of flux.

While community debates may be of great scholarly interest, their significance rests in their practical impact on policy and administration. The products of community interaction are transformed into public policy and condition institutional evolution. The most direct and obvious channel of transmission is that of appointment. Executive appointees are often selected on the basis of community reputation. Status in the policy community should represent the prevailing orthodoxy. A second and related means of transmission is peer review. After appointment, agency officials remain participants in the community of expertise; their activities are at all times subject to the scrutiny of other community members. The performance of agencies and agency officials will be evaluated continuously on the basis of criteria developed within the community. These channels of influence are most apparent and have been long recognized.[10] A third means of transmission, while often unrecognized, may be the most important. Community members identify policy problems and formulate alternatives. They conceptualize policy in a particular manner, adopting certain metaphors, modes of analysis, and argumentation. This language of analysis and evaluation provides a basis for communication and discursive stability. However, the structure of discourse also favors certain policy alternatives while excluding others from serious consideration. As the medium of intellectual intercourse, the community-generated language defines the epistemological and normative boundaries within which all serious policy debate must take place. Changes in policy and administration must fall within these boundaries if they are to be viewed as authoritative and accepted by community members.[11]

In chapter 1, it was argued that expert administrators in professionalized agencies are characterized by their acute orientation to external academic communities. By virtue of their training, they seek to act within the confines of professional standards while working within the intellectual-disciplinary consensus. It is important, in this context, to note that in policy areas characterized by high levels of technical complexity—that is, those areas in which specialized knowledge is a necessary component of reasoned policy discourse—the line of demarcation separating the community of expertise and the relevant academic community may be blurred. When a particular form of expertise is most relevant to a given body of policy, its practitioners are often key figures in the debates. Biologists will be important participants in environmental policy communities; geologists will be actively involved in the energy policy debates. In these situations, academic communities may play a central role in structuring the discourse within communities of expertise. Assumptions, concepts, and methodological standards associated with a given discipline are transferred to the community of expertise and are appealed to when assessing the contributions even of those actors drawn from politics or a competing discipline.

The results of community interaction may also be translated into institutional change through indirect channels. Interest coalitions may form around particular policy options, seeking to promote them through executive, legislative, or judicial channels. Individual legislators may seek counsel in designing legislative initiatives; attorneys may appeal to dominant theories when constructing legal briefs. When norms generated by the community are introduced into networks of resource dependency, dominant governmental institutions may hold other agencies accountable to the community-recognized standards. Policy and performance may be evaluated through formal appropriation and oversight processes in accordance with these criteria. The availability of these indirect channels of transmission will be contingent on the position of the agency in the larger political-institutional environment, the centralization of resources, and the propensity of specialized constituencies to form around the policies in question. Where a policy area is highly salient, the indirect channels of influence may allow for a triumph of politics over expertise—or may force expertise to serve an advocacy function.

While this discussion has focused on the community of expertise and its effects on defining the activities of a given agency, it is important to note that the orthodoxy that emerges from community deliberations may play an important role in linking multiple institutions and promoting a greater coordination of policy and administration across a policy subsystem. Insofar as actors from multiple institutions are involved in a common community of expertise and subject to a common set of community-generated norms, their activities will reveal a degree of consistency. Broad-based interest coalitions are often necessary to coordinate the activities of political agents in systems characterized by high levels of institutional fragmentation. In highly complex issue areas, communities of expertise serve a similar function.

The Antitrust Community
and Changing Policy Norms

The antitrust community consists of past and present policymakers from the FTC and the Antitrust Division, executive branch agencies, congressional committees, and the courts. It also includes prominent members of the antitrust bar, legal scholars, and industrial organization economists. Movement in and out of the agencies and other official positions is quite common. While there are no empirical measures of circulation, a number of common paths can be observed. For attorneys, service in one of the antitrust agencies is tantamount to an apprenticeship leading to a lucrative position in a private antitrust practice. Other attorneys and economists may move from one of the agencies to staff positions in the relevant congressional subcommittees. Likewise, many of the more visible participants in the policy debates have served in a management capacity in one of the agencies, occupied a position in an official investigative committee, or have testified frequently before Congress. Typically, these same individuals assume leadership positions in the American Bar Association's Section of Antitrust Law and will remain prominent in the antitrust debates.[12]

Although most of the community members have been trained as attorneys, the policy debates are framed primarily in economic terms. Economics is the shared body of knowledge that unites the community of expertise and structures the interaction of its members. One could go as far as to tie the emergence of the antitrust community with the convergence of legal and economic reasoning. Before economics was adopted in policy debates, antitrust was understood primarily as law enforcement. Those who violated the laws as defined by the courts would be prosecuted, given sufficient evidence and resources. The Sherman and Clayton acts were applied on a case-by-case basis; agency officials and judges failed to pay rigorous attention to the economic aspects of cases and the impact of enforcement on prices and output. As the economic interpretation of antitrust became dominant, antitrust was recast as policy. It became possible to assess the economic consequences of various forms of business organization and conduct and thus to set priorities beyond the enforcement of the law. Likewise, economics provided a means of comparing alternative caseloads and evaluating performance.

For the past three decades there has been a strong consensus that economics, correctly applied, could be used to interpret industrial structure and business behavior, to formulate rules for the administration of policy, and to aid in the evaluation of enforcement actions. This general consensus often concealed an intense rivalry within the antitrust community between competing economic paradigms. For many years, two seemingly irreconcilable theoretical frameworks existed side by side. By the 1970s, however, the structuralist vision of industrial organization began to fade with the ascent of the Chicago school. This shift forced a rather significant redefinition of the policy debates. Before examining the shift in greater detail, it is necessary to review briefly the major features of the rival schools of industrial organization economics.

The competing doctrines of industrial organization are constructed in reference to a common neoclassical model of perfect competition in which the interaction of multiple economic agents determines the price of a given good and the quantity produced. Since resources are mobile and divisible, actors can enter and exit markets in response to changing levels of demand. Because economic actors are rational, they seek to realize efficiency gains in order to compete more effectively and realize greater profits. Under conditions of perfect competition, prices are equal to long-run marginal costs, supply is equal to demand, and all markets clear. A situation of perfect competition will cease to exist when one or more of these conditions has been violated. While this model is recognized as an ideal state, the central propositions are often accepted as if they were generally descriptive of reality.[13] Economic structuralism and the Chicago school are variants of neoclassicism. However, there are significant differences in their adherence to, and faith in, the model of perfect competition. Their willingness to relax the central tenets of this model has been a major source of conflict. While limitations of space require that the subtleties of the two frameworks be ignored, it is possible to identify the main areas of contention.

The Intellectual Context

The Structure-Conduct-Performance Paradigm

Economic structuralism rests on the assumption that concentrated industrial structures promote anticompetitive forms of conduct which affect the performance of the economy. While there may be no strict causal relationship, concentrated industrial structures provide firms with the ability to adopt a variety of collusive and exclusionary strategies designed to maintain or enhance their positions and realize monopoly profits. The model of perfect competition requires a diffusion of market actors such that individual decisions will not affect aggregate production or prices. The structuralists build upon this assumption to arrive at their fundamental prediction regarding the impact of concentration on conduct. Joe Bain summarizes this prediction: "The higher the degree of seller concentration, the greater should be the tendency toward cooperative action to establish a joint profit maximizing industry price and output. And the smaller should be the incentive for individual sellers to pursue independent competitive policies that are designed to enhance their market shares and profits at the expense of their rivals."[14] Collusion will not typically assume an explicit form—express pricing, production and market-sharing agreements are relatively rare. Far more common are tacit agreements such as price leadership and parallel pricing often facilitated by the exchange of information regarding costs, output, and pricing policies.

Although economies of scale may account for increased concentration in many industries, structuralists are skeptical that they can provide a sufficient explanation for existing levels of industrial concentration. Some objections are based primarily on logical grounds. Under conditions of oligopoly, firms are insulated from market forces and are no longer compelled to pursue efficiencies. Because they can exercise discretionary control over prices and industry output, they are not forced by the market to realize economies of scale. On the empirical side, the structuralists argue that economies of scale can be realized at fairly low levels of production. Existing concentration levels are many times greater than one can explain through an analysis of economies of scale. The efficiency gains associated with minimum-efficient scale production are thus most correctly associated with the vigorous competition of firms in unconcentrated markets.[15]

An additional component of market structure is product differentiation, which "results from the actions of sellers attempting to heighten inherent traits of a particular product in buyers' minds."[16] Product differentiation fulfills a positive function by conveying important information to consumers and allowing for more efficient market decisions. However, it may serve a strategic function in the quest to undermine competition. A positive relationship has been shown to exist between concentration, profitability, and advertising expenditures, suggesting that product differentiation is a form of nonprice competition employed in oligopolistic industries.[17] Rather than engaging in destabilizing price competition, firms engage in intensive promotion and advertising to increase their relative market shares. The SCP framework suggests that dominant firms will engage in intensive advertising to maintain concentrated market structures, especially when there are promotional economies of scale. Like products are differentiated to condition consumer behavior: consumers are often willing to pay a premium for a specific brand rather than purchasing a less-expensive substitute. These activities are not harmless. They entail a misallocation of resources, insofar as firms in concentrated industries devote a substantial portion of their revenues to advertising rather than research and development or efficiency-enhancing innovations.

Perfect competition requires free entry into markets. According to the structuralists, this condition is often violated as a host of factors limit the ability of potential competitors to enter markets. Barriers to entry are generally defined as the variety of advantages possessed by established firms in concentrated industries. Entry barriers may reflect the existence of large economies of scale, product differentiation advantages, and absolute cost advantages derived from control over production techniques, distributional networks, or necessary factors of production. These advantages allow dominant firms to raise the costs of entering a market, thus protecting their market shares. Industrial concentration would be of little consequence in the absence of barriers to entry. They allow established firms to elevate their prices above the minimum average costs of production without attracting new competitors to the market. They engage in limit-pricing strategies, setting prices as high as possible without inducing new entrants to begin production. An indication of the size of the barriers to entry is the extent to which the "maximum entry-forestalling price" or the limit price exceeds long-run average costs.[18]

The interplay of structure and conduct leads the structuralists to make a number of performance-related generalizations. First, concentrated industrial structures create an inflationary bias. Dominant firms in highly concentrated industries set prices above costs to maximize profits, thus contributing to cost-push inflation. Concentration also contributes indirectly to wage-push inflation, insofar as labor tends to be more organized in concentrated industries. During deflationary periods, firms in concentrated industries tend to lower their prices at a slower pace as a result of long-term contracting practices, thus contributing to the extension of inflationary periods. Some structuralists have argued that active antitrust enforcement could enhance the usefulness of existing macroeconomic policy tools. Price stability could be maintained, freeing fiscal policy tools to promote economic expansion without engaging the inflation-unemployment trade-off central to the Phillips curve.[19]

The SCP framework also suggests that large firms in concentrated industries may be relatively inefficient. At first glance, this claim appears somewhat counterintuitive. Large firms are commonly believed to realize efficiencies by exploiting numerous economies of scale. However, these economies are exploited at relatively low levels of production. Concentration allows oligopolists to limit output to maintain high prices. In doing so, they underallocate resources and fail to realize the welfare gains associated with large-scale production. In addition, oligopolists have little incentive to combine factors in the most efficient manner because they are insulated from competitive pressures. Both forms of inefficiency are presented as causally related to excessive concentration levels that shelter firms from market forces.[20]

High levels of concentration also place limits on technological innovation. Empirical analyses reveal that there is a positive relationship between concentration and innovation but that this relationship holds only until concentration rates exceed a certain threshold. At some point, the relationship becomes negative. The explanation is straightforward: as concentration increases, firms have greater revenues to devote to research and development. Because dominant firms are locked into tacit price-fixing agreements, they seek cost-saving technological innovations as forms of nonprice competition. Under high levels of concentration, however, interdependence becomes so great and agreements so easy to police that innovative strategies threaten to undermine the existing arrangement. As a result, they are largely suspended.[21]

The fourth and final relationship is between excessive concentration and a maldistribution of wealth. The extraction of monopoly profits entails a transfer of wealth from consumers to corporations and stockholders. As a result, nations with concentrated industrial structures will often be characterized by a sharp inequality in the distribution of wealth. Aside from questions of economic justice, the redistribution of wealth will affect the performance of the economy as a whole through its effects on savings and consumption. It was precisely this aspect of industrial concentration that led policymakers to identify antitrust policy as a means of coping with the underconsumption and recessionary forces of the late 1930s.[22]

The Chicago School of Industrial Organization

The differences between the Chicago school and the SCP paradigm are both subtle and striking. Both recognize the relatively high levels of concentration in the American economy but interpret it in very different ways. Whereas the structuralists focus on market structure and strategic business behavior, the Chicago school and antitrust analysis finds its foundation in price theory. Indeed, Richard Posner argues that the essence of the Chicago school is the position that "the proper lens for viewing antitrust problems is price theory."[23] Melvin Reder builds on this notion by noting that the essence of the Chicago view is "the hypothesis that decision makers so allocate the resources under their control that there is no alternative allocation such that any one decision maker could have his expected utility increased without a reduction occurring in the expected utility of at least one other decision maker."[24] Economic actors are characterized by their rationality and their common goal of profit maximization. Within the confines of the market they will combine inputs in the most efficient manner. As a result, markets are self-equilibrating and efficient. When left to function freely, markets will tend toward the Pareto optimum. Departures from this state of affairs are considered "random disturbances" which will prove insignificant in the long run.

Chicago school industrial organization embraces pure price theory. This logically coherent system of propositions is seldom compromised. The SCP framework is described by Posner as "particularistic and nontheoretical." He continues, "The powerful simplification of economic theory—rationality, profit maximization, the downward sloping demand curve—[are] discarded, or at least downplayed, in favor of microscopic examination of the idiosyncrasies of particular markets."[25] In contrast, price theory provides the foundation of Chicago school analyses. Quoting Reder once again, research is evaluated "by a standard which requires (inter alia) that the findings of empirical research be consistent with the implications of standard price theory. . . . Any apparent inconsistency of empirical findings with implications of the theory, or report of behavior not implied by the theory, is interpreted as anomalous." The theoretical hard core of the Chicago school is protected by a simple rule with respect to empirical research: "If inconsistent with what was previously believed, it must be wrong."[26]

The Chicago school appeals to price theory in its rejection of the structuralist interpretation of market concentration. Firm size and concentration levels are determined through the interplay of market forces and the technical demands of production. Firms operating at the most efficient scales of activity will drive their less-efficient rivals out of business. John S. McGee expands upon this assumption. "If any firm should be larger than efficiency requires, and charges higher prices than the costs of its present and prospective competitors, they and the market will shrink it. If any firm should innovate better techniques, or offer a superior product at the same costs as its competitors, the market will respond and it will grow. If any firm offers the same product as its competitors at lower costs, it will prosper and grow. If any firm is so large as to be inefficient, there will be internal and external challenges to put things right; if they are not righted, its present and prospective competitors will outstrip it."[27] This approach is best exemplified by George Stigler's survival test. To determine the most efficient scale of production, one need only observe the size of firms which have survived the competitive process. What exists is ultimately the best guide to what should exist.[28]

The Chicago school interpretation of market structure entails a relationship between concentration and profitability much different from that presented by the structuralists. The structuralist fixation on collusion and discriminatory practices promotes a misinterpretation of the concentration-profits relationship. As Harold Demsetz suggests: "Relatively large firms in concentrated industries produce at lower cost than their smaller rivals. It is difficult to explain how large firms in concentrated industries earn rates of return significantly higher than small firms in the same industries without attributing superior performance to the larger firms."[29] As will be discussed below, the Chicago school does not simply ignore the possibility of collusion. It expresses genuine concern over the short-term welfare losses associated with horizontal restraints, or price-fixing.

The Chicago school does not deny that anticompetitive conduct exists.

However, its long-term impact is interpreted through an appeal to actor rationality and market supremacy. If firms engage in nonmarket strategies, they will often do so in pursuit of further efficiency gains. If they execute their strategies successfully, they do so on the basis of efficiencies denied to their smaller counterparts. High levels of market concentration and the exercise of market power may be indicative of efficiencies. Robert Bork presents this thesis in his book *The Antitrust Paradox*. "If the leading firms in a concentrated industry are restricting their output in order to obtain prices above competitive levels, their efficiencies must be sufficiently superior to that of all actual and potential rivals to offset that behavior. Were this not so, rivals would be enabled to expand their market shares . . . and would thus deconcentrate the industry."[30] A faith in the efficiency of markets is used to support the conclusion that firms may successfully bypass the market if they are sufficiently efficient.

The Chicago school questions the importance of entry barriers and ultimately the validity of the structuralist position. As noted above, the structuralists present barriers to entry as the advantages of established sellers which allow them to maintain prices above competitive levels without attracting new entrants. Following Stigler, the Chicago school narrows the concept to refer to a cost of production "which must be borne by a firm which seeks to enter an industry but is not borne by firms already in the industry."[31] This refinement, while subtle, is of great significance. Barriers cannot arise from economies of scale because they reflect the objective technical demands of production and distribution. Product differentiation does not constitute an entry barrier because established firms and new entrants will realize comparable gains at equal levels of advertising. One might imagine that capital requirements could create entry barriers, given the substantial investments needed to enter at minimum-efficient scale or multiple levels. However, capital requirements are also objective factors and thus roughly equivalent for all firms operating at the same scale within an industry.[32] Once entry barriers are discounted, all firms are subject to the threat of potential competition: the market will prevail regardless of the number of firms or levels of concentration. In the absence of entry barriers, the significance of market structure is greatly diminished. The connection between structure and conduct becomes difficult to support. As Posner notes: "Once 'barrier to entry' was redefined . . . the plausibility of supposing that barriers to entry are common, or commonly substantial, diminished sharply. The deconcentrators are thus arguing from an abandoned premise."[33]

The power of the Chicago school is often attributed to its simplicity. The multiple facets of market structure and the variety of concentration thresholds are replaced with a single decision rule that can be applied to determine the competitive impact of any economic arrangement. William M. Landes explains this rule in terms that cut to the heart of the structuralists' populism. "Cartels or monopolies are objectionable not because higher prices for monopolized goods means more profits for sellers. As a first approximation, sellers' profits are transfers of wealth from one group to another. Wealth transfers may be desirable or not on political grounds. . . . A cartel is objectionable because it reduces output and increases price, creating a deadweight or efficiency loss. We now have a precise way from an economic standpoint to analyze the competitive consequences of a challenged business practice. If it restricts output and increases price, it is anticompetitive. If it expands output, it benefits competition."[34]

The Chicago school analysts argue that the horizontal cartel-like arrangement is the only form of business association that should be consistently addressed through enforcement. By their very design, such arrangements exist to earn monopoly profits by simultaneously fixing prices and reducing output. Cartels are inherently unstable: members have a propensity to defect when the association is unprofitable; new competitors are drawn to the market when the association is too profitable. Nevertheless, cartel-like behavior results in significant short-term welfare losses. Accordingly, Chicago is united in its support for policies prohibiting price-fixing. Indeed, the concern over horizontal restraints is so great that their prosecution is often justified regardless of market structure or ultimate impact. There is also support—albeit less than unqualified—for policies prohibiting horizontal mergers that would provide a structural basis for price-fixing.[35] The Chicago school reveals little if any concern over vertical restraints. They fulfill a positive function by allowing firms to minimize uncertainty: they can secure access to necessary resources and distribution sites. The Chicago redefinition of entry barriers largely undercuts the structuralist position that vertical restraints in concentrated industries deter new competition by forcing entry at multiple levels, thus increasing the capital requirements for entry. The only type of vertical restraint which may be of justifiable concern is that which combines a dominant producer and a monopolist in control of some necessary primary resource.[36]

In summary, the SCP framework and Chicago school provide coherent visions of industrial organization. The SCP framework is premised on the conviction that industrial structure predisposes firms toward certain forms of behavior. High concentration and protective entry barriers insulate dominant firms from market forces. They can act alone or in concert to manipulate prices and output levels to maximize profits and impede new competition, ultimately suppressing the performance of the economy as a whole. The Chicago school, in contrast, bases its vision of industrial organization on a simple theoretical premise: rational economic actors working within the confines of the market seek to maximize profits by combining inputs in the most efficient manner. A failure to act in this fashion will be punished by the competitive forces of the market. Once this premise is accepted, the relationships and problems identified by the proponents of the SCP framework appear questionable at best.

Charting the Changing Influence
of Competing Schools

The SCP paradigm was the consensus position in industrial organization for most of the postwar period. As antitrust policymakers and practitioners appealed to economics to interpret the complexities of business behavior, the disciplinary consensus found an expression in policy. However, during the 1970s, the Chicago school emerged to challenge the structuralist consensus. It is possible to discover evidence of the shift. As noted earlier, members of the antitrust community interact in informal settings. However, more structured debates take place at conferences and through a number of specialized policy and law journals. At any given time, the journals reflect the status of various groups and analytic frameworks within the community of expertise.

The two major journals in the antitrust community are the American Bar Association's *Antitrust Law Journal* and the *Antitrust Bulletin*. Using citation analysis, these journals can be examined for evidence of the convergence of law and economics and changes within the body of policy-relevant economic knowledge. Citation analysis is adopted by many scholars seeking to identify cleavages and sources of influence within an academic discipline. This methodology is most appropriate for examining communities of expertise, given their self-bounded and structured nature. Citations are significant indicators of authority. As George Stigler and Claire Friedland note in their citation study of the economics profession, "The quality of a scholar's work is properly related to the frequency of its citation by his colleagues."[37] Here we suspend questions of objective merit: influence and quality are not necessarily synonymous. Richard Whitley draws attention to the broader significance and function of citations. "Citations are a way of ritualistically affirming group goals and norms, of demonstrating group membership and identity."[38] They reveal the importance of individual scholars and schools of thought in structuring policy discourse.

For evidence of changes in the antitrust community, I analyzed the citations in the above-mentioned journals for two periods: 1965–70 and 1975–80. The indicator of the changing status of economics was the frequency with which articles in economics journals were cited in constructing legal arguments. As suspected, the analysis revealed an increasing reliance on economics across the two periods. In the period 1965–70, 27.5 percent of the citations were to economics journals, compared with 60.5 percent to legal journals. The remainder were to noneconomic, nonlegal sources such as trade association publications. When one examines the figures for 1975–80, the contrast is quite striking. In this period, 39 percent of all citations were to economics journals, compared with 27.5 in the first period. The increasing reliance on economics journals was almost perfectly matched with a decrease in citations to legal journals (from 60.5 percent to 50.5 percent).

The citation analysis also allowed for the construction of a reputational hierarchy for the antitrust community. The basic unit of analysis was the author-work. The number of primary citations to an author's works was multiplied by the number of years in which an author's works were cited within each period. Influence should be continuous, not sporadic. Accordingly, this system of scoring is intentionally biased toward those cited in multiple years. Each member of the reputational structure was identified as working primarily within an economic school or, where appropriate, strict legal analysis. By examining the changing status and relative strength of these groupings in the reputational structure, it is possible to trace changes in the body of economic expertise *as they influenced the policy debates*. The reputational structures for the two periods are presented in tables 4-1 and 4-2.

The Intellectual Context

During the 1960s, ten of the top fifteen figures in the antitrust community could be associated with a distinct economic position. Of this number, seven worked within the structuralist paradigm. Donald Turner, an economist, law professor, and assistant attorney general for antitrust, was the most frequently cited authority, followed by Joe Bain, an economist and the foremost proponent of the SCP framework. Only two of the ten figures adopting economic positions could be placed in the Chicago school: Robert Bork and George Stigler. While Bork has always been one of the most zealous advocates of the Chicago position, Stigler's early work had a more structuralist orientation. By the latter half of the 1970s, two changes were evident. First, the status of economics had increased: fourteen of the top fifteen authorities could be associated with a distinct economic position. More significantly, the Chicago school emerged as a dominant force in the policy debates. Turner, for example, was replaced by the Chicago school's Richard Posner as the foremost authority in the antitrust community. It is important to note that the figures for the structuralists provide an inflated representation of their influence, given the common practice of contrasting new doctrines with a fading orthodoxy.

While a citation analysis can provide a rough indication of the shifts between two distinct schools of thought, it cannot capture the movement of individuals between the schools. Some early advocates of the SCP framework subsequently joined the Chicago school. Perhaps the best example is that of William Baxter. During the 1960s he helped to draft the Neal Task Force Report, which recommended a program of economywide deconcentration. Within the next decade he recanted his support for the structuralist agenda and became associated with the Chicago school. As he noted before the American Bar Association in 1977: "As one of the original drafters of the deconcentration act . . . it seems particularly appropriate that I recant. The state of economic art has changed somewhat since 1968."[39] Subsequently, Baxter was appointed assistant attorney general for antitrust during the Reagan administration.

In addition, citation analysis cannot convey the kinds of shifts that have taken place within the schools. As Chicago gained influence within the antitrust community, many structuralists modified their positions in such a fashion as to remain closer to the new consensus. For example, vertical integration and a variety of vertical relationships were increasingly presented as benign if not beneficial. Barriers to entry, while still important, were

Table 4-1
Antitrust Reputational Structure, 1965–1970

Name	Score[a]	Position
1. Donald Turner	244	Structuralist
2. Joe Bain	180	Structuralist
3. Milton Handler	165	Legal analysis
4. Carl Kaysen	100	Structuralist
5. George Stigler	96	Chicago school
6. Frederick Rowe	90	Legal analysis
7. Corwin Edwards	80	Structuralist
8. Lee Loevinger	75	Legal analysis
9. Joel Dirlam	60	Structuralist
10. Jerrold Van Cise	55	Legal analysis
11. Robert Bork	54	Chicago school
12. John Galbraith	50	Institutionalist
13. Earl Pollock	50	Legal analysis
14. Sigmund Timberg	44	Structuralist
15. John Clark	40	Structuralist

[a]Scores are based on works of an author cited in the *Antitrust Law Journal* and the *Antitrust Bulletin*. To reflect levels of influence, the number of citations per the five-year period was multiplied by the number of years within the period an author's works were cited.

deemphasized; the list of relevant barriers continued to be shortened. While market concentration remains the most important aspect of the structuralist position, most structuralists attribute causal force to concentration only at the highest levels. Many admit that the critical-concentration thresholds advocated in the 1960s and 1970s were overly restrictive and resulted in unnecessary prosecutions.[40] Richard Posner, while not unpartisan, may be correct when he observes that "the debate is no longer one between schools that employ consistently different and ideologically tinged premises to render predictably opposite results."[41] While the extreme Chicago school and structuralist positions remain easy to differentiate, the differences between mainstream structuralists and Chicago school economists is a matter of degree. Whether the convergence reflects the power of persuasion or the requirements

Table 4-2

Antitrust Reputational Structure, 1975–1980

Name	Score	Position
1. Richard Posner	340	Chicago school
2. F. M. Scherer	330	Structuralist
3. George Stigler	270	Chicago school
4. Donald Turner	220	Structuralist
5. Robert Bork	215	Chicago school
6. Oliver Williamson	195	Transaction cost
7. Harold Demsetz	140	Chicago school
8. Joe Bain	135	Structuralist
9. Milton Handler	125	Legal analysis
10. Phillip Areeda	116	Structuralist
11. Yale Brozen	115	Chicago school
12. Kenneth Elzinga	105	Chicago school
13. Leonard Weiss	100	Structuralist
14. John McGee	95	Chicago school
15. Carl Kaysen	80	Structuralist

of retaining influence is unclear. However, it is difficult to identify any concessions on the part of the Chicago school.

Models of the Market and the Limits of Public Authority

There is ample justification for examining economic models as political doctrines. The manner in which markets are conceptualized directly influences the positive role attributed to the state. If the market is presented as a policy-based mode of economic governance, an expression of public authority, one may freely question whether the market is the most appropriate mechanism for realizing a given set of goals. If, in contrast, markets are seen as efficient, self-equilibrating, and prepolitical in origin, one is predisposed to assigning the state a secondary role. State "intervention" will be cast as unnecessary, if not counterproductive.[42] As variants of neoclassicism, both the SCP framework and the Chicago school accept the vision of the state and market as constituting separate spheres. Nevertheless, there is significant disagreement over the self-sufficiency of markets and the positive role of the state in manipulating business organization and industrial structure to shape conduct and economic performance. Let us consider the two schools as competing visions of the state-market interface, focusing on their impact on policy and institutional change.

The SCP framework has distinct implications for policy. By virtue of the priority it attributes to concentrated economic power, its assumption that this power promotes abusive forms of conduct, and its reaffirmation of open markets with multiple small actors, the framework provided technical support and justification for the political and social goals which were long central to antitrust. This correspondence promoted the convergence of law and economics. As Donald Baker and William Blumenthal suggest: "The precise objective of antitrust policy was unimportant, for populist and economic approaches yielded consistent results. Few were troubled, then, as the dialect in which antitrust enforcement was conducted grew increasingly economic."[43] Members of the antitrust community found industrial organization economics an attractive guide to policy partly because of the shared conceptions of economic power. Thus, the SCP framework served an important function insofar as it justified an expansive definition of public authority. Policies governing the growth and conduct of large business enterprises were presented as necessary if the multiple abuses associated with monopoly power were to be avoided. The structuralist framework forced a new understanding of normal market behavior and, in doing so, of the relationship between the state and business. It was argued that in an age of large corporate entities and complex managerial strategies, rational business behavior may have an adverse effect on competition, economic stability, and the efficient allocation of resources. Because the market has lost its self-sustaining capacity, public policy must invigorate and protect competition.

Economic structuralism also influenced administration, in part because it fulfilled important practical needs, in part—as will become clear in the following chapters—because it was adopted as a keystone of judicial decision making. The willingness of attorneys to employ structuralist doctrines rested less on broad questions of state-economy relations than on the nature of antitrust and the potential functions which economics could serve. Economics promised to provide the technical means for identifying violations and assessing the economic consequences of a variety of business strategies. Moreover, it was believed that an antitrust informed by economics could transcend the incoherence of existing court precedent. Frederick Rowe explains: "Notably, law's yen for abiding principle was met by the axioms of an economic science that unveiled fate in buxom curves, fit chaos into squares, and fused the future with the past. Timeless economic models . . . promised to end antitrust law's toils and troubles of prediction, resolve its hard choices, and regain that lost paradise where general principles do decide concrete cases."[44] The ambiguity of court doctrine and the quest for certitude motivated policymakers, analysts, practitioners, and, indeed, jurists to appeal to the laws of economics for logical decision rules and simple tests of legality. As court doctrine evolved, complex legal problems were transformed into economic-structural problems which could be resolved with the assistance of economic models.

As the courts were forced to determine the legal status of complex economic arrangements and strategies, judges increasingly looked to economics to derive objective principles that could guide the enforcement of the Sherman and Clayton acts. Judge Stephen G. Breyer explained the attraction of economics in the following fashion: "Lawyers and judges desperately need clear standards when they try to apply vaguely worded statutes. No one likes to be at sea with a vague statutory word that seems to leave every decision to the discretion of the judge. The law cries out for objectivity. And the body of economic principle, consistent with the statute's language and consistent with its history, offers objectivity—terra firma—upon which we can base decisions."[45] Judges accumulated economic knowledge from a variety of sources, including prior cases, articles and books, legal briefs presented by the parties to the litigation, and their own basic understanding of microeconomic theory; they applied the knowledge to clarify and simplify difficult legal questions. Most of these sources were affected by the shifting status of competing economic schools within the debates.[46]

The gradual convergence of antitrust law and economics can be illustrated by general trends in judicial decision making.[47] In a number of cases in the early postwar period, the Court faced two questions when addressing violations of section 2 of the Sherman Act.[48] First, did the corporation possess a monopoly position? Second, was the corporation guilty of attempting to monopolize? The first question was typically resolved through an examination of economic market-share data. The second question, however, could be answered only by determining the "intent and purpose" of the corporation in question. Did it actively seek to gain and exercise market power to limit competition, or was it merely following a normal path of industrial development? The Court answered the question of intent by examining company histories. The separation of the two issues was quite important, for while an arithmetic representation of market power was sufficient to determine whether a monopoly position existed, this data carried no implications with respect to purpose. However, the relationship between the two questions quickly changed. The Clayton Act was amended in 1950 to bring mergers directly under the jurisdiction of the antitrust agencies. Reflecting the growing force of economics structuralism, the act was designed to prevent monopoly by placing limits on industrial concentration. Mergers that substantially increased concentration would be prohibited, on the theory that market concentration provided the structural basis for monopolization. As policy evolved in the agencies and courts, the illegality of a merger could be determined solely on the basis of market structure data, trends toward concentration, and levels of corporate integration.[49] As a general rule that quickly influenced the bulk of antitrust, behavior and intent could be implied from economic data because the SCP framework suggested that structure and conduct were necessarily related.

The changing status of economics in the antitrust community and courts had a significant impact on the evolution of institutions and policy.[50] Throughout the latter half of the 1960s and into the next decade, critiques of antitrust increasingly focused on the economic merits of established doctrines, major cases, and the economic-analytic capacities of the two agencies. Judicial decision making increasingly placed primary emphasis on the economic merits of cases. This shift had a considerable impact on institutional change. Since the events of this period are the subject of the following chapters, a few words here must suffice. At the Antitrust Division, attorneys had been using economic evidence to bolster legal arguments for some time. However, the changes in the policy debates and court doctrines suggested that this use of economics was no longer sufficient. A series of agency officials sought to provide economics with a more meaningful role in agency affairs to enhance both the economic argumentation underlying the case filings and the allocation of agency resources. From the mid-1960s on, efforts were made to improve the division's economics staff and provide economists with an organizational presence in policy planning and case selection. Policy increasingly reflected the dictates of economic structuralism. Cases were being evaluated, in part, on the basis of their economic merits. Attempts were made to define agency priorities based on the predictions of the SCP framework. By the end of the 1970s, the agency had been professionalized; economists had come to exercise an influence over policy equal to that of the attorneys.

A similar set of events took place at the Federal Trade Commission, albeit under different circumstances. In the late 1960s, a number of agency critics argued that the FTC was without direction and was failing to fulfill its mission in antitrust and consumer protection. It was found lacking in the capacity to establish priorities and select cases according to some objective measure of impact. The agency was wasting resources on trivial cases and fruitless investigations. While the critiques were reminiscent of past agency evaluations, the response was so resounding that the very existence of the FTC was threatened. Consumer groups joined with a congressional-executive coalition to force a major reorganization and reorientation. There was a consensus that professionalization and a greater emphasis on economics in policy planning, case selection, and development could solve the commission's long-standing problems. Structural decision rules were regularly relied upon in setting priorities and defining the caseload.

As the policy process became dependent on economic expertise, shifts in the body of economic knowledge were sufficient to force the redefinition of policy. Chicago school doctrines were substituted for the structuralist theories at the staff level, with a notable impact on the composition of the caseload. The shift toward Chicago had a practical effect on policymakers. Unlike the SCP framework, the Chicago school fails to provide simple decision rules other than the insight that business arrangements are anticompetitive if and only if they result in a decline in output and an increase in prices. The causal chain linking market structure with anticompetitive behavior and suboptimal performance provided structuralists with clear guidelines for the interpretation of industrial structure. Market concentration and the existence of substantial barriers to entry carried with them the presumption of illegality. Once this causal chain was broken, the presumption of illegality was replaced with a presumption of legality—or more to the point, a presumption of efficiency. Rather than assuming on the basis of structural measures that a particular form of activity would undermine competition, it was necessary to recognize and address a host of complex efficiency considerations. Thus, the shift in the economic consensus created a demand for more detailed economic analysis and a greater reliance on economists within the policy process.

The ascendence of the Chicago school also shaped the prevailing understanding of policy by virtue of its faith in the self-sufficiency of markets and its distinct antistatism. As noted earlier, the fundamental assumption underlying this position is that the most efficient level of activity is the market. Managers tend to act rationally, seeking out new and greater efficiencies as a means of maximizing profits. As a movement away from market interaction, state activism necessarily entails added inefficiency. The differences between state actors and market actors are quite striking. Public officials are difficult to monitor and direct toward specific goals; they are unaccountable and subject to the pressures of special interests. In contrast, business managers are rationally engaged in the pursuit of profits, at all times subject to the discipline of the market. If the goal of antitrust is to promote the realization of efficiencies and to maximize consumer welfare, the role of the state must be minimized.[51]

Beyond the question of sound economic policy, the Chicago school eschewed the populism of the SCP framework. For most Chicagoans, the use of antitrust to realize grand political, social, and even macroeconomic objectives was nothing short of perverse. In a biting critique of structuralist enforcement, Yale Brozen remarked: "We are no longer subject to the kind of superstitions that led the early colonists to hang witches. . . . Instead, in this enlightened age, when we seek to rid ourselves of inflation and other mysterious ailments, we pillory dominant firms or the Big Fours in concentrated, and not so concentrated, industries."[52] The central goal of policy must be the promotion of business efficiency. Given the unquestioned assumptions of the Chicago school, efficiency will be the natural and necessary product of unfettered economic interaction. Public policies manipulating business behavior and organization will be required only on the rarest of occasions. Policymakers must acknowledge the capacity of business and markets to answer questions of structure and conduct; deregulation and disengagement should be among their central goals.

Once Chicago school models were adopted, the political, economic, and social goals traditionally associated with antitrust came into question within the policy debates. Some argued that business efficiency was the only legitimate policy goal—that a concern with the efficiency question was at the heart of the original policy debates. Even if other goals could be identified, they were better realized through other means. The same policy could not be used to maintain a diffusion of economic power and promote efficiency—the goals were clearly in conflict. As the core of economic, political, and social goals disintegrated, the consensus which for so long protected antitrust began to fade. Because antitrust had been long defined in economic terms, the purely economic goals of policy assumed a primacy that would have been denied in an earlier period.

Largely because economic criteria had assumed a central role in the policy process, the question of competing policy goals was not as intense as one would otherwise expect. The goals not related to efficiency simply failed to find a concrete expression. The Antitrust Division and the FTC increasingly selected cases that reflected Chicago enforcement priorities: horizontal restraints and price-fixing arrangements were emphasized, other violations were ignored. These changing priorities were not a product of political design or executive-driven policy agendas. They did not emerge as a product of debate over the most appropriate goals of policy. Rather, they were an unintended expression of institutional changes which provided economics with a more central role in the policy process and of subsequent changes in economic doctrine. While the officials at the two agencies called for cases more in keeping with the the SCP framework, their calls went unanswered. The organizations evolved in such a manner as to contain a conservative bias against most forms of state intervention.

The traditional goals of policy have not been abandoned by all members of the antitrust community. Some analysts remain supportive of the populist aspirations of antitrust. However, their arguments increasingly appear to be lacking economic foundations. To justify the noneconomic goals through an appeal to the SCP framework is to argue from a set of models and theoretical premises which have been substantially modified, discredited, or dismissed. Even members of the structuralist vanguard have conceded defeat, seeking to accommodate the tenets of the new orthodoxy while retaining some remnants of the SCP framework.[53] In many ways, concessions have been necessary. Arguing from outside the body of dominant doctrines severely limits the influence of those seeking to affect policy. If the adoption of economic analysis has

The Intellectual Context

made policy vulnerable to changes in the relevant expertise, it has simultaneously created a bias against the noneconomic. For policy recommendations to be recognized as authoritative, they must find technical support in the school of economics which is presented as authoritative. In short, influence is contingent on the acceptance and utilization of doctrines which question the very foundations of policy.

CHAPTER FIVE

The Integration of Law and

Economics at the Antitrust Division:

From Planning to Process

During the decades of the 1960s and 1970s, the evolution of antitrust policy
was driven by the force of ideas. As policy discourse came to embody economic theory, economic theories and analysis found an expression in court
decisions and reform proposals. It is no coincidence that division officials
appealed to economics when attempting to create the capacity to plan policy
and manage agency affairs. The debates in the antitrust community suggested
that economics must provide the cornerstone of policy. The courts were responsive to the shifting conceptions of policy. However, it is difficult to
attribute direct causality to the courts, since judicial decision making and
agency policy-making drew on the same sets of debates. While economic
theory provided the basis for shifts in policy, its impact was contingent on
organizational changes designed to give economists and economic analysis a
key role in the policy process. After a number of false starts, agency officials
provided economic expertise an organizational presence through a professionalization project and related changes in structure and process. While these
innovations stimulated conflicts between the legal and economic staffs, the
attorneys gradually accepted the new role attributed to economic analysis. By
providing a means of identifying violations and assessing the merits of cases,
economics could serve an important managerial and policy-making function.
However, it is questionable whether attorneys and policymakers could have
made any other choice: an antitrust policy that denied the importance of
economic theory would be questioned by the courts and challenged and discredited by the antitrust community.

In this chapter I present a selective history of the Antitrust Division from
1960 to 1980, detailing the series of events that promoted the convergence of

law and economics in the policy process. Moreover, I explore the way in which the interplay of institutions and ideas resulted in the establishment of new values and a new antitrust enforcement agenda. Policy was redefined at the staff level in the terms provided by the Chicago school—a development that was unanticipated and to a large extent undesired by those responsible for initiating the professionalization process and encouraging the appeal to economic analysis in the implementation of antitrust.[1]

Toward Policy Planning and Evaluation: The 1960s

The legal professionalization of the 1950s invested the division with a new prosecutorial zeal. The attorneys brought into the agency through the honor program often sought to gain experience that would propel them into lucrative positions in the private antitrust industry. Without mechanisms for planning policy and managing agency affairs, authority was delegated to the staff. In the end, policy was a reflection of the sum of individual cases generated by the division's internal dynamic. The caseload revealed a strong reliance on price-fixing prosecutions because these cases were the easiest to litigate under existing per se rules. The division once again entered a period of transition in the 1960s. Division officials sought to build the capacity to establish and pursue distinct policy priorities. In essence, the goal was to bring a new rationality to policy and practice. Reflective of the debates in the antitrust community regarding the relationship between law and economics, agency officials looked to economic expertise as a guide to policy planning, case selection, and evaluation. While the initiatives of this decade were only partially successful, they were nonetheless significant. Before examining the events of this period and their influence on public policy, we need to place them in their proper context.

The early years of the 1960s witnessed another expansion of agency authority. A recommendation of the National Committee to Study the Antitrust Law resulted in new investigative powers. The committee recognized that although the division could use the grand jury system to investigate criminal violations, no such power existed for building civil cases. The committee recommended that the division be authorized to issue civil investigative demands, administrative subpoenas that could be used to gain access information and corporate documents. The Antitrust Civil Process Act was passed in 1955, granting this authority to the division. The new powers were not as great as those granted the Federal Trade Commission under its organic act. For example, the Antitrust Division could not use the CIDs to gather information unrelated to an investigation. Nonetheless, it guaranteed access to information which had been lacking. The first CID was issued in 1962. Soon thereafter, the CID became a much-used tool in investigating civil complaints and gathering evidence.[2]

A series of court decisions was of even greater importance in shaping the authority of the division and the understanding of antitrust. As noted in chapter 3, the Celler-Kefauver Act amended section 7 of the Clayton Act in 1950. However, the new jurisdiction over mergers remained relatively undefined. In 1955, the division filed the first of many merger cases under the new section 7. And yet, cases like *United States v. Bethlehem Steel Corp.* (1958) only revealed the obvious: the new law could be used to challenge mergers between dominant firms in oligopolistic markets.[3] In 1962, the Supreme Court handed down its first full-length decision on a case based on the amended section 7. In *Brown Shoe Co. v. United States*, the Court ruled on a merger between Brown Shoe and Kinney.[4] This case was of critical importance for two reasons. First, the merger had both horizontal and vertical dimensions: both firms were involved in production and retail sales. Second, *Brown Shoe* truly tested the limits of Celler-Kefauver by addressing a merger in a relatively unconcentrated market. Combined, the two companies produced only 4.5 percent of the industry output and controlled 8 percent of the retail sales.

The Court resolved the vertical aspect of the case through an examination of trends toward concentration and manufacturer-retailer integration. These trends suggested that the merger would contribute to the lessening of competition in the industry. The horizontal aspect was addressed through an appeal to trends toward concentration and the resulting market share in various geographic submarkets. Based on these factors, the Court decided in favor of the government. While it was clear that the merger could promote consumer welfare through the creation of an integrated operation, this benefit was seen as secondary to the broad implications for industrial concentration. Chief Justice Warren's decision stated: "We cannot fail to recognize Congress' desire to promote competition through the protection of viable, small, locally owned businesses. Congress appreciated that occasional higher costs and prices might result from the maintenance of fragmented industries and markets. It resolved these competing considerations in favor of decentralization. We must give effect to that decision."[5]

The *Brown Shoe* decision expanded the scope of antitrust policy and the division's jurisdiction by acknowledging the authority to bring both horizontal and vertical merger cases under the revised section 7. Moreover, it revealed that the section 7 prohibition was not strictly limited to oligopolistic industries but could be used even in relatively unconcentrated industries as long as there were trends toward concentration. The expansion of government authority in bringing merger cases when combined with the Court's support for such cases subsequently prompted Justice Stewart to remark, "The sole consistency that I can find is that under section 7 the Government always wins."[6]

Economic theory had long been central to merger analysis. Its importance was enhanced as courts embraced economic structural decision rules to resolve complex questions of industrial organization. For example, in *United States v. Philadelphia National Bank* (1963), the Court relied primarily on concentration figures to determine whether to enjoin a merger.[7] Drawing on "scholarly opinion" to establish appropriate concentration thresholds, the Court suggested that a detailed examination of a merger's effects on the competitive process (the method adopted in *Brown Shoe*) could be bypassed through a reliance on quantitative measures of market power. The decision is worth quoting at length.

> This intense congressional concern with the trend toward concentration warrants dispensing, in certain cases, with elaborate proof of market structure, market behavior, or probable anticompetitive effects. Specifically, we think that a merger which produces a firm controlling an undue percentage share of the relevant market, and results in a significant increase in the concentration of firms in that market, is so inherently likely to lessen competition substantially that it must be enjoined in the absence of evidence clearly showing that the merger is not likely to have such anticompetitive effects. Such a test lightens the burden of proving illegality only with respect to mergers whose size makes them inherently suspect in light of Congress' design in §7 to prevent undue concentration. Furthermore, the test is fully consonant with economic theory. That

"competition is likely to be greatest when there are many sellers, none of which has any significant market share," is common ground among most economists, and was undoubtedly a premise of congressional reasoning about the antimerger statute.[8]

In essence, market-share data could be used as the primary factor when determining whether or not a merger would substantially lessen competition. Moreover, this decision revealed the importance of maintaining a deconcentrated industrial structure.

In a decision handed down the next year, the Court expressed once again its concern with concentration and its willingness to rely on simple arithmetic representations of market power as a basis for judicial decision making. In *United States v. Aluminum Co. of America* (1964), the division challenged a merger strictly on the basis of market-share data and overall market concentration. ALCOA possessed 27.8 percent of the combined aluminum and copper cable market; the acquisition was a small but highly innovative independent with 1.3 percent of the market. Because the market was characterized by its oligopolistic structure, the Court decided to protect the small aluminum company and find against the merger. The majority decision, handed down by Justice Douglas, was based, in part, on the importance of maintaining a deconcentrated industrial structure. Quoting *Philadelphia Bank*, the decision stated, "If concentration is already great, the importance of preventing even slight increases in concentration and so preserving the possibility of eventual deconcentration is correspondingly great."[9] Significantly, Justice Stewart's dissent was based on the problem of determining the competitive ramifications of a merger involving firms in what could be considered distinct industries (e.g., copper and aluminum).

The expanded investigative and prosecutorial powers of the division compelled agency officials to recognize the need for organizational reforms. It was necessary to find a means of promoting the greater consistency and coherence of policy. The general intellectual climate was supportive of this effort. The debates in the antitrust community and the courts' increasing reliance on economic decision rules combined to suggest that a credible antitrust policy had to be built upon a foundation of economic theory. This conclusion had a distinct and well-understood implication for institutional change. Economics, if given a greater presence in the policy process, could rationalize policy and enhance the probability of winning cases in court. The task of reorienting the agency was not, however, a simple one. As division officials searched for a means of applying economic theory to enforcement activities, they were both empowered and constrained by a host of organizational and political factors. Clearly, organizational subunits could be expanded and rearranged; new sections could be created to supplement or replace those already in existence. However, the opportunities for change were not unlimited. The discretionary arena of division officials was defined by the agency's own historical legacy, the limitations imposed by the prosecutorial dynamic that had long characterized what was essentially a litigating agency. Attempts to reconstitute the division and its internal processes would be thwarted both by the resistance of the staff and the agency's limited economic-analytic capacities.

Institutional Innovations: Building on the Past

Lee Loevinger's tenure as assistant attorney general (1961–63) was unremarkable in terms of both the division's evolution and the nature of the cases filed. Loevinger's division filed a large number of cases. As in the past, they were primarily minor price-fixing violations. Loevinger's behavior was in many ways structured by the striking successes of the electric-utilities cases filed under the previous administration. These filings were a point of reference during congressional oversight. Although a handful of major cases were contemplated, they were never filed. Consistent with past administrations, questions of planning and evaluation were rarely raised and never addressed. While there was little case review within the Antitrust Division, an evaluation process was imposed from above. Division activities were closely monitored for fear that they would negatively affect the Kennedy administration's troubled relationship with the business community. The attorney general instituted an ad hoc review process in which three Justice Department officials (the solicitor general, the head of the Civil Rights Division, and the deputy attorney general) evaluated the division's cases prior to filing. Although division filings had required the final approval of the attorney general since the early 1940s, approval was usually automatic and entailed little if any evaluation. The review process imposed by Attorney General Kennedy was a striking departure from the intradepartmental management of the past. The general dissatisfaction with Loevinger resulted in his rather sudden removal from the

The Antitrust Division

division in 1963, when he was appointed to the Federal Communications Commission.[10]

In 1963, William Orrick assumed the position of assistant attorney general. He lacked the specialized competence in antitrust shared by his immediate predecessors, resulting in a certain naïveté that was best exhibited by his surprise when he discovered a lack of enforcement priorities and standards. Orrick later recalled: "When I first came to office, I had hoped I would find some place a little booklet entitled 'Policies of Enforcement–Antitrust Division.' And I was so certain it was there that I ordered a thorough search of all the Department's files, but I came up with no such booklet."[11] Of course, no standardized criteria existed to assist in planning, case selection, and evaluation. The lack of criteria had distinct results: a majority of cases addressed minor restraints that were of little economic consequence. Large structural cases would be more difficult and resource intensive because of both their complexity and the Court's adherence to the rule of reason. However, they held the promise of being of greater economic significance.

In response, Orrick created a team to investigate the dozen most concentrated industries in the United States and to gather the data necessary for setting division priorities and generating monopolization and divestiture suits in sectors of the economy where they would have the greatest impact. Planning would be meaningless unless some organizational mechanism existed for promoting a correspondence between enforcement priorities and the caseload. In recognition of this fact, new policy-planning and evaluation sections were created and linked through a new review process. Its functions were enumerated in the following manner: "The Group has been given responsibility for formulating proposed general statements of this Administration's antitrust policy, for assessing the Division's enforcement activities, for making special studies on questions which arise from time to time involving basic policy considerations, and for proposing recommendations to the Assistant Attorney General regarding means by which to achieve an effective and well balanced enforcement program. . . . It will play a significant role . . . in developing a program which will have the broadest possible economic significance and will most efficiently utilize the limited resources of the Division."[12]

The Policy Planning Group consisted of a director of policy planning and the directors of a number of sections including the Economics Section, the Legislative Section, and the Evaluation Section. A subunit of the section was responsible for evaluating new and existing cases on the basis of their technical merits, resource requirements, and overall correspondence with division policy. Unfortunately, a lack of resources and severe understaffing necessarily limited its impact on the division's enforcement activities. Nevertheless, the Policy Planning Group was an important if symbolic event in the history of the division in that it established a role for economic analysis in defining policy, thus providing an institutional foundation for future innovations.

Economic Evaluation and Advice:
A Revolution from Above?

Substantial changes in policy and practice were imminent when Donald Turner was appointed assistant attorney general for antitrust in 1965. Turner was perhaps the most qualified individual ever to assume the position. He was a law professor with an economics Ph.D. and was a coauthor of one of the decade's most influential volumes on antitrust law and economics.[13] This work was a pure application of economic structuralism. It urged the use of economic analysis in antitrust. The volume argued for an antitrust policy designed to lower concentration levels in the economy. Most striking, the volume suggested the benefits of using antitrust to force the dissolution of monopolies and oligopolies on an economywide basis. Dominant firms in highly concentrated industries could be broken up unless the level of concentration reflected efficiencies or other objective factors. The new antitrust program would be enforced by an independent commission, while cases would be adjudicated by a special economic court. The deconcentration program would be facilitated by a streamlined process and limited judicial review. While Turner subsequently revised his position on deconcentration, this volume and a series of articles made Turner the most frequently cited authority in the decade's antitrust debates.[14]

Turner brought a new sense of mission to the Antitrust Division. He argued that "it is the duty of the Department of Justice not to bring a case simply on the basis that it thinks it *can* win, but to bring only those cases that it thinks it *should* win."[15] Turner's conviction reflected his legal and economic training and the structuralist policy consensus to which he had contributed. He believed that the division had to appeal to economic analysis to establish goals and to manage the caseload. To this end, he created a rather complex policy review and planning process that built upon the foundations of the old Policy Planning Group and review process. The Policy Planning and Evaluation Section was upgraded and staffed with twenty attorneys. It was charged with the duty of reviewing CIDs, complaints, and briefs to maintain quality and promote consistency with predefined policy goals. The process, however, was both repetitious and time consuming, often demanding up to one year to run its course. The initial goal was to review all matters. In practice, the process concentrated on the more important civil cases, which addressed major economic problems or dealt with complex issues or facts.

The revitalized Policy Planning and Evaluation Section was established to promote a greater consistency and standardization of agency activities. Its ultimate impact, however, was limited by the division's organizational legacy. The division had long functioned as a litigating agency. Its organizational culture was defined by the professional orientations of the legal staff. The economists were relatively isolated as members of a technical support staff. Moreover, their number was small, their qualifications limited. The description of the section provided by an economist in Turner's division is quite suggestive. "There may have been twenty people who called themselves economists, but they were mostly folks with B.A.'s in economics who had learned a lot in one form or another about specific industries. Ninety percent of them were incapable of anything resembling sophisticated analysis. They were experts in particular industries, but only in a descriptive sense. They knew the facts and where to get the data. But if you asked them how to evaluate markets, most of these folks would have thrown up their hands. They simply were not analysts."

The section's lack of economic expertise and the institutionalized exclusion of economists from the policy process forced Turner to bypass it altogether in the planning and review process. He relied instead on the advice of a small group of special economic assistants and his own economic knowledge when reviewing existing and proposed cases. When economic theory was offered as a guide to case selection, it was imposed from above. Because economic analysis had a new and limited presence in the policy process, agency officials could only request that attorneys attempt to find violations with certain characteristics—cases that addressed economic theories that were foreign to the lawyers. In response, attorneys often selected cases in hope that they would fulfill the little-understood requests of the front office.

For obvious reasons, these initiatives were often unsuccessful. The assistant attorney general's role in determining the composition of the caseload was limited by his position in the policy process. While Turner and his economic assistants possessed the authority to reject, modify, or approve case recommendations, this power could not extend to the universe of potential cases. Many violations—some of which may have been appropriate test cases based in economic theory—were simply excluded from consideration during the early stages of the case-selection process by staff attorneys applying legal reasoning and decision rules, or economic theories that seemed, at best, nebulous. As had been the case throughout the division's history, cases were generated by the legal staff, often in response to industry complaints. The lawyers' training and career incentives created a bias favoring cases that could be won, regardless of their impact on the economy or their correspondence with division objectives. Potential cases were pursued when there was sufficient evidence and supportive court doctrines. There was little incentive to bring cases on the basis of unfamiliar and little-understood economic principles, especially if they had not been explicitly recognized by the courts. Requests that cases be brought to further goals of economic policy went largely unmet.[16]

A related problem could be tied to the conflict between the evaluation process and the division's dynamic. The prosecutorial zeal and career goals of the Antitrust Division's litigators were difficult to reconcile with the lengthy review process. The delays in the enforcement process had a negative effect on morale. The protracted review resulted in a decline in the number of cases filed. Many attorneys had some negative experiences with the planning and evaluation system. In the words of one division attorney: "Most of us had experience with cases that went in but never came out. At times it was frustrating; at times, downright mysterious."

The goal of promoting an economically based antitrust also found official expression in merger guidelines that the Department of Justice released in 1968.[17] In 1965, Attorney General Katzenbach announced that the division was formulating merger guidelines, to be released the next year. The guidelines were to serve a dual purpose as a statement of enforcement criteria for administrators and a clarification of merger policy for members of the business community. While the guidelines undoubtedly served the second purpose, they were a significant innovation because of the first. In the process of preparing the guidelines, agency officials—many of whom were actively involved in the planning and evaluation process—were forced to define policy in specific terms. The difficulties associated with this task may explain the fact that they were delivered two years after the announced date of release. Once completed, however, the guidelines provided the division with standard—if ultimately imprecise—criteria which could be used in selecting, developing, and evaluating merger cases. Given the historical lack of standardized criteria, this was an event of central importance.

For present purposes, the significance of the guidelines exists less in the policy they presented than in the manner in which it was articulated. Reflecting Turner's goal of promoting the synthesis of antitrust and contemporary economic thought, merger policy was defined in the conceptual framework provided by the dominant economic expertise. As clearly stated in the guidelines: "The primary role of Section 7 enforcement is to preserve and promote market structure conducive to competition. Market structure is the focus of the Department's merger policy chiefly because the conduct of the individual firms in a market tend to be controlled by the structure of that market. . . . Thus, for example, a concentrated market structure where a few firms account for a large share of the sales, tends to discourage vigorous price competition by the firms in the market and to encourage other kinds of conduct."[18]

The merger guidelines were a pure expression of the structure-conduct-performance framework, the dominant analytical reference point in industrial organization economics at the time. As noted in chapter 4, this framework posits a direct causal relationship between the structure of a market and the conduct of the firms within the market. The greater the level of concentration (i.e., the greater the market shares of the largest firms), the greater the capacity of the dominant firms to create and monitor cartel-like relationships and engage in a host of exclusionary practices. This is particularly the case when concentration is combined with barriers to entry. The policy implications of the structuralist framework were clear: the state must not defer to business over questions of organization and market structure. Policy must be designed to maintain relatively low levels of concentration and low barriers to entry.

The guidelines established concentration thresholds which were to be used in determining the legality of a horizontal merger. In highly concentrated markets with a CR4 of 75 (i.e., the top four firms control 75 percent of the market), most significant mergers would be enjoined. The division provided maximum allowable mergers in terms of market share. In such markets, a firm with 15 percent of the market would not be able to acquire a firm unless its share of the market was 1 percent or less; firms with a market share of 10 percent would be questioned if they sought to acquire a firm with more than 2 percent of the market. A set of somewhat more permissive examples was provided for markets where the CR4 was less than 75. Even if the concentration threshold was not exceeded, mergers might still be questioned if there were significant trends toward concentration. Such a trend would be acknowledged whenever the market share of the eight largest firms increased by 7 percent or more within the past decade. In a market with trends toward concentration, any merger between one of the top eight firms and a firm with a 2 percent market share would be challenged.

Based on the predictions of the structure-conduct-performance framework, the guidelines argued that integration into concentrated and semiconcentrated markets could promote conduct that would limit future competition. Accordingly, the department would generally challenge vertical mergers that might raise barriers to entry or disadvantage existing nonintegrated or partly integrated firms in either market. The guidelines identified a number of problems that could be associated with vertical mergers. First, the integrated firm could limit access to potential suppliers and markets, thus seriously constraining the capacity of other firms to operate at an efficient level. Second, excessive levels of integration could force potential competitors to enter at multiple stages (e.g., as a producer and a distributor), thus increasing the capital barriers to entry. Once again, the guidelines established market-share criteria for enforcement. In each case, the department reserved the option of challenging vertical mergers, even if they did not violate the market-share criteria. In particular, mergers would be challenged if there was a significant trend toward vertical integration by merger that would probably raise barriers to entry or impose disadvantages on unintegrated or partly integrated firms.[19]

Conglomerate mergers were a concern of many policymakers in the late 1960s because of their predominance in the growing merger wave. The guidelines helped to clarify division policy in the relatively untested area of conglomerate mergers. They stated that "the purpose of . . . enforcement activity regarding conglomerate mergers is to prevent changes in market structure that appear likely over the course of time to cause a substantial lessening of competition . . . or to create a tendency toward monopoly." The guidelines expressed a concern with growing aggregate concentration of the American economy and the potential for the transference of monopoly power across sectors. Reflecting structural concerns, the guidelines stated that an acquiring firm would come under scrutiny if it possessed a substantial market share and could be considered a potential entrant (i.e., a firm which possessed the ability to enter on "a competitively significant scale" and had the economic incentive to do so). In addition, the guidelines warned that the division would likely intervene if the merger would facilitate the creation of tying arrangements or allow the acquiring firm to transfer monopoly power from one market to another. The rather tenuous discussion of conglomerate mergers reflected the difficulties of constructing strict criteria for enforcement in this area, given the limitations of scholarship and relevant court doctrine.[20]

The guidelines did not make an efficiency or economies defense available for firms merging above the established concentration thresholds, although firms might profit from operating at larger scales. The rationale behind this decision was clearly presented by Turner as being applicable to other areas of antitrust. "There is no reason whatsoever to suppose that vigorous antitrust policy, either in the anti-merger area or even in some other areas, would pose any threat whatsoever to economic efficiency. We have a great many companies that are far larger than economies of scale would dictate. We have a great many companies which have probably got in the range where they have dis-economies of scale, particularly in management."[21] The department's explicit rejection of the efficiencies defense rested on the belief that mergers provided a less-than-optimal means of realizing economies of scale. They necessarily resulted in the elimination of one or more competitor. The department's position was simple. "Where substantial economies are potentially available to a firm, they can normally be realized through internal expansion."[22]

Although the release of the guidelines marked a genuine departure in division policy, it did not constitute a major redefinition of antitrust. Rather, the guidelines presented an economic translation of enforcement criteria that had evolved over the course of the decade in a number of important court decisions. They were, in this respect, a codification rather than an innovation. The real significance of the guidelines was to be found in their standardization of enforcement criteria and the status they accorded economic thought. However, it was precisely these aspects of the guidelines that limited their impact. Some of the staff believed that the release of the guidelines allowed corporations to evade prosecution for section 7 violations. Given their political origins as a means of strengthening the Johnson administration's relationship with business, these suspicions may have had some basis. But of greater relative concern to the staff were the constraints they placed on the activities of the division attorneys. Because the guidelines required that cases be selected—or at least justified—in accordance with specific economic criteria, they engendered resistance. By stating the enforcement standards in economic terms, they forced a marginally greater reliance on the economic staff and stood at odds with the division's well-established legal culture.[23]

With the election of Richard Nixon, Richard McLaren was appointed assistant attorney general for antitrust. Unlike Donald Turner, McLaren was a practitioner rather than a scholar. He did not actively promote an economic interpretation of antitrust, nor did he seek to bring about substantial changes in agency structure and process to promote the further integration of law and economics. Under his direction, the division became much more accommodating to the traditional concerns of the legal staff; emphasis returned to questions of evidence and precedent. Nevertheless, McLaren made some noble attempts to test the limits of section 7 in the area of conglomerate mergers.[24] Ultimately, his persistent support for a large conglomerate merger case cost him his job, through the direct intervention of President Nixon.[25] While the guidelines and extensive review process established by Donald Turner remained in place, their presence in the policy process was deemphasized as attention returned to law enforcement.

The Enforcement Record of the 1960s

The decade of the 1960s was a period of substantial change in the organization of the Antitrust Division. My goal here is to assess the impact of the changes on policy and performance. The attempts to create a policy planning and evaluation capacity were unprecedented in the agency's history. From the 1930s on, a series of division officials acknowledged that economic analysis could play a role in antitrust enforcement. Since the 1940s, division economists commonly contributed to the efforts of the legal staff, both in case selection and development. Yet they were restricted to a support function. Economic analysis was commonly grafted on to legal arguments. In the 1960s, the status of economics in the policy process was dramatically enhanced. Economic analysis was given an explicit—if limited—role in the formulation and pursuit of the division's policy goals.

Division officials explicitly sought to create a capacity for defining enforcement priorities and promoting a correspondence between these priorities and the caseload. Assistant Attorneys General Orrick and Turner expressed the specific goal of redirecting the agency away from the minor price-fixing violations that had dominated the caseload throughout its history. Contemporary economics suggested that the division could have a greater economic impact if it focused on the problems associated with or contributing to industrial concentration. An examination of the caseload over the span of the decade reveals that this objective was partially realized. In 1962, the year before Orrick established the policy planning and evaluation system, 66.7 percent of the cases filed addressed price-fixing violations. After 1963, this category of violations declined as a proportion of the caseload, often falling well below 50 percent. While the trend in price-fixing cases suggests that the division realized some success in altering the composition of the caseload, the fluctuation in the caseload provides evidence that the priorities were not clearly established or consistently imposed. A comparison of caseload composition is presented in figure 5-1. Although the annual number of cases filed had been increasing throughout the latter half of the 1950s and the early 1960s, the number began to decline and then remained fairly stable once the policy planning and evaluation system was engaged.

Figures from the same period provide the basis for interpretation of this trend. Over the decade of the 1960s, the number of investigations conducted on an annual basis more than doubled, going from 253 in 1960 to 555 in 1969. During the same period the number of cases filed remained relatively stable. As a result, the number of investigations per case filed went from 3.12 in 1960 to 10.05 in 1964, fluctuating between roughly 7 and 11 investigations per case filed for the remainder of the decade. These trends are presented in table 5-1.

There are a number of possible explanations for the trend in these figures. First, they may reflect the point at which the new enforcement priorities and economic criteria were introduced into the policy process. The policy planning and evaluation process was superimposed upon a policy process that had existed for decades. Cases were evaluated at a final stage in the policy process.

Figure 5-1

Antitrust Division Case Filings, 1960–1970

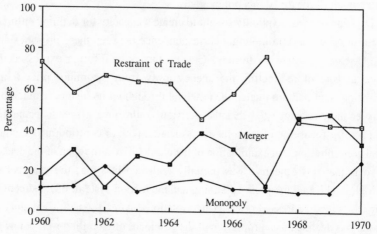

Source: Caseload data collected from appropriations hearings and Department of Justice, *Annual Report of the Attorney General*, various years.

Table 5-1

Antitrust Division Case Filings and Investigations, 1960–1969

Year	Investigations (I)	Cases Filed (C)	I/C
1960	253	81	3.12
1961	249	50	4.98
1962	336	87	3.86
1963	376	52	7.23
1964	432	43	10.05
1965	486	44	11.05
1966	449	45	9.98
1967	444	55	8.07
1968	446	43	10.37
1969	555	54	10.28

Source: Figures compiled from appropriations hearings and Department of Justice, *Annual Report of the Attorney General*, various years.

Activities at the staff level were largely unaffected; the dynamic which had come to characterize the agency continued. Second, the figures may simply reflect the inefficiency of the evaluation process, the scholarly approach adopted by the economic assistants, and the limited staff of the evaluation section. The evaluation system was a bottleneck in the policy process that could not accommodate the number of case recommendations generated by the staff. Of course, these explanations are not mutually exclusive. Third, because the legal staff was unacquainted with economic theory, it was difficult to direct their activities toward specific ends. As one division veteran noted: "The front office would tell the attorneys to look for a certain kind of case. Since most of them didn't know anything about economics, it was more-or-less trial and error. Through observation, some of them began to figure out what Turner was looking for. Most of them didn't." The economic theories upon which cases were to be based were relatively foreign to the division attorneys, thus stimulating resistance and creating the basis for an uninformed selection of potential cases. Economics could not provide a basis for division activities if it was simply imposed upon the prosecutorial dynamic. It had to be integrated into the policy process. This was a lesson of the 1960s that would be applied in the early years of the next decade.

Integrating Economics at the
Process Level: The 1970s

The 1970s are often remembered as the decade of the big cases. While the cases against IBM and AT&T were filed in the final years of the 1960s, they claimed a large share of division resources and were the source of much publicity, both good and bad, throughout the 1970s. The apparent populism of Carter's appointees and the fanfare surrounding the cases against two of the nation's largest corporations drew attention back to an earlier and largely mythical era when the government headed crusades against the great trusts. Behind this facade, significant changes were taking place in the division at the organizational level. In the end, the organizational changes, rather than any of the big cases, would be critical to the definition of antitrust policy well into the next decade.

In 1972, Thomas Kauper was placed in charge of the Antitrust Division. He was a law professor who shared Turner's belief that sound antitrust policy had to find a basis in economics. This position was explicitly stated in a 1969 essay where he urged, "Continued reliance on the knowledge of economists is essential to the antitrust practitioner, and lawyers who continually assert that they cannot understand economics or economists must go back and learn."[26] Unlike Turner, however, Kauper was not an economic structuralist. While sympathetic to some of the predictions of the SCP framework, he was more correctly associated with the Chicago school. Of course, it was precisely in these years that economics as a discipline and the antitrust community were actively scrutinizing the tenets of the structuralist orthodoxy, identifying its weaknesses and the implications for policy. The theoretical linkages between structure, conduct, and performance were disintegrating, in part as a product of the Chicago school critique of the concentration-profitability relationship discussed in chapter 4.

Kauper, as many before him, was troubled by the limited presence of economic knowledge in the division and policy process. As he would later recall: "In substantive terms, the Division needed help in economic terms. It lagged in knowledge of contemporary developments in economic thinking and was still relying on assumptions concerning economic behavior that were already under severe attack."[27] The division's failure to adopt contemporary economic theory was part of a much larger problem regarding the organizational status of economic expertise in the agency. In earlier years, economic analysis had been imposed from above through the planning and evaluation mechanisms. However, it had not been integrated into the policy process and thus exerted a limited influence. Kauper's assessment was straightforward. "A greater capacity for economic analysis was needed both in terms of the development of specific cases, where the courts themselves were beginning to force the issue, and in the development of an overall program that made economic sense. Whether put in terms of the development of doctrine, or simply the proper allocation of Division resources . . . the Division at least needed to know the economic costs of its conduct, a need which was critically important even if non-economic values continued to receive some recognition in the formulation of rules."[28]

Kauper searched for a means of increasing the presence of economic analysis at all stages of the policy process. He notes that he purposefully steered away from the models presented by the division's special economic assistants and the Federal Trade Commission's Bureau of Economics. The special economic assistants first employed by Turner tended to be assigned to cases in an ad hoc fashion, and only after substantial resources had been devoted to investigations. They served what was essentially an advisory function. The economic assistants were generally quite well qualified, but there was little continuity of analysis because they concentrated on a relatively small number of cases and tended to be drawn from university settings for a limited term of service in the division. These factors placed limits on the extent to which an expansion of this model could resolve the division's problems of planning, evaluation, and management. The FTC's Bureau of Economics provided an equally unacceptable model. Because it was a separate entity in the agency, direct interaction with the litigating bureaus was limited. The Bureau of Economics conducted numerous ongoing investigations and market studies, many of which had important potential implications for policy. Its analyses and enforcement recommendations had little impact on the agency, however, because of the almost insurmountable institutional barriers presented by the commission's structure. Because Kauper sought the integration of economic expertise, not its organizational isolation, this model could not be emulated.

The needs of the division and a recognition of the above-mentioned constraints led Kauper and his economic assistant George Hay to create the Economic Policy Office (EPO). The central goal underlying the creation of the EPO was to form an economic staff that was large enough and of high enough quality that an economist could be assigned to every case at an early stage. Rather than merely providing the attorneys with technical assistance, economists would work as independent analysts. The difference between these two roles was quite significant. As members of a support staff, economists offered economic analysis, only to have it supplement noneconomic evidence when building a case. Legal reasoning and simple structural decision rules that were easily employed by attorneys continued to shape the decision to prosecute. As independent analysts, economists would assume a much different position in relationship to the lawyers. They could engage in ongoing detailed analysis, thus affecting change at the process level and having a significant impact on case selection.

The division's legalistic culture was strong, a defining force in the determination of policy, as had been the case throughout the history of an agency that was primarily devoted to litigation. The legal staff would ultimately determine whether any organizational innovation would succeed. Kauper needed to maintain the support of the agency attorneys; their resistance could undermine the experiment. As George Hay notes, this dimension of the division helped shape the way in which economic analysis was introduced. "As a way of avoiding revolution among the lawyers, the process was quite deliberately structured so that the EPO would not be seen as having any formal role. . . . The whole idea was to convince the lawyers that it was in their interest to have us work with them, not to shoot down their cases."[29]

With the organizational realities in mind, Kauper and Hay sought to enhance the influence of the EPO economists in subtle but meaningful ways. Their strategy had several components.[30] First, the Economic Policy Office would have to promote analytic consistency; internal conflicts would erode the cohesion of the economic staff and limit the EPO's influence in the division. Second, since many of the attorneys were either unfamiliar with or hostile to economic analysis, the EPO would succeed only if the legal staff could be made more accepting of and competent in economic analysis. In accordance with the original design and the realities of the division, the EPO's only power was that of persuasion. Since attorneys were to remain the primary actors in the case-selection process, the economists would have an impact on policy only to the extent that the attorneys were convinced that economic analysis could serve a positive function. The economists could not restrict their efforts to the prevention of cases lacking in economic merits; they had to assist in the identification of sectors of the economy where significant violations would be prevalent. Moreover, they had to assure the attorneys that attention paid to economic criteria would enhance the chances of subsequent success both within the agency and in the courts.

Impediments were many, at least in the early days of the EPO. First, it was difficult to attract a sufficient number of high quality economists because the division was not well known for its economic proficiency. As noted earlier, staff economists had little if any graduate training; they typically carried bachelor degrees and had some experience working in a particular sector of the economy. When the EPO was created, it was forced to absorb the old Economics Section, thus continuing the reputational problems. The kinds of economists that were needed at the EPO often wanted to conduct detailed and sophisticated analysis, an activity that had received little appreciation over the division's history. George Hay was able to attract a number of quality economists to the agency because of his connections with the university and the limited career opportunities associated with shrinking academic markets. Nonetheless, staffing remained insufficient for some time; the goal of assigning an economist to each case remained out of reach.

Second, conflicts between the attorneys and economists grew in frequency and intensity, reflecting the normal tensions which accompany professionalization and the different disciplinary orientations of the two staffs. The attorneys sought to identify cases that could be litigated to a successful conclusion within a relatively short period of time. To this end, they often selected cases which rested on firm points of law and were supported by sufficient evidence. The economic staff, on the other hand, did not share the attorneys' career goals, professional orientation, or prosecutorial zeal. They typically discounted cases that lacked economic merits, even if there was proof that the laws had been violated and cases could be won. This is not to say that the economists were objective analysts—division litigators are quick to point out that the economists often promoted their own conservative enforcement agendas, albeit in a subtle fashion. While the attorneys initially saw the economists as conservative case-killers and academics removed from the concrete demands of litigation, this perception faded as experience accumulated.

Third, the goal of providing a consistency of analysis was partially undermined by the lack of consensus within the EPO. During the 1970s, industrial organization was in a period of redefinition. The conflicts between the structuralists and the Chicago school were reproduced in the EPO through the recruitment process. As a result, there was greater variation in analysis than might otherwise had existed. As a consensus developed in the discipline, the theoretical center was reconstructed in Chicago school terms. A similar consensus emerged in the EPO, in part through recruitment, in part through the economists' knowledge of changes within their discipline. While the economics staff could not be described as monolithic, disagreements were relatively insignificant and tended to involve marginal issues. The desired analytic consistency was achieved.

Initially, the Economic Policy Office did not explicitly recommend or reject cases. It did not have a formally defined role in the policy process. Individual economists worked closely with the attorneys, using economic analysis to identify the important aspects of each case. This partnership commonly resulted in jointly authored recommendations. The EPO's role in division activities was enhanced as the legal staff came to understand economic analysis and appreciate the positive functions it could play in the policy process. The EPO's role was often a negative one: during the initial investigation, economists would reveal that a potential case lacked economic merits, even if it could be won before the courts. It was not uncommon, even at this early date, for economists to prevail in such disputes. The negative role, while important, was quickly overshadowed by a more positive function. By the middle of the decade, economic analysis was being used to generate cases by identifying sectors of the economy where various competitive problems were likely to be found. The attorney general was able to report that "the Economic Policy Office . . . undertakes studies to identify possible collusive situations by relying upon objective economic data such as regional price differences rather than specific complaints."[31] For an agency which had long been dependent on industry complaints as the primary source of cases, this new independence was significant in itself. With this new capacity and the degree of autonomy it entailed, the division leadership could actively define priorities and seek out appropriate cases.

By 1978, the Economic Policy Office assumed responsibilities in virtually all aspects of the division's antitrust activities. As stated in the *Annual Report*, "The Economic Policy Office is staffed with professional economists whose skills are used from the preliminary investigative stage through to actual litigation and final judgment enforcement."[32] The duties of the EPO economists went well beyond the daily involvement in investigations and case selection. Since the Appellate, Evaluation, and Judgment Enforcement sections and the Office of Policy Planning did not have their own economic staffs, they relied heavily on the EPO as a source of expertise. By the end of the decade a listing of the EPO's major duties and functions included evaluating the competitive effects of various forms of business organization and activity as part of division investigations; analyzing the competitive effects of proposed mergers; identifying price-fixing, bid-rigging, and other anticompetitive activities which increase the costs of goods procured by the federal government; assisting in the design of antitrust remedies; analyzing the justifications for and competitive impact of proposed consent decree modifications; examining the economic impact of government regulation and designing proposals for regulatory reform that would increase competition; and testifying as expert witnesses before courts and regulatory agencies. The significance of these duties is apparent when one reflects back on the historical role of economists in the agency. In a relatively short period of time the division economists went from serving merely a support function at the discretion of attorneys to fulfilling critical functions in all of the agency's activities and thus constituting a locus of power within the agency.[33]

The growing organizational presence of the EPO in the 1970s was not merely a product of incremental change. Although the strategy of gradualism was highly successful, the EPO's influence in agency affairs was magnified and its evolution was accelerated by a number of factors that were beyond the control of the division leadership. These factors created a greater demand for economic expertise in the Antitrust Division and promoted the continued integration of the legal and economic staffs. In the end, these forces combined to provide economic expertise and organizational presence unanticipated by (but not unwelcome to) those responsible for the creation of the EPO.

As in the past, division affairs were shaped by changes in Court doctrine. Throughout the postwar period, the Supreme Court recognized the multiple goals of antitrust. However, when weighing competing goals—particularly competing economic goals—the Court often limited or denied the relative importance of efficiency considerations. The Court advocated limiting the trends toward economic concentration and deemphasized the potential merits of a host of horizontal and vertical restraints. In part, this was tied to the Court's reliance on the behavioral postulates of economic structuralism. Because large firms in concentrated industries were predisposed to collusionary and exclusionary forms of behavior, the courts could not sanction corporate autonomy when addressing questions of organization and intercorporate relations. Moreover, the Court contended that Congress had explicitly weighed competing economic values and decided that maintaining a deconcentrated industrial structure was to be a central objective of public policy.

While no other conclusion could be derived from the Celler-Kefauver Act of 1950, the debates surrounding the bulk of antitrust legislation revealed little recognition of the potential conflicts between the multiple goals of policy. As a generalization, Robert Bork is correct when he notes, "For years the Court . . . denigrated business efficiency either as irrelevant to antitrust analysis or as a factor weighing on the side of illegality."[34] Indeed, the Court's position was clearly presented in the series of section 7 decisions reviewed above, including *Brown Shoe Co. v. United States* (1962), *United States v. Philadelphia Na-*

tional Bank (1963), and *United States v. Von's Grocery Co.* (1966). In *Von's Grocery*, the dissenting opinion of Justices Stewart and Harlan went as far as to accuse the majority of establishing a rule of per se illegality for mergers in industries with trends toward concentration.[35] This antiefficiency bias was not exclusive to merger decisions: the Court had made clear its position that efficiency considerations could not justify any of a variety of market restraints. Many of these restraints were covered by explicit or implicit per se rules, despite their possible economic benefits. Their capacity to contribute to economic efficiency or reduce transaction costs was rarely considered.

The primacy of economic decision rules in judicial reasoning was a necessary preface to the changes in the 1970s. As industrial organization economics and the antitrust community began to challenge the tenets of economic structuralism, the Court followed suit: it increasingly recognized the importance of detailed economic analysis and efficiency considerations. The shift in the Court's use of economics was obvious in a series of decisions. The Antitrust Division challenged the acquisition of the United Electric Coal Company by General Dynamics in a case originally filed in 1967. The case reached the Supreme Court in *United States v. General Dynamics Corp.* (1974).[36] While primarily involved in the defense industry, General Dynamics had recently expanded into mineral extraction. The division argued that the merger should be enjoined on the basis of General Dynamics' market share and existing concentration levels. The top four firms in the two relevant markets (the eastern interior and Illinois) controlled 63 percent and 75 percent of the output. The acquisition increased General Dynamics' market share from 7.6 percent to 12.4 percent in one market, and from 15.4 percent to 23.2 percent in the other. In framing the decision, the Court admitted that this evidence would have been sufficient for a prima facie case of illegality in an earlier era. However, a more detailed analysis of the industry revealed a number of factors that showed the limited utility of concentration figures. Because trends in consumption of coal demonstrated the prevalence of long-term contracting with electric utilities, the Court found that the best indication of competitiveness was the amount of uncommitted reserves of recoverable coal. Since the acquired firm had limited reserves and had already committed most of its capacity, the merger had no perceptible competitive effect. The division lost its case.

In other cases such as *United States v. Marine Bancorporation* (1974), the

Supreme Court appealed to more detailed economic analyses to expose the limitations of concentration figures that would have been most persuasive during the Warren Court.[37] The government's case rested on the fact that the merger would result in the elimination of a potential entrant in a highly concentrated market. Following its approach in General Dynamics, the Court considered a host of factors that limited the importance of structuralist relationships. A detailed examination of the economic background of the industry and legally established entry barriers forced the Court to discount concentration levels and the potential-entrant argument.[38]

The most explicit and consequential statement of the Court's new position regarding the economics of antitrust and the importance of business efficiency was formulated in the decision of a 1977 case, *Continental T.V. Inc. v. GTE Sylvania Inc.*[39] In this case, the Supreme Court overturned the per se illegality of territorial and customer restraints, established a decade earlier in *United States v. Arnold Schwinn & Co.* (1967).[40] Justice Powell's decision suggested that the Court had revised its interpretation of competition and had become quite sympathetic to the arguments put forth by the Chicago school. "Vertical restrictions promote interbrand competition by allowing the manufacturer to achieve certain efficiencies in the distribution of his product. These 'redeeming virtues' are implicit in every decision sustaining vertical restrictions under the rule of reason."[41] After noting that "economists have identified a number of ways in which manufacturers can use such restrictions to compete more effectively," Powell went on to explore the efficiency-promoting aspects of vertical restraints, citing authorities such as Richard Posner, Robert Bork, and Paul Samuelson. Powell noted that "economists . . . have argued that manufacturers have an economic interest in maintaining as much interbrand competition as is consistent with the efficient distribution of their products."[42] The importance of this case is found not only in its sophisticated approach to economic analysis and the unwillingness to appeal to structural decision rules but in the belief that businesses rationally adopt those arrangements best suited to the realization of greater efficiencies. This case and others provided evidence that the simple structural relationships of the past were no longer sufficient to guide judicial decision making and provided, at best, a tenuous basis for future prosecutions.[43]

One can hardly overstate the significance of *Sylvania*. As the Court adopted a more complete consideration of economic issues and explicitly recognized the importance of efficiency considerations, it became necessary to redefine once again the authority of the state to intervene in questions of organization and intercorporate transactions. Implicit in the Court's position was the belief that the efficiencies best recognized by market actors may be only partially appreciated by antitrust policymakers. In this case, business adopted nonmarket restraints because they were of great economic utility. Although Powell noted that "the view that the manufacturers' interest necessarily corresponds with that of the public is not universally shared," the decision noted that restrictions are "widely used in our free market economy" and are usually efficiency promoting.[44] In the wake of *Sylvania*, division attorneys were compelled to examine in greater detail the economic aspects of their cases. Rather than grafting economic factors onto an existing body of noneconomic evidence or relying on simple structural decision rules, economic analysis would have to be given a primary role in case development. This fact, in turn, required that the attorneys grant greater relative importance to the work of the division's economists.

The relationship between the economic and legal staffs was further redefined as the responsibilities of the division changed. With the passage of the Hart-Scott-Rodino Antitrust Improvements Act of 1976, a premerger screening system was created. Firms anticipating a merger were required to provide the antitrust agencies with information regarding the acquisition before its consummation. Under this system, the Antitrust Division assumed a regulatory posture with respect to mergers. Once the division received information regarding mergers or acquisitions, it could terminate the waiting period if it is believed that the transaction would not have an anticompetitive impact. When a question arose as to the competitive implications, the division could request additional information. If there appeared to be a competitive problem after the new information was received, the division could seek an injunction to stop the merger. However, the division increasingly worked closely with corporations to restructure mergers to minimize competitive problems (the so-called fix-it-first approach).[45] Merger analysis is primarily an economic task combining market studies with detailed analyses of internal economies. The premerger notification program promoted the integration of the legal and economic staffs by forcing their regular interaction in a new context. While premerger filings were cleared by the parallel efforts of the EPO and the appropriate litigation unit, in practice, there was much interplay between the economic and legal staffs in the course of analyzing potential mergers.

The importance of economics in the intellectual and political environment of the 1970s contributed to the EPO's new status within the division and in Washington. Presidents Ford and Carter, important congressional committee leaders, officials from a host of executive departments and independent agencies, and nongovernmental policy specialists were engaged in a debate over the competitive deregulation of the economy. There was a general consensus that many existing regulations created an inflationary bias, placed limits on growth, and affected the distribution of wealth in society. Whereas there were many unresolved questions regarding the form and extent of future regulations, there was bipartisan agreement that competitive regulatory reform was necessary. The economic analyses of regulation were central to the policy debates.[46]

The activities of the Antitrust Division were directly relevant to the deregulation movement in two senses. First, although antitrust can be presented as a form of regulation, it differs from other regulatory policies in that its goal is to maintain markets and competition. Policymakers saw vigorous antitrust enforcement as part of a broader strategy to promote competitive deregulation. Once government-imposed prices and entry barriers were eliminated, antitrust could provide a means of ensuring that they were not replaced by a new set of private restraints. Second, the Antitrust Division had long articulated its concern for the competitive impact of government regulations. During the 1970s, the Antitrust Division was relied on to provide economic analysis of existing regulations and proposed remedies.

The division's systematic intervention in the policies of regulatory agencies dated back to the middle of the 1960s. These activities came to demand a greater proportion of division resources throughout the 1970s. The goals of the division were quite straightforward. The first goal was to eliminate existing regulations where unnecessary. A second and related goal was to limit or prevent the growth of unnecessary new regulations. Third, the division sought "to minimize the competitive distortions caused where regulation is necessary by advocating the least anticompetitive form of regulation consistent with the defined regulatory objective."

In 1976, the importance of competition advocacy was formally recognized with the creation of a Special Regulated Industries Section. The section was charged with the task of representing the division before a number of regulatory agencies, including the Federal Reserve Board, the Federal Home Loan Bank Board, the Federal Deposit Insurance Corporation, the Federal Maritime Commission, the Office of the Comptroller of the Currency, the Department of Energy, the Interstate Commerce Commission, the International Trade Commission, the Nuclear Regulatory Commission, the National Credit Union Administration, the Security and Exchange Commission, the Commodities Futures Trading Commission, the Federal Communications Commission, and the Postal Rate Commission. The Special Regulated Industries Section (in combination with the Energy Section) and the Transportation Section were involved in the analysis of regulation at the federal and state levels. In 1978 alone, the division participated in regulatory agency proceedings on 134 occasions.[47] Because the regulatory filings dealt with complex economic issues, increased activity in this area forced a greater reliance on the division economists. The EPO economists participated in planning and implementing the division's regulatory interventions and in designing proposals for regulatory reform. As the EPO's proposals were circulated and economists appeared before various regulatory bodies, its analytic quality and role in the deregulation movement became well known and contributed to the status of the division as a whole.[48]

The Enforcement Record of the 1970s

In the course of less than a decade, the economic-analytic capacity of the Antitrust Division was considerably enhanced. Through the creation of the Economic Policy Office, the economic staff was expanded and professionalized. More important, economists and economic analysis were introduced into each of the division's internal processes. The organizational realities of the Antitrust Division forced officials to pursue a strategy of gradual change. However, the factors reviewed above accelerated the convergence of law and economics. While conflicts between the economists and attorneys were not completely eliminated, by the end of the decade economists were genuine participants in the policy process. Economic criteria were integrated into case selection and evaluation; they became central in framing investigations and building cases. As a general rule, cases would not be contemplated unless the prosecution could be defended both on legal and economic merits.

Under Turner, economic analysis was imposed from above through the planning and evaluation system. While this method of introducing economics affected the definition of policy, it could not be viewed as a success. This heavy-handed approach was not adopted in the 1970s. As this brief discussion of the Economic Policy Office reveals, economic analysis was introduced at the staff level, where it could have a greater impact on process. The interaction of economists and lawyers in investigating and building potential cases had a natural effect on division policy. As Kauper explains, "Proceeding from models and a generalized perception of economic behavior, the economic analysis employed in specific cases inevitably moved back in the direction of generalization and thus into the formulation of Division policy with respect to a broad range of conduct."[49] As economic analysis was introduced into the organization at the process level, the organization was transformed along with the dynamic which for so long characterized the division and defined policy. Economic criteria were embodied by the organization at each level; the division began to generate cases which reflected the dictates of contemporary economic thought. This development was, however, both a source of strength and, ultimately, a profound vulnerability. The Antitrust Division gained a degree of political autonomy, while losing its capacity to determine which goals would be pursued by the division. The goals and values embedded in the expertise determined which goals would be pursued by the agency.

The assistant attorneys general who headed the division in the 1970s shared the explicit goal of bringing only those cases that had economic merits. Throughout the decade of the 1970s, however, changes in industrial organization economics forced a reassessment of the anticompetitive significance of various types of business activity. As shown in chapter 4, the structure-conduct-performance framework presented a direct relationship between the structure of a given industry and the conduct of its constituent firms. As concentration and barriers to entry increased, so did the ability of corporations to create and monitor collusive arrangements. The structuralists suggested that an effective antitrust policy would focus on structural problems and seek to limit increases in concentration or even promote deconcentration. In the 1970s, the central pillar of the SCP framework was challenged by the Chicago school. Rejecting the strict relationship between structure and conduct, the Chicago school argued that high levels of concentration reflected the objective demands of producing in specific industries, past successes, and the availability of various economies of scale. The positive relationship between concentration and profits reflected these factors rather than the exploited opportunities for collusion. A sound and effective antitrust policy would leave questions of organization and conduct to the market, where they were most efficiently resolved, and focus primarily on horizontal restraints which could have a substantial short-term negative effect on consumer welfare insofar as they result in a restriction of output and an increase in prices.

These debates were not restricted to the scholarly community but found an immediate expression in the antitrust community. By the mid-1970s, the Chicago school had come to play a central role in structuring policy discourse. The emergence of Chicago found an equally apparent expression in Court decisions. As the economics of antitrust changed, so changed the way in which the Court conceptualized policy and agency authority. Because economics had been given a central role in the Antitrust Division's policy process, the shift in economic knowledge had a notable effect on agency priorities and policy. At the same time that economic analysis was becoming a foundation for the decision to prosecute, the forms of corporate organization and conduct regarded economically problematic were changing as well. An examination of the caseload for the 1970s reveals rather dramatic evidence that policy was evolving to conform with Chicago school priorities. Price-fixing cases increasingly dominated the caseload, whereas merger and monopolization cases were deemphasized. An annual comparison for the 1960s and 1970s is presented in figure 5-2.

These priorities were established by the organization; they were not a product of political control. Indeed, they were often at odds with those presented by presidents and pursued by agency officials. President Gerald Ford, for example, endorsed an antitrust policy conceived in structuralist terms. "It seems to me that through [antitrust] we can make certain, in the business world at least, that there will be a proper governmental role in making an environment where free enterprise can operate without a monopolistic development. . . . The strength of our free enterprise system depends on competition. We can't have big business, big labor—or big government, I might add—dominating our economy."[50]

A similar position was adopted by President Carter. John Shenefield, assistant attorney general during the Carter administration, assumed a structuralist position to argue that concentration provided the best single indicator of

Figure 5-2

Antitrust Division Case Filings, 1960–1980

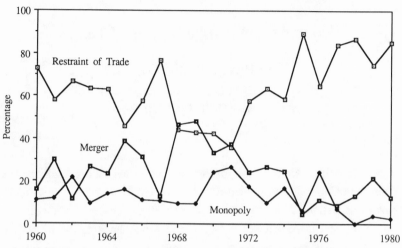

Source: Caseload data collected from appropriations hearings and Department of Justice, *Annual Report of the Attorney General*, various years.

collusion. While promising to continue to address price-fixing violations, he made known his resolve to bring more structuralist initiatives in concentrated industries and merger cases and to test the limits of existing law with cases in the relatively untested areas of shared monopoly and conglomerate acquisitions. While Shenefield held that economic analysis was an important basis for antitrust, he rejected the purely economic interpretation of policy, suggesting that the populist tradition and popular suspicion of large corporations could not be ignored.[51] Despite the structuralist declarations of the Carter appointees, one detects little movement in this direction during the second half of the decade. The reason is clear: once economic models and criteria were given a presence in the division's processes, the organization tended to generate only those cases which had distinct economic merits. Since the economics in question failed to recognize the causal significance of market structure, excluding the highest levels of market concentration, the organization contained a bias in favor of cases involving horizontal restraints. The organization, not the division leadership, came to play the central role in the definition of priorities. In essence, policy became an institutional artifact.[52]

CHAPTER SIX

Economics and Organizational Change:

The Revitalization of the

Federal Trade Commission

The Federal Trade Commission was for decades a stagnant organization. The Court and Congress had limited its authority and punished its activism. Its narrow discretionary arena was compatible with its problems of internal co-ordination and management: both promoted a bias favoring the trivial and inconsequential cases that were easiest to prosecute. During the late 1960s and 1970s, the convergence of multiple factors—a concern over growing inflation, the rise of the consumer movement, and clear evidence of poor agency performance—promoted organizational change and agency revitalization. More-over, there was a common understanding of policy and the potential role of public authority which gave the movement for organizational change a certain coherence.

In this chapter, I present a selective history of the Federal Trade Commission, covering the decade of the 1970s. During this period, many observers believed that the commission was finally gaining the authority and administrative capacities necessary to fulfill its broad mandate. Reflecting the broad acceptance of industrial organization economics and the central role of economics in structuring the antitrust debates, policymakers promoted an expansion of administrative capacities through a professionalization project and a series of organizational changes designed to integrate law and economics within the policy process. However, the decade ended as the earlier history of the commission would have predicted. Members of Congress joined once again to respond to the demands of a business-based interest coalition and limit the authority of the FTC.[1]

Economics in Agency Affairs:
Expertise in Isolation

The organizational problems that plagued the FTC were deep seated. Indeed, agency critiques spanning over four decades displayed great consistency. With few exceptions, they urged the commission to develop mechanisms for long-range policy planning, evaluation, and caseload management and suggested that a major reorganization would facilitate these efforts and improve coordination. Many critics suggested that the commission's economists be provided more central positions with respect to these activities. Economic analysis, it was believed, could provide a technical guide to determining policy priorities and managing resources. By the 1960s, economics was playing a greater role in agency affairs. However, an important distinction must be made by type of violation. In the area of mergers, economists had long exerted some influence over the caseload. In 1955, eleven economists were placed in the Bureau of Investigation to analyze mergers. Even after subsequent reorganizations, a close working relationship continued to exist between the legal and economic staffs in this enforcement area. The Division of Mergers in the Bureau of Restraints of Trade regularly interacted with the Division of Economic Evidence in the Bureau of Economics. Indicative of this relationship, merger analysis claimed up to 90 percent of the resources available to the Division of Economic Evidence in the 1960s. Economists were involved in each stage of the section 7 enforcement process. They often informed the Mergers Division and engaged the process when their analyses identified questionable acquisitions. Economic advice was often solicited before recommending that the commission issue a complaint. Finally, the economists were frequently requested to play a role in designing remedies; they also contributed to the determination of the content of cease-and-desist orders and became involved in negotiating settlements.[2]

The close interaction of economists and attorneys allowed for the formulation of several merger statements describing policy on an industry-by-industry basis. There were statements covering mergers in dairy products, food distribution, the cement industry, tire production, and textiles. In addition, the coordination of legal and economic staffs allowed for some rather innovative merger cases. For example, in *Federal Trade Commission v. Proctor & Gamble Co.* (1967),[3] the commission successfully forced Proctor & Gamble to divest itself of Clorox, a conglomerate acquisition allowing the former to enter the bleach industry. The case was based, in part, on a potential competition argument. Proctor & Gamble was a likely entrant in the bleach industry. The question was whether it would enter the market through merger or expansion. The latter path, it was argued, would make the industry more competitive and was thus more attractive from a public policy position.

There is no evidence that economists played a significant role outside of merger enforcement. Complaints filed under section 5 of the Federal Trade Commission Act and the remainder of the Clayton Act were brought with little input from the Bureau of Economics, although the economists often interpreted financial statistics and provided evidence. Outside of merger enforcement, the Bureau of Economics was primarily involved in conducting investigations and compiling reports that were largely unrelated to existing cases.

The Federal Trade Commission was conceived to bring specialized expertise to bear in the regulation of business. Throughout its history it has contained an active economics staff. And yet, the influence of the economists has been limited. Potentially, economists could contribute to the resolution of long-standing organizational and managerial problems. Why did they continue to occupy such a limited position in agency affairs? In part, the answer was tied to the organization of the commission. One of the central problems that characterized the commission during the half-century following its creation was the lack of internal coordination. No mechanism existed for integrating the efforts of the separate bureaus within the policy process. The rigid organizational divisions created barriers to the coordination of activities, particularly with the Bureau of Economics. Since the creation of the commission, the bureau (or its functional equivalent) remained isolated from the other bureaus.

One must, however, appreciate the subtle interplay of organizational factors and individual incentives. The organizational isolation of the economists reinforced and was reinforced by the divergent professional orientations and career goals of the two staffs. As with the Antitrust Division, the staff attorneys in the FTC were concerned with bringing cases and gaining the experience necessary to strengthen their future career opportunities. The economists, in contrast, were trained to base decisions on strict economic criteria. This orientation often led them to discount matters that might otherwise have a firm legal basis. The potential for conflict led attorneys to protect their monopoly over the authority to recommend enforcement efforts. Because the attorneys viewed the

FTC as a law enforcement agency, the decision to recommend a complaint was understood as a legal decision best left to the discretion of the legal staff. The comments of the chief of the Division of General Trade Restraints at the time of the 1961 reorganization are quite enlightening in this context.

> It would not be feasible nor desirable for economists to participate in the decision to issue a complaint. The Commission is an enforcement agency and is charged with the responsibility of correcting unfair methods of competition and unfair and deceptive acts or practices in commerce. Is the Commission to be guided by an economist and substitute his economic theories as grounds upon which to issue or not issue a complaint or is the Commission to rely on its staff members who are trained in the law and who have advised that a violation of law does or does not exist? The Commission must, under its organic act, prosecute where it has reason to believe the laws it enforces are being violated. Its only discretion in this respect is the limitations of its budget and manpower and the weighing of one violation against another as to the amount of public interest involved.[4]

The decision to recommend a filing remained the responsibility of the Bureau of Restraint of Trade. Commission economists might advise the attorneys as to the economic effects of a particular action or make their concerns known to the commissioners, but—with the exception of merger enforcement—they had no formal role in the case-selection or evaluation processes. In the end, the decision to prosecute was a legal decision made by attorneys.

Finally, the isolation of the commission economists was promoted by the growing status of economic structuralism in judicial decision making. On the surface, this statement appears counterintuitive. As detailed in chapter 5, during the postwar period the courts increasingly adopted economic and structural decision rules. The cases responsible for bringing about a reliance on economic decision rules were initiated by the Department of Justice and decided by the courts—both institutions dominated by attorneys. Attorneys are trained to build on rules when constructing cases. Although the new rules drew on industrial organization economics, they remained rules. A dependency on simple rules—whether legal or economic—reduces the role for detailed analysis. Once embedded in precedent, the rules created an institutional bias against careful analysis of industrial structure. Jesse Markham, former chief economist at the FTC, argued this point in a 1964 essay. "Since FTC cases are finally settled in the courts, it is not surprising that the legal doctrines the courts adopt become powerful determinants of the approach taken by the Commission in discharging its responsibilities. In the recent case work of the Commission legalistic rules appear to have triumphed over the analysis of economists and other professionals whose expertise theoretically has always distinguished the Commission from the courts."[5]

Organizational Impotence and the Pressure for Change

The FTC's miserable performance was long tolerated, even sustained, through its relationship with Congress. The autonomy of staff attorneys when combined with the isolation of economists contributed to the FTC's incapacity to plan and manage its own affairs. By the late 1960s, congressional tolerance faded. Attention turned, as in the past, to problems of policy planning and internal coordination. In 1969, a number of law students working under the direction of Ralph Nader released *The Nader Report on the Federal Trade Commission*. One month later, the *Report of the Task Force on Productivity and Competition* (the Stigler Report) was released. Although not primarily concerned with the FTC, the report was critical of its antitrust activities. President Nixon reacted to the severity of the Nader Report by requesting the American Bar Association to conduct an investigation of its own. The *Report of the ABA Commission to Study the Federal Trade Commission*, compiled by sixteen influential attorneys and economists, identified many of the same problems emphasized by "Nader's Raiders." A few months later, the Budget Bureau released its own critical review of the FTC. The concerns were raised once again with the 1971 release of a Nader report on antitrust enforcement, entitled *The Closed Enterprise System*. When taken together, the substance of the critiques and the resulting recommendations was quite familiar, in many ways a restatement of earlier critiques. However, the response was quite singular: the FTC was reorganized and was given an expanded budget and unprecedented rule-making powers.[6]

The primary problem identified by the ABA and recognized by the other critics was the lack of priorities and planning. Rather than pursuing definite policy objectives, enforcement appeared to be "ad hoc and unordered responses to individual problems as they arise." The caseload was characterized by its incoherence, the agency by its inefficiency. As the report noted, "The failure of the FTC to establish and adhere to a system of priorities has caused a misallocation of funds and personnel to trivial matters rather than to matters of pressing public concern." Despite the magnitude of the merger wave, section 7 merger enforcement claimed a mere 9 percent of the commission budget. More resources were devoted to regulating the labeling of textiles and furs than were used in the area of mergers, although the Bureau of Economics had been quite active in analyzing the merger wave, stressing the importance of merger enforcement, and stimulating debate in Congress over this very issue.[7]

Because the commissioners lacked the capacity to impose priorities, the caseload reflected the aggregate activities of the agency attorneys. As the ABA report noted, "The consequence of a lack of direction from the top has been de facto delegation of a good deal of authority to the staff." This was highly problematic because there were no established and standardized criteria for case selection and evaluation. There were "no institutional devices of agency-wide standards available . . . for comparing the relative merits of allocating FTC resources to proceedings against possible violations of the law handled by different divisions or bureaus." Priorities were not consciously established but emerged in the course of selecting cases according to idiosyncratic decision rules.[8]

The lack of standard criteria was troublesome in and of itself. Its negative impact was magnified by the low quality of the agency's staff. While the federal government as a whole encountered difficulties in hiring and retaining qualified attorneys, it appeared to all that the FTC had made a policy of seeking the least qualified. The ABA report quoted a senior staff member who claimed to hire attorneys "who had been out in the world for ten years or so and had come to appreciate that they were not going to make much of a mark." Perhaps Chairman Dixon had the same thing in mind when he stated: "Given a choice between a really bright man, and one who is merely good, take the good man. He'll stay longer." The discounting of law-school grades and promoting from within the agency contributed to the low quality and morale of the agency's legal staff.[9] The Nader Report attributed the poor quality of the legal staff to the regional biases of Chairman Dixon, a native of Tennessee. A majority of applicants from Kentucky and Tennessee were offered positions, while a majority of applicants from the better eastern and northern law schools were simply denied interviews. Regional biases aside, the Nader Report presented another reason for the poor quality of the staff attorneys: the bureau chiefs "prefer new attorneys who will not underscore their elders' mediocrity or disturb the work patterns of their bureau."[10]

The poor quality of the legal staff and the inadequacy of leadership were exacerbated by the lack of mechanisms for monitoring and evaluating investigations. Once investigations were initiated, the commission simply lost track of them. The ABA report described the problem in quite suggestive terms. "Frequently, investigations or studies disappear into the lower levels of the FTC, and reappear only after many years have elapsed." Long delays and a growing backlog of investigations were inevitable products of this system. At the time of the study, 54 percent of the 644 pending antitrust investigations were over two years old. Some 40 percent of the complaints pending litigation in the Bureau of Restraint of Trade were between two and four years old. This lethargy found an expression in agency performance. Throughout the 1960s, there was a dramatic downward trend in pending enforcement matters in both the antitrust and consumer protection areas. In 1962 and 1963, there were 179 and 142 complaints pending litigation. Within five years the number had dropped to 20.[11]

The reviews of the commission economists commonly noted their limited qualifications: only one-fifth of the economists held Ph.D.'s. Since the leadership was considered to be of the highest quality, the ABA report placed the blame on civil service hiring requirements and urged their suspension. A number of additional options were put forth to ensure the quality of economic analysis in the bureau. These options included economic internships to bring "top-flight economists" into the agency for limited terms of service, outside advisory panels, and programs allowing bureau economists to serve in academic positions on a rotating basis. In addition, the studies recommended an expansion of the bureau, since its growth had fallen well behind that of the litigating bureaus. These recommendations aside, the review of the Bureau of Economics was generally favorable; there was no presumption that the training of the economics staff had a negative effect on the quality of analysis.[12]

The central problem with respect to the Bureau of Economics was its isolation within the agency and policy process. As the *Closed Enterprise*

The Federal Trade Commission

System noted, "Economists—the basis for the FTC's vaunted economic expertise—have a second-class status in the budget and operations." Although the
economists in the Division of Economic Evidence worked with the legal staff
on all cases brought by the commission, there was little interaction outside the
area of merger litigation. The ABA noted that the Merger Division in the
Bureau of Restraint of Trade could be distinguished within the agency by the
quality of its work. As the report noted, the performance was partly attributed
to "the participation of economists from the Bureau of Economics in the
planning process." The ABA report explicitly sought to remedy this situation
by recommending greater coordination of the economic and legal bureaus in
agency affairs. In calling for the expansion and revitalization of the Office of
Program Review, the report suggested that the office be staffed with five to ten
lawyers and economists with appropriate support personnel. The office would
be charged with eliminating the backlog of pending matters and "reporting to
the Commission on ways and means of coordinating future agency operations
. . . tak[ing] advantage of modern budgetary techniques."[13]

Additional recommended reforms were direct extensions of the problems
discussed above. At the level of the organization, the ABA report emphasized
the importance of policy planning and internal management. The FTC's planning system had to be transformed and expanded to allow for the establishment
of priorities and long-term goals. The costs and competitive impact of potential and existing cases and programs would have to be assessed as a guide to
the rational allocation of resources. Once long-term goals were established,
the agency would be able to adopt a more active stance in the identification of
potential cases by creating standardized criteria to guide case selection and
evaluation at the staff level. The ABA report suggested that these duties be
concentrated in a revitalized Office of Program Review. "We suggest that the
Office of Program Review prepare, for each separate category of business
conduct regulated by the FTC, reasonably specific criteria . . . with respect to
opening and closing of investigations, accepting assurances of voluntary compliance, filing complaints, and recommending in favor or against settling
cases once brought as well as the range and scope of acceptable compromises
or remedies."[14]

There was general agreement that Chairman Dixon had to be replaced,
along with the type of leadership he represented. The Nader Report noted

Dixon's "alacrity in filling the Commission with his cronies" and his success in turning the FTC "into a patterned and intricate deceptive practice unto itself." The report concluded by suggesting that "Mr. Dixon's chief and perhaps only contribution to the Commission's improvement would be to resign from the agency that he has so degraded and ossified." The ABA implicitly assessed Dixon's performance in the same way when it called for "the appointment of a Commission Chairman with executive ability, knowledge of the tasks Congress had entrusted to the agency, and sufficient strength and independence to resist pressures from Congress, the Executive Branch, or the business community that tend to cripple effective performance by the FTC." Since the chairman was a presidential appointee and Nixon had only recently assumed office, Dixon's replacement was all but inevitable.[15]

The reports also called for measures to enhance the quality of the agency's legal staff. The Nader Report called for a hiring system that would overcome the institutional bias against qualified law-school graduates. The ABA concurred, identifying professionalization as critical to agency success. "It will be impossible for [the FTC] to implement present programs effectively, let alone institute the programs proposed in this report, unless it attracts new personnel of high quality." As noted above, the report also recommended that the economic staff be expanded and upgraded.[16]

By virtue of its organization, duties, flexible procedures, and unique investigative powers, the FTC has always been presented as an agency with great potential. And yet, each critic has noted that this potential has gone unrealized. As the ABA report noted, "If the measure of the quality of FTC performance in the antitrust area is whether the agency has broken new ground and made new law by resort to its unique administrative resources, it seems clear that the record is largely one of missed opportunity." This assessment only reinforced the findings of the Stigler Report, which concluded, "Little that the Commission undertakes in the antitrust area can be defended in terms of the objectives of maintaining and strengthening a competitive economy." The Stigler Report recommended "substantial retrenchment by the Commission in the antitrust field," an end to increases in the agency's appropriations, and a redeployment of resources away from antitrust and into consumer protection and economic investigations. In contrast, the ABA called for the revitalization and rationalization of the FTC's antitrust activities. In specific terms, it called for a reduction of Robinson-Patman cases, a critical examination of the compatibility of existing antitrust prohibitions, and increased activity in the merger area.[17]

Given the long history of poor performance and the internal problems of the Federal Trade Commission, it was unfit to fulfill its primary function as an antitrust agency. Only two options were presented by its critics: reform or elimination. The ABA report could not have presented this position in clearer terms. "The case for change is plain. What is required is that the changes now be made, and in depth. Further temporizing is indefensible. Notwithstanding the great potential of the FTC in the field of antitrust and consumer protection, if change does not occur, there will be no substantial purpose to be served by its continued existence."[18]

It is surprising that the reports of this period, unlike those of earlier decades, resulted in rapid and significant change in agency organization and procedure. Their influence can be attributed to the interplay of a number of factors. If Paul Rand Dixon could dismiss the Nader Report as "a hysterical, anti-business, diatribe" and a "summer vacation smear project," a similar strategy would be ineffective in minimizing the impact of a report requested by President Nixon and conducted by the American Bar Association. Indeed, the ABA report legitimized the Nader Report and supported its findings. Since the ABA commission combined many of the most important members of the antitrust community, its influence with the relevant congressional committees could not have been more pronounced.[19]

There is, however, a key factor that must not be overlooked. Concern over the increasing concentration of the American economy, the swelling merger wave, and rising inflation rates led to a renewed interest in antitrust. Reminiscent of the late 1930s, antitrust was being presented as a policy which could address changing industrial structures and the major macroeconomic problems to which they contribute. In 1968, a White House Task Force on Antitrust Policy (the Neal Task Force) proposed a Concentrated Industry Act that would force divestiture until no firm possessed a market share in excess of 12 percent. The task force recommended the creation of new antitrust agencies and a special economic court to manage deconcentration. National deconcentration had been a topic of debate throughout much of the 1960s. However, this bold policy initiative gained greater support in the late 1960s and 1970s, finding its ultimate expression in Senator Philip Hart's Industrial Reorganization Act. When the critiques of FTC organization and performance were presented in this context, their influence was magnified.[20]

Reforming the Federal Trade Commission

The critical reports and the economic structuralist consensus unified actors across the institutional network and promoted rapid and consequential innovation. As in the case of the Antitrust Division, great emphasis was placed on changing the agency's internal organization, professionalizing the staff, and improving the capacity for policy planning. This process was driven by a coalition that united members of Congress, the executive branch, the antitrust community, and leaders of the consumer movement who saw economics as a key to expanding the agency's capacities and rationalizing policy. President Nixon initiated the process with his appointment of Casper Weinberger as chairman. Weinberger was chosen, in part, as a response to the ABA recommendation that an outsider be brought into the commission to supervise its reform. Although Weinberger's tenure was short—from January 13 to August 6, 1970—the changes he initiated were quite extraordinary. He was replaced by Miles Kirkpatrick, the head of the ABA committee that had only recently completed the study of the Federal Trade Commission. These appointments provided a sign to the commission's critics that attempts were being made to solve the problems which had long characterized the FTC.[21]

While presidential appointees were instrumental in promoting change, Congress was truly the driving force. The relevant committees generally supported the recommendations of the ABA report and viewed it as a blueprint for agency transformation. During a Senate oversight hearing, Senator Kennedy stated Congress's position in terms that were unequivocal. After noting the limited impact of past critiques, he warned that Congress would not allow the new proposals to "become grist for the mill of future students of the FTC." He went on to state that should the ABA proposals be ignored, the Congress would "consider abolishing the agency and starting it from the ground again."[22] At successive hearings, congressional leadership promoted organizational change and activism, going as far as to state, "The mistakes you are to make ought to be mistakes in doing and trying rather than playing safe in not doing."[23] The support for an activist FTC was best expressed by Senator Frank Moss. Discussing the accomplishments of Weinberger and Kirkpatrick, he noted: "Under their direction, the commission has not shied away from tangling with the giants of American commerce. . . . The commission has stretched its powers to provide a credible countervailing force to the enormous economic and political power of huge corporate conglomerates which today dominate American enterprise. . . . The commission has sought and vigorously pursued legislative authority to make its writ run firmly to reach and irradicate market abuses. That is as it should be."[24] In hearing after hearing, commission initiatives were reaffirmed by members of both chambers and parties. Moving beyond the level of rhetoric, Congress appropriated ever-greater sums of money for the FTC. Over the decade of the 1970s, the budget for the FTC increased from $19.9 million in 1970 to $62 million in 1979. Adjusted for inflation, the budget more than doubled.[25]

Congressional support was not limited to appropriations. Throughout the decade, Congress passed legislation which dramatically amplified commission powers. The first legislative expression of commission authority came in 1973, with the passage of the Trans-Alaska Pipeline Act. The act increased the sanctions available to the FTC by doubling the fines for violating commission orders to $10,000. Moreover, it granted the commission greater access to the courts. The commission was allowed to represent itself and to seek temporary or permanent injunctions and restraining orders when there was reason to believe that the law had been or was going to be violated. The act also provided the district courts the authority to grant mandatory injunctions and seek relief in equity in accordance with FTC orders. Finally, the act strengthened the commission's ability to gather information.[26]

In 1975, Congress passed the Federal Trade Commission Improvement/ Magnuson-Moss Warranty Act, forcing a dramatic expansion of agency authority in a number of areas. First, it extended its jurisdiction from activities in interstate commerce to activities *in or affecting* interstate commerce. Second, the act established the commission's power to issue substantive industrywide rules addressing unfair or deceptive acts and practices. Third, it provided the commission with the authority to recover civil penalties in federal or state courts for violations of the FTC Act. It is important in this context to note that violators could be penalized even if they were not themselves subject to a commission cease-and-desist order for the given practice. The significance, of course, was that the FTC could effectively legislate for an entire industry with each cease-and-desist order. Fourth, the FTC had the power to sue in court to obtain consumer redress. Finally, the Magnuson-Moss Warranty Act granted the FTC the additional authority to promulgate regulations for written and implied warranties.

The new legislation created dramatic new powers on the consumer protection side, giving rise to what was commonly referred to as the second most powerful legislature in Washington. However, the new power carried considerable administrative costs. Through the provisions of the Federal Trade Commission Improvement Act, Congress required that the FTC observe procedural norms beyond those required by the Administrative Procedures Act. The FTC was required to announce the proposed rule making along with a detailed justification for the rule, allow for the submission of comments and data which would become part of the public record, and provide informal hearings on the rule. Once the rule was promulgated, the FTC was required to publish a statement of "basis and purpose," noting the prevalence of the practices addressed by the rule, the manner in which such practices were unfair or deceptive, and the economic impact of the rule on small businesses and consumer welfare. Thus, rule making became an excessively complex and lengthy affair.[27]

Finally, Congress passed the Hart-Scott-Rodino Antitrust Improvements Act of 1976. This law has been discussed in some detail above. Suffice it to say that the act required that firms contemplating a merger provide financial data regarding the firms and changes in the postmerger market. This information not only enhanced the capacity of the FTC to conduct section 7 enforcement proceedings in a more rational manner but provided access to additional economic information which would prove valuable in policy planning. Since the threat of prosecution was usually sufficient to prevent a merger, the act strengthened the FTC's capacity to regulate industrial consolidation. Significantly, the act was modeled on past FTC practices. Since 1969, the FTC had conducted a limited premerger notification program for grocers.

The Court played an equally important role in remolding commission authority. In an earlier case, *Federal Trade Commission v. Motion Picture Advertising Service Co.* (1953), the Court determined that the prohibition of "unfair practices" in section 5 of the Federal Trade Commission Act "was designed to supplement and bolster the Sherman Act and the Clayton Act—to stop in their incipiency acts and practices which, when full blown, would violate those Acts as well as to condemn as 'unfair methods of competition' existing violations of them."[28] For two decades, the FTC's authority had been defined within the restrictive boundaries of this decision. Section 5 had to be interpreted in light of, and as an extension of, the specific prohibitions in the other antitrust laws.

In 1972, the Court had the occasion to reconsider the section 5 prohibition. In *Federal Trade Commission v. Sperry and Hutchinson & Co.*, the Supreme Court reviewed an unfavorable decision issued by a court of appeals. The Court affirmed the commission's authority to use section 5 to address practices that fail to fall clearly under the other antitrust prohibitions. The decision stated, "Legislative and judicial authorities alike convince us that the Federal Trade Commission does not arrogate excessive power to itself if, in measuring a practice against the elusive, but congressionally mandated standards of fairness, it, like a court of equity, considers public values beyond simply those enshrined in the letter or encompassed in the spirit of the antitrust laws."[29] This decision greatly expanded the agency's powers. Section 5 could be used to reach practices that were beyond prosecution under the other antitrust statutes.

The Reorganization of 1970

Agency reorganizations are often acts of political symbolism used by new political executives to herald a break with the past. Reorganizations seldom have a greater impact than the rhetoric with which they are accompanied.[30] Nevertheless, the 1970 reorganization was much more than political drama. The new leadership assumed power with a clear mandate. Using the ABA report as a guide, the agency was reorganized to deemphasize activities which had been the object of criticism, to eliminate sources of parochialism, to create a centralization of authority for management purposes, to enhance subunit coordination, and to expand the capacity for policy planning.

The reorganization addressed the decentralization of authority by eliminating a number of formerly separate bureaus and bringing their operations under the control of the remaining bureaus. Three existing bureaus (Field Operations, Textiles and Furs, and Industry Guidance) were discarded. The Bureau of Restraint of Trade was replaced by a Bureau of Competition with seven divisions: evaluation, accounting, compliance, general litigation, industry guidance, small business, and special projects. The Bureau of Deceptive Practices was replaced by a Bureau of Consumer Protection with nine divisions: evaluation, compliance, consumer education, food and drug advertising, general litigation, industry guidance, scientific opinions, special projects, and textiles and furs. The Bureau of Economics was retained in more or less its original form. The reorganization of the antitrust bureau was most significant. The new Bureau of Competition retained the central functions of the old Bureau of Restraint of Trade: it was charged with conducting investigations, recommending commission action where violations have been identified, litigating cases and negotiating consent orders, and enforcing compliance with commission orders. Despite the common functions of the two bureaus, the reorganization addressed an important organizational problem which had played a central role in undermining the commission's antitrust efforts.[31]

The leadership of the old Bureau of Restraint of Trade faced a number of organizational impediments when attempting to manage and define the caseload. The bureau was composed of highly specialized litigation units—such as the Division of General Trade Restraints, the Division of Mergers, and the Division of Discriminatory Practices—responsible for bringing specific kinds of cases. The high level of specialization and the rigid separation of divisions fostered a certain parochialism. Attorneys resisted any attempts on the part of the bureau officials to set priorities or evaluate caseloads. An additional problem was the ability of attorneys to initiate investigations at will. Because the termination of an investigation could be interpreted as a sign of error, investigations were commonly abandoned informally, creating a large backlog of cases. Staff autonomy combined with professional incentives to shape a caseload which revealed an infatuation with minor violations.

As Robert Katzmann details in his fine study of the FTC, the bureau's internal cleavages had to be addressed before any meaningful attempt could be made to affect the composition of the caseload and the contents of antitrust policy. Katzmann explains, "The new leadership . . . believed that their efforts to change the nature of the case load—to bring innovative, economically oriented cases—would have little chance of succeeding if structural units, which posed obstacles to the regulation of their plans, remained in place."[32] The reorganization eliminated the special litigation units and created a Division of General Litigation. As part of the professionalization process (to be discussed in greater detail below), specialists were replaced by generalists of a much higher quality. This aspect of the reorganization allowed bureau officials to set policy priorities without first having to overcome the resistance of the attorneys seeking to protect their specialized subunits. An Office of Policy Planning and Evaluation was created to conduct studies and make recommendations with respect to long-term policy goals and the allocation of agency resources. In addition, a deputy executive director for operations and a deputy executive director for management were established to increase the executive director's capacity to manage the agency. An economic adviser position was created to increase the chairman's access to economic expertise.

The agency's critics were united in arguing that the FTC was plagued by the poor quality of its staff. Weinberger and Kirkpatrick immediately sought to transform the agency's personnel resources. Basil Mezines, an experienced commission attorney, was appointed executive assistant to help direct this endeavor. First, eighteen of the top thirty-one staff members were replaced, thus removing one source of commission lethargy. However, the personnel problems ran much deeper. Thus, attention quickly turned to the large legal staff. The strategy adopted was relatively simple. Using the powers granted to the chairman in the 1950 reorganization, the chairman eliminated the positions occupied by the incompetent attorneys. Because veterans were granted "preference eligible" status by the civil service system, they had the right to reassignment. In these cases, the commission leadership convinced the individuals that resignation or retirement was preferable to a transfer to one of the field offices. Overall, one-third of the almost six hundred attorneys at the middle and lower levels of the organization were dismissed. By the end of 1971, the first stage of the process was completed: the so-called "deadwood" had been removed from the commission.[33]

The purge complete, an effort was initiated to fill the new openings with talented graduates drawn from the better law schools. For a number of reasons, recruitment was relatively easy. First, the leadership instilled a new sense of mission, thus overcoming the agency's reputation for passivity. Second, Chairman Kirkpatrick was an influential member of the ABA Antitrust Law Section. His presence combined with that of a number of impressive appointments at the bureau level made the FTC an attractive place to work. Finally, with the rise of the consumer protection movement and the increased salience of antitrust, many well-qualified attorneys were motivated by nonprofessional concerns to seek positions in the agency. As always, the FTC remained one of the few agencies that could provide attorneys with extensive experience in antitrust, thus increasing their value in subsequent employment in the private sector. These factors combined to draw a sufficient number of qualified graduates into the FTC.[34]

A parallel effort was launched to professionalize the Bureau of Economics. The FTC's critics identified the limited training of the economics staff as one of the problems to be addressed. As in the case of the Antitrust Division, few economists in the bureau had more than a minimum of graduate education. Although the bureau's budget had increased during the 1960s under the active leadership of Willard Mueller, the quality of the staff remained a problem which needed to be resolved. At the time of the reorganization, only one-fifth of the bureau's forty economists had their Ph.D.'s.[35] The Bureau of Economics' professional staff was both enlarged and upgraded. By 1980, the bureau had a professional staff of eighty economists, twice the size of the staff only a decade earlier. Numerical comparisons veil a critical difference: the new economists tended to be better qualified for their duties. Under the leadership of prestigious economists such as H. Michael Mann and F. M. Scherer, the bureau assumed an academic character that made it an attractive place to work for economists trained for employment in universities. The bureau bypassed the civil service system to recruit Ph.D. economists at American Economics Association meetings. By the mid-1970s, about half of the economists had their Ph.D.'s; the remainder were doctoral candidates. The majority of new recruits were trained in advanced microeconomics and industrial organization. By the decade's end, a majority of economists had their Ph.D.'s.[36]

As the bureau actively recruited economists at professional meetings, it increasingly attracted graduates from the top-ranked economics departments. Indeed, the FTC—along with the Council of Economic Advisers, the Federal Reserve, and the Antitrust Division—became one of the most attractive places for economists to work within the federal government. As the status of the Chicago school increased in the subdiscipline of industrial organization economics, a new understanding of policy was transmitted to the bureau through the recruitment process. This influence would have an impact on policy, for as in the Antitrust Division, the economists increasingly assumed a key position in the case-selection and evaluation processes. As economic expertise was provided an organizational presence in the policy process, the theoretical orientations of the economic staff came to play a greater part in developing priorities and defining the caseload.

Policy Planning: Economics
as a Guide to Enforcement

The commission's inability to establish priorities or long-range goals was a source of criticism throughout its history. The 1970 reorganization partially addressed this problem with the creation of an Office of Policy Planning and Evaluation (OPPE), designed to advise the commission in the definition of policy goals. Chairman Kirkpatrick portrayed the duties of the OPPE in the following manner: "It guide[s] the Commission in the important area of the allocation of its resources, [and] the statement of priorities. . . . It has developed guidelines, and we seek advice as to which cases are indeed important to bring, where, when and why. They are the planners of the Commission's activities, subject always to the approval of the Commission."[37] The OPPE differed in a significant manner from its organizational predecessor, the Office of Policy Review, which had a professional staff of four on those rare occasions when it was operating at full force. Without resources, it accomplished little over its ten-year existence. In contrast, the Office of Policy Planning and Evaluation had a professional staff of thirteen and an annual budget approaching half a million dollars. The OPPE quickly assumed an active role in agency management.[38]

Commission officials also addressed questions of planning and evaluation at the bureau level. In the Bureau of Competition, an assistant director for evaluation was charged with the task of evaluating existing investigations and supervising the opening of new cases. The magnitude of this task focused attention on the need for an organization and procedures for case evaluation and planning. In 1972, an Evaluation Office was created in the Bureau of Competition to assess potential cases in the setting of an evaluation committee. This committee initially consisted of Bureau of Competition officials, meeting on a weekly basis. They formulated goals and evaluated cases and potential investigations. The evaluation process was facilitated by the introduction of a computerized case-tracking system which provided bureau officials with access to information regarding the status of existing investigations, resources committed to individual cases, and staff assignments. With this information, bureau officials had the potential to exercise greater control over the composition of the caseload, the allocation of agency resources, and the match between the caseload and larger policy objectives.

During this period, the OPPE was engaged in a related enterprise. It worked closely with the Bureau of Economics' Division of Industry Analysis to develop a formal econometric model to determine where enforcement efforts would reap the greatest benefits. The resulting Prototype Resource Allocation Model (PRAM) used data on industrial concentration, imports, and barriers to entry to estimate losses in consumer welfare in given industries. PRAM was a pure expression of economic structuralism. It generated a rank-ordering of one hundred industries which was, in essence, a list of industries characterized by high concentration and profit levels. Although PRAM was ultimately rejected by the commission, it represented the agency's first comprehensive attempt to use economic analysis as the basis for policy planning and apply cost-benefit criteria to antitrust enforcement. The OPPE also worked with the bureaus to create standardized criteria for case selection and evaluation.[39]

In 1974, the OPPE assumed a central role in the FTC's budgetary process, furnishing the commission with an independent evaluation of bureau requests. The importance of the budget as a tool of planning increased with the commission's decision to employ a program-based budget. The separation of the various programs conducted by the bureaus allowed for the separate evaluation of resource allocations. This function expanded when midyear reviews were adopted to appraise changes in agency activities and budgetary requirements. As the evaluations began to influence commission decisions and limit bureau discretion, the conflicts between the litigating bureaus and the OPPE intensified.

Under the leadership of Wesley Liebeler, the OPPE produced an evaluation of the proposed 1976 fiscal year budget and a subsequent midyear review. Liebeler received his legal training at the University of Chicago, a fact that found a distinct expression in the assumptions underlying the budget overview. The overview began by establishing that a survey of economic costs and benefits was the sole acceptable guide for evaluating priorities and programs. The introductory section of the overview established this point with great clarity. "We submit that the basic objective of these laws is to maximize consumer welfare. Success or failure in accomplishing this objective should be measured in terms of the consumer's economic well-being. We are not aware of any other operationally viable objective available to the Commission in setting priorities. The choice as to which programs should be undertaken, which given priority and which deferred, should be made on the basis of their expected economic impact on the consumer in dollars-and-cents terms. Those programs which will produce the greatest economic benefits for consumers should be given the highest priority."[40] The review provided a cost-benefit analysis of all existing and proposed initiatives and called for the end of a number of established programs which could not be justified on the basis of these criteria. The negative assessment rested on the economic theories adopted by the OPPE.[41]

The review of the Bureau of Competition was highly critical of the industrywide enforcement programs and their theoretical foundations. Central to this critique was a lengthy Chicago school interpretation of the structure-conduct-performance framework and a denunciation of the "market concentration doctrine." The review concluded: "Neither profits nor concentration are the problem. The problem is collusion. While this might be thought to be obvious, there is a tendency for the proxy (concentration and profits in this case) which economists use to seek the underlying problem (collusion), gradually to become thought of as the problem itself. . . . These findings strongly suggest that efficiency is the most plausible general explanation for any observed correlation between concentration and profit rates. They make it essential that the efficiency hypothesis be given great weight in the case selection process of this Commission."[42] Once the concentration-profits relationship was undermined, deconcentration and cases based on structuralist assumptions were, at best, ill advised. In the area of antitrust, the OPPE recommended that a number of existing programs be discontinued and resources focused on new programs addressing state regulation in milk marketing, occupational licensure, and horizontal price-fixing arrangements—"undoubtedly among the most important transactions to which the Commission can devote its resources."[43] The OPPE's policy evaluations and recommendations met with great resistance from the officials in the litigating bureaus. This resistance was recast as partial compliance when it became clear that the OPPE's recommendations had influenced the commissioners. As a result of the three-volume midyear review, the commission adjusted the expenditures for half of the bureaus' programs for fiscal year 1976. A number of the OPPE's recommendations found an expression in the commission's programs.[44]

The OPPE stimulated changes in the case-selection and evaluation processes at the bureau level, which were designed to force a standardization of process and a greater reliance on economic analysis. Under the direction of Chairman Lewis Engman, the OPPE began working with the bureaus to develop "policy protocols," standardized guidelines to be employed by the bureaus when determining whether to initiate a preliminary investigation or recommend the filing of a formal complaint. The protocols established standard criteria by type of offense. Officials in the two bureaus argued that formal protocols were unnecessary because criteria were already being used by the bureaus, albeit in an unwritten and unstandardized form. Despite their objections, the bureaus provided draft protocols to the OPPE for consideration. The Bureau of Competition's recommendations were initially rejected because they lacked the necessary specificity and did not place a great enough emphasis on economic criteria. Final protocols were officially accepted by the commission in 1976.[45]

Attempts were made to advance the integration of law and economics at the bureau level in another way. As noted above, the Bureau of Competition began using an evaluation committee in 1972 to conduct short-term planning and evaluation. By 1975, a similar committee had been created for screening mergers. The OPPE approved of these evaluation committees—indeed, it advised the Bureau of Consumer Protection to utilize a similar mechanism. Nonetheless, Liebeler suggested changes in the committee's composition and decision-making processes that would enhance the role of economic analysis in the definition of the caseload. First, he recommended that the evaluation committee include representatives from the Bureau of Economics and the OPPE. This suggestion met with little opposition; economists were already occasional participants in committee meetings. The same cannot be said of the role which the new participants would play under Liebeler's recommendation. Under the existing arrangements, the bureaus had the authority to initiate preliminary investigations. Liebeler recommended that this authority be exercised only with the approval of the Bureau of Economics and the OPPE. If a potential case addressed significant economic problems and could be justified by cost-benefit criteria, the bureau would be authorized to initiate the investigation. The OPPE and Bureau of Economics would exercise limited veto power. Their dissent would force the bureau to receive special authorization from the commission.[46]

While the OPPE's recommendation was rejected, Bureau of Economics officials were granted permanent positions on the evaluation committee. As the evaluation committee evolved, Bureau of Competition officials were accompanied by the deputy director of the Bureau of Economics, the assistant director for economic evidence, and a number of staff economists. Although the economists were never granted equal influence, they were guaranteed access to the evaluation process. The bureau acknowledged the potential power of the OPPE by consulting with its officials on a regular basis.

Despite the impact of the OPPE in agency affairs, its evaluative responsibilities were eliminated in 1977. In part, the decision reflected the evolution of the evaluation committee. Under the direction of Chairman Michael Pertschuk, the OPPE was reconstituted as the Office of Policy Planning (OPP) and placed under the direction of Robert Reich. The OPP was organized into task forces to plan policy in a number of major issue areas and industry groupings. The commission responded to congressional will by creating task forces in food, health care, energy, and enforcement. The task forces combined representatives of the litigating and economics bureaus, coordinated and led by the OPP. The new office allowed for a partial realization of a long-standing organizational need, namely, the coordination of the various bureaus. Within the context of the task forces, the members of formally separate staffs were working together in the definition of agency goals.[47] At the same time, evaluation responsibilities were devolved upon the bureaus. The Bureau of Competition underwent a minor reorganization to place greater authority in two deputy directors for evaluation and operations, with similar changes in the Bureau of Consumer Protection. The bureau officials' knowledge of investigations and programs was superior to that of the old OPPE. Likewise, bureau personnel had gained greater skill in evaluation and short-term planning. However, these changes left the commission without an independent source of expertise when evaluating bureau programs and budget proposals.[48]

Prior to the 1970s, there is little evidence that economic criteria played a significant role in agency affairs outside of section 7 enforcement. The Bureau of Economics was isolated and relatively unintegrated into agency activities. The same could not be said by the end of the 1970s. Economists were regular participants on the evaluation and merger screening committees and were directly involved in the definition of the caseload. Enforcement decisions were guided by policy protocols which were heavily influenced by economics. Finally, the commissioners increasingly accepted the position that the question central to its legislative mandate—whether a case was in the public interest—was best resolved through an appeal to economic analysis. Through an evolutionary process, economic knowledge assumed an institutional presence which would have been unimaginable only a decade earlier.

Data for Planning and Enforcement

Despite the conflicts that characterized the first half of the 1970s, there was general agreement on at least two points. First, the commission had to devote more attention to policy planning and the allocation or resources. Second, there was general agreement that economic analysis could provide a technical guide to these activities. The antitrust policy debates continually reinforced the belief that a credible antitrust policy would rest on economic theory. Economic analysis was viewed as a keystone of agency reform. It would allow for an expansion of industrywide enforcement programs, the establishment of priorities, and an assessment of the relative costs and benefits of agency initiatives. The commission's ability to use economic analysis remained contingent, however, on its capacity to gather reliable data. To this end, the FTC initiated the Line of Business (LB) program in 1973, a program designed to generate a comprehensive data base on the American economy.

The Federal Trade Commission's annual report noted that the information from the LB program would "permit, for the first time, profitability comparisons between meaningful economic markets and between firms in these markets" and would allow for "an application of cost-benefit analysis to decision-making in the antitrust area."[49] Under the LB program, the FTC would use its investigative powers to require selected firms to supply annual figures on sales, direct costs, research and development outlays, promotional expenditures, and profits by line of business and plant. These data would provide information unavailable through gross estimates of corporate profits or other public information. The availability of this information for each sector of the economy would allow the commission to target for investigation industries with abnormally high profits. It was argued that the program would provide "the data necessary to help plan a rational allocation of its antitrust resources."[50]

By August 1974, the Line of Business program was formally underway. At this time, 345 companies were ordered to file data for the last fiscal year. In the next year, 453 companies were directed to report on their activities. Reflecting the concerns of the SCP framework, the Bureau of Economics required information from the nation's largest firms, companies with assets of over $1 million as well as the 250 largest firms in terms of domestic manufactured production sales. In order to acquire economywide data, it demanded information from at least five companies in each of 260 product categories, including the two leading firms in each category, and from companies representing over 20 percent of the industry sales. Given the prevalence of conglomerate organization, these criteria could be met with a relatively small sampling.[51]

The LB program was an immediate source of controversy. Following the first mailing, eight corporations filed a class action suit on behalf of all other corporations being forced to comply. They were soon joined by a majority of the firms involved in the LB program. They called for the commission to quash the order, arguing that the program exceeded the FTC's legislative mandate, raised problems of self-incrimination, and violated the Administrative Procedure and the Budget and Accounting Procedure acts. The request also expressed fears that compliance would be costly and that disclosed data could be obtained by competitors. The motions were denied, and restrictions were placed on the scope of subsequent complaints. Ultimately, the limits of commission authority in this area were determined by the courts, in a manner favorable to the FTC.[52] Nevertheless, the commission made some concessions: extensions were granted, the reporting process was simplified to reduce costs, and restrictions were placed on availability and use of the individual reports. Access was restricted to the Bureau of Economics and the Division of Management. Reports would not be made available to the Bureau of Competition and outside agencies, including Congress and the courts. They would be used only for studies within the Bureau of Economics and for policy-planning purposes on a sectoral basis.[53]

The LB program generated a substantial body of data, while failing to fulfill the ultimate expectations of its creators. The program's problems were many. Costs of compliance were minimized by allowing firms to report accounting figures—data that failed to correspond with economic markets. The individual categories were broad enough to capture products which were not clearly substitutes; other substitutes were placed in separate categories. It was also difficult to estimate costs and profits with any accuracy, given the number of multipurpose plants. Because the reporting firms were usually the larger firms in the sector, the sample was biased to overstate concentration levels. As William Breit and Kenneth Elzinga note: "The selection of LB segments is oriented to sectors of the economy with relatively high four-firm concentration ratios. . . . If only successful firms are designated as respondents (or the sample is biased toward them), even 'accurate' data from these firms would bias upward the profit figures of the line of business and not portray the true returns being made by suppliers as a whole." As a result, the LB data "erroneously attract[ed] the attention of the antitrust authorities and new investors."[54] Given the genesis of the program and the reliance on the structuralist framework as a guide to enforcement, one may question whether the bias was unintended.

With the passage of the Hart-Scott-Rodino Antitrust Improvements Act of 1976, another source of information was made available to the commission. Through the notification process the FTC was provided with extensive information on firms planning a merger. The premerger notification forms required firms to disclose much of the information required by the Line of Business program. When the LB data and Hart-Scott-Rodino data were combined, the FTC possessed a most extensive collection of economic figures on American industry. These figures were used as a basis for industry studies and ultimately to establish commission enforcement priorities and inform enforcement decisions.[55]

The Limits of Agency Autonomy and Activism

As a product of the decade's reforms, the agency acquired a greater ability to manage resources, define specific policy goals, and pursue them with vigor. The new capacities were employed to generate a number of innovative initiatives. Performance was most impressive under the direction of Michael Pertschuk, chairman during the Carter administration. Pertschuk recognized the importance of economic analysis but rejected the assertion (already in vogue) that the primary goal of antitrust was the promotion of business efficiency. His statement before a Senate subcommittee made clear his understanding of his mission.

> All of the most important questions antitrust policymakers must decide are ones on which reasonable men, applying legal and economic theory to the facts, can and will differ. . . . The decision to be made in antitrust policy will, after vast efforts at factual documentation and economic prediction, be an assertion of values. The values I bring to these decisions include a pervasive distrust of concentrations of power in a few hands. I believe that Congress intended in the antitrust laws to secure to a democratic society the dispersal of economic and political power, diversity, and innovation. It is to that end, through every available means, that I intend to direct my efforts and those of the Federal Trade Commission.[56]

Under Pertschuk, attempts were made to generate important cases and expand agency authority through the application of largely untested economic and legal doctrines. In testing the limits of the law, he also tested the limits of congressional tolerance. While initially supportive, Congress's response ultimately threatened the agency's very existence. Before examining the response, it is necessary to address briefly some of the initiatives brought about under Pertschuk and his immediate predecessors.

The legislation of the 1970s increased the sanctions available to the FTC while expanding its authority, particularly in the area of industrywide rule making. The new rule-making authority was immediately employed. The FTC announced thirteen new rules in 1975, a level of activism that would continue over the next half-decade. The rules (proposed and enacted) addressed practices in a wide variety of industries, often focusing on activities coordinated by trade associations. The objects of concern included cost disclosures in insurance and undertaking, generic substitutions in pharmaceuticals, price advertising and competition in optometry, and mechanical disclosures in automobile sales. The commission also opened a number of important investigations. One was directed at the major cigarette producers. Another, more publicized investigation addressed television advertising aimed at children. In the "kid-vid" investigation, the FTC argued that such efforts were tantamount to the exploitation of minors. The agency threatened to place substantial restrictions on broadcasting. A final effort involved eliminating the Formica trademark, since the name had become the general term used to refer to an entire class of products.[57]

The commission's activities were no less bold in antitrust. It charged Sunkist Growers with monopolizing the citrus industry in the western United States through exclusive-dealing contracts with distributors. The case challenged the antitrust exemption granted agricultural cooperatives under the Capper-Volstead Act. A major suit was also brought against Exxon, in an attempt to test the law in the area of vertical restraints. The FTC addressed professional self-regulation by challenging the American Medical Association's prohibition against price advertising. The commission argued that this prohibition was but a glorified price-fixing arrangement. Similar challenges were made against the American Bar Association. Finally, the commission constructed an innovative shared-monopoly case. It charged that the major ready-to-eat cereal producers had effectively limited competition and raised prices through collusive arrangements governing advertising, pricing, and allocation of shelf space. Some of these cases, such as the shared-monopoly case, held the promise of extending the reach of the antitrust laws and expanding agency jurisdiction.[58]

Taken individually, the cases, rules, and investigations might not have provoked much of a political reaction. Indeed, some of these activities were initiated at the request of Congress, which—at least for the past several years—had promoted agency activism and in some cases suggested investigations and enforcement activities. The congressional support of the early 1970s, however, began to disintegrate by the latter half of the decade for three reasons. First, there were significant changes in Congress. Beginning in 1976, the core of the Senate coalition that had supported the FTC and encouraged its activism was weakened as death, retirement, and electoral defeat claimed some of its most influential members. Between 1976 and the elections of 1978, thirteen senators were replaced. Because they had occupied important positions in the Senate committees most relevant to the FTC, their absence eroded the base of agency support.[59] Second, there is reason to believe that Congress simply underestimated the powers that it granted to the FTC with the legislation of the 1970s. The enhanced industrywide rule-making power was literally unprecedented; in the early 1970s no other agency, barring Congress, possessed as broad a grant of authority. Third, and related, the exercise of the new powers generated stiff political opposition. Individually, firms that had been objects of the FTC's investigations, rule-making, and enforcement activities would have been quite weak. Combined, they constituted a considerable political force. With industrywide rule making and the broad applicability of cease-and-desist orders, each case automatically created its own constituency. As a response to agency activism, multiple business interests—from the cigarette producers to the American Medical Association to the undertakers—demanded that Congress intervene to provide individual exemptions and restrictions on FTC authority. The Chamber of Commerce and the National Association of Manufacturers organized a broad-based business coalition, the former working to unite members in the society of "victims of the FTC."[60]

As an electorally based institution, Congress has always been highly vulnerable to the pressures of organized constituencies, an exposure that rendered the autonomy and activism of the FTC contingent on congressional approval. Congress has rewarded the FTC for mediocrity, penalized it for fulfilling its mandate. No better example exists than the events of the late 1970s. The intensive business lobbying combined with turnovers in the Senate to stimulate the formation of a new coalition devoted to limiting the commission's authority and meeting the short-term demands of business. During the 96th Congress, debates over the commission's authority turned increasingly hostile. Congressman Bereuter's comments are most suggestive of the origins of congressional discontent.

> I can think of few Federal agencies that rival the Federal Trade Commission in their ability to rouse both concern and downright outrage on the part of my constituents. . . . [I] have seen first-hand the extent to which this agency has interfered with, complicated and harassed a variety of constituent groups. Whether it is funeral directors, life insurance salesmen, the cereal industry, or used car dealers, the story is the same over and over again. The heavy-handed, arbitrary, arrogant manner by which this agency and its staff pursue a mission makes one wonder whether the charter for the agency should be extended, let alone without clear evidence that Congress intends to exercise considerably more influence over the direction of that agency's activities.[61]

While a few members of Congress spoke in support of the FTC, the overall mood was warlike. The FTC was described as "a king-sized cancer on our economy," "a virulent political and economic pestilence," "a dangerous and tyrannical entity," and "a propaganda machine." The FTC's staff were labeled "the masters of conceit in the Federal Government" and "a pack of interventionists," guilty of applying "extra-legal criteria for harassment" and engaging in "demagoguery and social experimentation at the expense of the American consumer and taxpayer."[62]

The congressional backlash was not confined to rhetoric. Congress contemplated various ways of limiting agency powers. Some argued that all of the rules put forth in recent years should be nullified, and pending investigations and litigation terminated. Others sought to subject all future rules to a one-house legislative veto. Symbolic of the FTC's uncertain future, the agency repeatedly failed to receive authorization; funds were allowed to lapse, forcing the commission to close down for brief periods in May and June 1980. The symbolic importance of these events was not lost on commission personnel.[63]

The conflicts found their final expression in the mislabeled Federal Trade Commission Improvements Act of 1980. Although substantially modified as a result of consumer-group lobbying and presidential intervention, the act restricted the agency's authority and further reduced its autonomy. The act contained a number of reasonable reform measures: it required that relevant parties be notified in advance with respect to rule making and that the commission meet with concerned parties. Moreover, it required that cost-benefit analysis be applied to all proposed rules. The remainder of the act, however, was correctly described by Pertschuk as "spurious regulatory reforms: naked political sorties by the affected industries to evade public accountability for commercial abuse and consumer injury."[64] The act put an end to an insurance investigation and limited future investigations by requiring that they take place only at the request of a majority on either the Senate or House Commerce Committee. The Lanham Act proceeding to cancel the Formica trademark was completely disallowed. Although the children's advertising proceeding was not formally terminated, the commission was restricted to seeking evidence of deception, rather than using its authority over unfair practices. As a final limit on the future activities of the commission, all rules were made subject to a two-house legislative veto within a ninety-day period. The other proceedings went unaffected, despite attempts to amend the act to force their termination. With the passage of the 1980 legislation, the period of rapid transformation drew to a close.[65]

It would be easy to attribute the FTC's difficulties solely to a Congress that was hyperresponsive to the demands of local interests and pressure groups. While this cannot be minimized as a causal force, the commission's troubles also reflected, in a curious fashion, the conflicts between competing economic paradigms. Although the FTC economists increasingly called for cases in conformity with contemporary economics, the activism of the legal staff and the agency leadership reflected a continued adherence to economic structuralism—or more correctly, a political structuralism. After the central tenets of the SCP framework had been discredited, they continued to exert political influence. Thus, a growing concern with price-fixing and a skepticism regarding vertical restraints prosecutions—both in keeping with Chicago doctrine—were combined with ambitious structuralist initiatives such as the shared-monopoly investigation of the cereal manufacturers. The bold structuralist experiments were driven by political agendas and only reinforced by now-suspect economic theories. They were adopted, one can only conclude, to extend the reach of the antitrust laws and expand agency authority.

Enforcement decisions supported by economic structuralism were increasingly out of step with a policy community seeking to invigorate markets through deregulation and affirm economic efficiency as a positive value.[66] Moreover, this structuralism opened the door for growing conflicts with the courts which, in the wake of cases like *General Dynamics* and *Sylvania*, were increasingly adopting Chicago school doctrines in antitrust decision making. Accordingly, the FTC's success rate in defending appealed antitrust decisions fell from 88 percent in the first half of the decade to a mere 43 percent from 1976 to 1981. The continued adherence to structural decision rules at the commission level and within the Bureau of Competition placed the FTC at odds with the courts, Congress, and the evolution of antitrust law and economics.[67]

Organizational Innovation and Policy Change

The decade of the 1970s was one of rapid and extraordinary change. Although the FTC's statutory authority and budget were expanded, the resources would have been of little consequence without significant change at the organizational level. Through a major reorganization, professionalization, and the creation of mechanisms for planning and evaluation at the commission and staff levels, the agency was transformed. The economic and legal staffs increasingly worked together in the definition of priorities and the caseload. The interaction was initially conflict ridden because of the divergent goals and professional orientations of the two staffs. By the decade's end, however, the tensions had lessened. One commission official recalled:

> As things ended up, the lawyers went out and did the investigation, and the economists' role was to critique it. Institutionally, that created tensions: if this is your job, you had better find something wrong. The lawyers were less likely to have found the facts that the economists thought were important because of the lack of communication beforehand. By the end of the 1970s, economists were increasingly less the people who waited until after the lawyers had done the investigation and then attacked it. They became participants in the investigation. As the economists worked along with the lawyers, the conflicts decreased. There was just better overall understanding.

In the span of a decade, organizational isolation had been exchanged for integration in the commission's central processes. The conflicts between the professional staffs were partially eliminated through a process of convergence, largely reflecting the demands of the new organization and the changing position of economics in the antitrust community. As economists and economic criteria came to claim an organizational presence in the FTC, the agency's priorities were gradually transformed. These changes were expressed in the composition of the caseload. The enforcement record for the period 1970–80 is summarized in figure 6-1.

Before the decade of the 1970s, the caseload revealed few priorities other than a fixation on Robinson-Patman cases. Throughout the 1970s, the number of Robinson-Patman cases decreased dramatically, reflecting the common belief that these cases were of little or no economic concern. A more important trend must be recognized. In the first half of the decade, the FTC caseload reflected a concern with horizontal and vertical restraints. Economic structuralism suggested that both were sources of competitive problems, particularly when employed in concentrated markets. By the second half of the decade, however, the proportion of vertical cases was in clear decline. As with the

Figure 6-1

Federal Trade Commission Complaints, 1970–1980

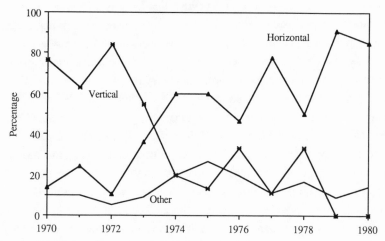

Source: Complaints data gathered from *Federal Trade Commission Decisions: Findings, Opinions, and Modifications*, vols. 77–96.

Antitrust Division, these changes corresponded with the evolution of the policy debates and the rise of the Chicago school. As noted in chapter 4, the Chicago school differed from the structuralist perspective by presenting vertical restraints and mergers as efficiency promoting. With an increasing reliance on economic expertise, Chicago criteria were integrated into the policy process. The only area where antitrust found consistent support was in the area of horizontal restraints.

This trend toward a Chicago-based enforcement agenda is evident. However, the transformation was less than complete because of the persistence of organizational problems. Although the 1970s brought a greater integration of the legal and economic staffs and provided economic criteria with an established position in the policy process, economics did not dominate the policy process. The authority to recommend an investigation or case remained vested in the Bureau of Competition, much as before the reforms of the 1970s. One bureau veteran explained the organizational barriers to convergence as follows: "Investigations were opened by the director or deputy director of the Bureau of Competition. The economists couldn't stop that. They provided input, but they had to defer judgment to the Bureau of Competition director.

Opening cases was done by lawyers. As a matter of policy they listened to what the economists had to say. But the economists had no vote, they had no veto. The decision to open a case or investigation was a legal decision and remains a legal decision." Structural divisions continued to reinforce professional divisions, placing limitations on the extent to which the economic criteria could find an expression in the caseload. Undoubtedly, attorneys were increasingly willing to consider the economic merits of potential cases. Given the changes in judicial decision making, this was imperative. But the role of economics in the decision to initiate enforcement proceedings remained indeterminate, subject to the discretion of the bureau's leadership and staff.

A second organizational problem must be recognized. Recommended proceedings find an ultimate expression in complaints only when they receive the support of a majority of commissioners. A majority of commissioners must apply economic decision rules before the caseload will come to be a pure expression of the dominant expertise. While the attorneys are concerned with prevailing before the courts, success before the commission is the proximate goal. The evidence and economic analyses are of little importance if the case fails to receive the support of the commission. In the end, one should expect to find a caseload that reveals much compromise between the goals of the bureau leadership, the interests of the commissioners, and the demands of economic expertise. The movement of the caseload toward a Chicago agenda and the simultaneous pursuit of structuralist initiatives are best interpreted as expressions both of the extent of legal and economic convergence and of the limitations imposed by the structure of the agency itself.

When seen in historical perspective, the 1970s was a period of dramatic organizational change. Unlike past agency critiques, the Nader Report and the American Bar Association study resulted in significant organizational and administrative reforms. The findings of the study were combined with the demands of the consumer movement, broader concerns over inflation, and a strong consensus regarding the nature of antitrust. If the 1970s was a decade of change, it was also a period of continuity. As in past decades, the commission's autonomy was limited by external institutional forces in its environment. Congress, while initially supportive of change, revealed its own vulnerability once this organizational revitalization found an expression in agency activism.

The Federal Trade Commission

As affected businesses mobilized against the FTC, the coalition that had supported change disintegrated. It was replaced by a coalition devoted to placing new restrictions on the commission and providing for greater corporate autonomy. In the end, the Federal Trade Commission Improvements Act of 1980 would stand, along with the Packers and Stockyards Act of 1921, as an expression of congressional vulnerability to business and the institutional constraints on agency authority.

CHAPTER SEVEN

A Reagan Revolution in Antitrust?:

Economics, Ideology, and the

Limits of Institutional Change

The Reagan administration came to Washington with the mission of redefining the relationship between the government and the market. The basis for the Reagan policy agenda was clearly presented in the *Economic Report of the President*. The report noted the coincidence of political and economic freedoms. "All nations which have broad-based representative governments and civil liberties have most of their economic activity organized by the market." Moreover, market supremacy, national wealth, and political liberty were presented as being causally related. "All nations in which the government has dominant control of the economy are run by a narrow oligarchy and in most economic conditions are relatively poor. In the absence of limits on the economic role of the government, the erosion of economic freedom destroys both political freedom and economic performance."[1]

The interventionist state, so the administration argued, undermines individual economic incentives and entrepreneurial initiatives. Welfare policies make citizens dependent on the state and eliminate the economic compulsion to reenter the market. The high rates of taxation required to fund these policies place downward pressures on profits and create penalties for innovation and economic success. The "regulatory burden" creates inefficiency and forces a misallocation of resources. On the societal level, it establishes barriers to investment that undermine growth. The welfare state failed to fulfill its social objectives: it introduced new sources of privilege, while subverting market forces and rendering American firms incapable of competing in an international economy. The cure seemed as evident as the ills. By contracting the role of the state in the domestic sphere, market mechanisms could be revitalized, thus reestablishing the foundations of a strong, vital, economy.[2]

A Reagan Revolution?

The Reagan revolution extended to antitrust policy with good reason. Of all regulatory policies, antitrust has the broadest scope. The vast majority of firms in the American economy fall under the jurisdiction of the antitrust agencies. While relatively few firms are actually prosecuted in any given year, the threat of prosecution structures business behavior and strategies of corporate expansion. Appealing to Chicago school doctrines, the administration's appointees rejected most of the traditional goals and objects of antitrust enforcement and promised that cases would be brought only when there was clear evidence that they would result in efficiency gains. Since the market was depicted as efficiency promoting and self-sustaining, there were few circumstances that could be used to rationalize intervention. This vision of antitrust conformed with the broader agenda. As one observer noted: "Mr. Reagan had promised to restore the economy to its former vigor by getting out of the business of business. A vision of antitrust as conservative microeconomic policy, which would sanction antitrust only when it could create a more efficient allocation of resources . . . fit nicely with the political philosophy and campaign commitment of the administration."[3]

There is a common depiction of the antitrust policy change of the 1980s. According to this explanation, President Reagan initiated a grand reorientation of antitrust policy. He appointed Chicago school lawyers and economists to leadership positions in the antitrust agencies. They redefined antitrust by refusing to enforce it or establishing new policies that had little support or judicial precedent. It was a policy revolution executed through administrative means. This is the common interpretation of the events of the 1980s, and a common explanation of policy change.[4] On both counts, it is also incomplete. While there is no doubt that this strategy was adopted by the administration, the histories presented in this book suggest that the redefinition of policy had already taken place. The policy changes attributed to the administration were in fact a product of an evolutionary process initiated well before the elections of 1980. Despite their rhetorical elegance and analytic rigor, the Reagan appointees were preaching to the converted. Indeed, it is questionable whether any enforcement agenda other than that supported by the administration could have been possible.

It is important, in this context, to note that the Supreme Court was generally accommodating to the agenda put forth by the administration. While the Court remained a potential threat, the changes in the judicial use of economics which were so clear in the wake of *Sylvania* and the elevated importance of efficiency considerations continued to shape its position toward antitrust. In the area of naked price-fixing, the Court continued to apply a strict per se rule.[5] However, related activities that would have been quickly denounced as per se violations in the past were increasingly examined under the rule of reason. With one notable exception, to be discussed in greater detail below, the Court consistently examined the efficiency rationale underlying a questioned form of business conduct and proved quite willing to circumvent established judicial rules on this basis.

Following the approach adopted in *Sylvania*, the Court continued to examine the economic effects of restraints that might have been easily cast as per se violations. In *Broadcast Music Inc. v. Columbia Broadcasting System Inc.* (1979), the Court decided that a system of blanket licensing for the use of copyrighted materials did not constitute a price-fixing violation vulnerable to per se rules. Rather, the appropriate approach was deemed to be the application of the rule of reason.[6] The Court decided that a joint selling arrangement could be so efficient that it could actually increase aggregate output. This chain of reasoning came to be common during the 1980s. In another private case, *National Collegiate Athletic Assn. v. Board of Regents of the University of Oklahoma* (1984), the Court decision stressed the necessity of examining the efficiency aspects of price-fixing arrangements, rather than addressing them through existing per se rules.[7] Justice Stevens's decision was quite revealing. "Horizontal price fixing and output limitations are ordinarily condemned as a matter of law under an 'illegal per se' approach because the probability that these practices are anticompetitive is so high. . . . Nevertheless, we have decided that it would be inappropriate to apply a per se rule to this case. . . . What is critical is that this case involves an industry in which horizontal restraints on competition are essential if the product is to be available at all."[8] The Court went on to apply a rule-of-reason approach. While the Court rejected the efficiency argument because of the reduced levels of output and the inability of member institutions to respond to consumer demands, the essential point was clear: the need to search out the economic rationale for adopting a given business practice could be so compelling as to limit the applicability of per se rules.

The Court was supportive of an economically based antitrust that derived legal conclusions from the detailed economic analysis of competitive effect. The agencies and antitrust law had evolved in such a fashion that this approach had become imperative. Economists and economic criteria could not be excluded from, or marginalized within, the policy process. Even if there is reason to exercise skepticism when assessing the administration's impact on antitrust priorities, the Reagan presidency must not be neglected. This period clearly revealed the extent and the limits of the organizational changes initiated in earlier decades. The new economic-analytic capacities were applied in a most creative fashion to shape policy and condition the activities of other actors in the political-institutional environment.

The Antitrust Division

The Reagan administration appointed Chicago school lawyers and economists as political executives to the Antitrust Division. They explicitly rejected the traditional goals of policy and promoted a well-defined enforcement agenda. Drawing on microeconomic theory, they declined to enforce the prohibitions against price discrimination, reciprocity, and monopolization. Because mergers were presented as manifestly efficiency promoting, there was little activity in this area. The appointees supported the enforcement of section 7 of the Clayton Act only in the area of horizontal mergers and only when the mergers would dramatically increase the probability of horizontal restraints. Indeed, antitrust enforcement was justified only when it addressed horizontal price-fixing or cartel-like arrangements that reduced output: the vast majority of cases were filed against these violations.[9]

When the 1980s are seen in historical context, it becomes clear that the Reagan revolution at the Antitrust Division was largely driven by rhetoric. To be certain, the administration was successful in realizing its goals; performance by most accounts was quite impressive, despite dramatic reductions in staffing. The caseload was in complete conformity with the stated goals: the lion's share of cases addressed horizontal restraints. Within a year of assuming charge of the division, the Reagan appointees settled the AT&T case on terms agreeable to the company. On the same day, the IBM monopolization suit was dismissed—after the division had invested twelve years and some tens of millions of dollars in investigation and litigation. The decision to drop the case was based, as one might expect, on the "flimsy" and "extremely tenuous" economic evidence.[10]

My main point is relatively simple: this revolution in antitrust was at most a coup. The majority of changes had already taken place as a product of the convergence of a decade-long process of organizational evolution and critical shifts within the economics discipline. Economic expertise was given an organizational presence at each stage of the policy process, creating an institutional transmission belt. The shift to Chicago forced the reevaluation of established policy goals and a redefinition of the role of the state in a market economy. As the new economics of antitrust was given a presence in the policy process, the caseload came into conformity with the concerns of the Chicago school. The successes of the Reagan administration can be explained through the correspondence of elite demands and organizational imperatives.

The 1980s remain a intriguing era in the history of the Antitrust Division. Tensions which emerged in earlier decades were largely resolved; the integration of the legal and economic staffs was all but complete. As the evolutionary process detailed in earlier chapters found an expression in complete integration of law and economics in agency affairs, the extent and limitations of change became clear. The events of the 1980s also revealed the extent to which the new economic and analytic capacities of the division could be directed toward the realization of distinct goals, once engaged by political elites with compatible visions of policy. The period was one of great and perhaps unparalleled agency activism. However, the agency deferred to business in questions of organization and conduct.

The first and most consequential Reagan appointment was that of William Baxter as assistant attorney general for antitrust. Baxter's desire to redefine policy in the terms suggested by the Chicago school was as striking as his faith in economic analysis. According to Baxter: "Economic efficiency provides the only workable standard from which to derive operational rules and by which the effectiveness of such rules can be judged. Efficiency gains or losses from mergers are at least theoretically calculable, and economic theory provides a basis for making a priori determinations as to the circumstances under which mergers are likely to reduce economic efficiency. The same cannot be said for social and political standards. . . . There is no objective measure for valuing social and political costs and benefits."[11] The established policy goals—while

A Reagan Revolution?

clearly a product of political will—could not be reconciled with the economic goals of policy. When the two came into conflict, Baxter's advice was simple. "To the extent that [the traditional goals] are inconsistent with increased consumer welfare or operate through some manner other than improved market or firm efficiency . . . they have no part in the objectives of antitrust law."[12] Basing policy on efficiency doctrines was not, for Baxter, truly a redefinition of policy. Rather, it was a return to the original ideal of antitrust. Indeed, in a 1982 essay he argued that efficiency was "the only legitimate objective that [could] be distilled from the fundamental congressional goals of the antitrust laws." Following the line of reasoning, antitrust policy had lost sight of its original mission. The division could play a positive role in reestablishing the integrity of antitrust through the selective enforcement of the laws. Drawing on the broad discretion of the executive branch, he argued that the division had no duty to prosecute cases involving illegal conduct if the economic merits and legal foundations were questionable. He concluded his essay on a confident note. "By selecting the cases it prosecutes and the arguments it makes with care, the executive branch will fulfill its potential as an independent force in the evolution of the antitrust laws."[13]

This activist orientation and economic interpretation of antitrust characterized the tenure of Baxter and his successors in the Antitrust Division. With few exceptions, Reagan's assistant attorneys general—William Baxter, Douglas Ginsburg, J. Paul McGrath, and Richard Rule—coupled an academic's faith in the tenets of pure microeconomic theory and a conviction that the division could be used to bring about substantial and permanent changes in antitrust policy. Through their activities, economic analysis came to play a dominant role in the definition of division objectives at the executive level; the political goals were, in essence, reconciled with those already established at the organizational level.

Toward the Convergence of Law and Economics

Though subtle, the conflicts between the attorneys and economists grew both in frequency and severity during the early 1970s. The conflicts were the predictable expressions of the professionalization process: they reflected the divergent norms and career orientations of the staffs and the growing influence of economists in an agency traditionally monopolized by attorneys. The tensions diminished as the staffs gained experience working together; changes in antitrust doctrine and court decisions forced close interaction throughout the policy process. During the 1980s, the conflicts between the economists and attorneys were largely resolved—in favor of the economists. Attorneys adapted to the new role of economic analysis in the policy process. As a result, the economic merits of a case increasingly found an expression in the enforcement recommendations, regardless of their origin within the division.

Reflecting the Reagan administration's pessimism regarding the role of regulation in a market economy, the Antitrust Division was subjected to unprecedented reductions in support. The Reagan budgets forced substantial cuts in the division's staff. In 1980, the Antitrust Division had a professional staff of 352 attorneys and economists stationed in Washington, D.C., with another 122 attorneys in the division's field offices. Six years later, the numbers had been reduced to 166 and 95, respectively. Beneath these aggregate figures, the presence of the staff economists was actually increasing relative to the legal staff. In 1980, there were 1.5 economists for every 10 Washington attorneys. With the staff reductions falling disproportionately on the attorneys, there were 2.9 economists per 10 attorneys by the end of the period. In less than a decade, the relative strength of the economic staff almost doubled.[14]

The staff reductions, combined with a high turnover rate, affected morale and accelerated a change in the orientation of the legal staff. Economics increasingly came to play a central role, structuring the activities even of the division's attorneys. As one deputy assistant attorney general explained:

> You've got to remember that we have been cut in half since the beginning of this administration. The ones who are left are not exactly a random sample of those who were here before. . . . I think that a lot of the people who left were good litigators, but they didn't want to be restricted by the economics. In hiring, more and more attorneys have learned economics, and we have increasingly tended to hire people who are in the Chicago tradition. It's a much more attractive place for them to be for the same reason that these other people were leaving. I don't really think that it was so much a bloodletting process as simply a natural evolution of the legal staff, a case of natural selection.

The new attorneys differed from their predecessors in their sophisticated knowledge of economic theory and their belief in the relevance of economics in antitrust. Much of the increasing influence of economic analysis in the legal staff was derived from this source. However, it was also forced by an important change in the policy process.

The case-selection process that emerged over the course of the past decade had three stages. First, an attorney and economist worked as a team to determine whether or not significant anticompetitive problems existed in a given sector. If problems were identified, the lawyer and economist compiled separate recommendations regarding the merits of a potential case. The two recommendations were formally separate: the legal memo provided a statement of fact, the economic memo provided the analysis. In practice, however, there was a great deal of informal coordination at this stage of the process. The two recommendations were subsequently sent through the litigation unit and the Economic Policy Office, approved by the unit leaders, and submitted to the assistant attorney general. Under William Baxter, it became division policy that cases would be filed only when there were firm legal and economic underpinnings. Even if there was evidence that the law had been violated and reason to believe that the division could triumph before the courts, a case would not be approved unless economic analysis revealed that enforcement would be economically beneficial. The division economists and attorneys each exercised what amounted to veto power in the enforcement process.

It is necessary to be clear on two related points. First, the legal and economic staffs were in agreement as to the vast majority of recommendations. Economists categorically agreed that bid-rigging and price-fixing arrangements should be prosecuted, regardless of the magnitude of the offenses. This opinion fit well with the attorneys' own professional training: Section 1 violations were seen as simple cases of white collar crime. Moreover, their per se illegality reinforced the decision to file. Since the mid-1970s, the bulk of cases addressed section 1 offenses. The instances in which the economists might veto a case decision (e.g., in a civil matter) were rather limited.

Second and more important, because the law and economics were closely interwoven, the legal and economic merits were not easily differentiated. In the words of one of the division's policy planners, "If the case has legal merits, it has economic merits; if it has economic merits, it has legal merits. It is difficult to think of a case where the two questions can be addressed separately." In practice, this may be an overstatement of the fact. Certain vertical restraints, for instance, retain their per se illegality, despite substantial economic evidence suggesting that they are benign or yield distinct economic benefits.[15] Except for certain strands of court doctrine, the law and economics of antitrust are largely inseparable. Significantly, in areas where cases may have legal merits without having economic justification (e.g., vertical restraints), the division has been relatively inactive.

The integration of the legal and economic staffs reflected the changes in the antitrust debates detailed in chapter 4. However, it remained in many ways an organizational adaptation to changes in process and judicial reasoning. The new emphasis on economic analysis in the policy process forced the legal staff to adopt economic reasoning when preparing case recommendations. As one division official noted: "As it became quite clear that nobody would get a case through the division which didn't make economic sense, those people who were here who said 'this is the law, we can win this case because its illegal' found life here very unpleasant. They would stay up all night working on briefs, only to get trashed because they were lacking in economic theory." Because the economic merits of a potential case often proved definitive, the attorneys had reason to increase their economic analytic skills and work closely with the EPO economists in the preparation of case recommendations. The Economic Policy Office played an important role in promoting this integration. At the request of agency officials, the office conducted courses in microeconomic theory and industrial organization as part of what was affectionately referred to as EPO-U. Because these courses were mandatory, they engendered the resentment of some of the attorneys. Nonetheless, given the importance of economic criteria in case selection, attorneys had a great incentive to attend.[16]

The increasing economic sophistication of the legal staff was undisputed. As the division's chief economist noted, "Some of the best economic analyses I've seen here were written by attorneys." We should not, however, exaggerate the degree of convergence. Professional differences still exist. While the prosecutorial spirit was restrained, it was not exorcized.[17] The attorneys have become more sensitive to the economic merits of a case and more accepting of the role of economic analysis in the policy process. However, many attorneys continue to conceive of the Antitrust Division as a law enforcement agency with the central mission of prosecuting those who violate the law. They have merely adapted to the growing importance of economics. The comments of the chief of one of the litigation units is most revealing in this respect.

A Reagan Revolution?

There is always pressure to work within the consensus. We are soldiers in that sense. If the rules of the game are that you have to know economics, we will know economics. We have our own views, but ultimately someone makes a decision, and we go to war and bring a case. We do the best we can to litigate it within the existing constraints. . . . We are oriented to litigation. That's how we keep our best people. It's hard to get good people to work on a section 7 investigation if they feel it is going to be analyzed to death when they want to bring the case. They will take any rules you or anybody sets and work with them. The best of them will understand the rules and marshal the facts to do it. But get rid of the case quickly.

The analytic and organizational distance separating the legal and economic staffs has been reduced, not eliminated. The key factor to explaining the greater convergence of the two staffs is found in the evolution of the division and of the policy process. The two staffs can no longer operate as distinct entities.

Organizational Change

The convergence of law and economics was partially reflected in, and partially promoted by, organizational changes in the 1980s. The formal organization of the division was not altered significantly during the first years of the decade. The structure of the division changed in dramatic fashion in 1984, however, when it was reorganized under the direction of Assistant Attorney General Douglas Ginsburg. The changes were partly designed to streamline the organization: staff reductions left some of the existing units unable to function, while creating an overabundance of management positions. With respect to the functions and jurisdictions of the various sections, the division had evolved in a somewhat incoherent manner. The reorganization consolidated existing units and redistributed duties when appropriate. In the end, the reorganized division consisted of two parallel units reflecting the principal concerns of the agency: antitrust litigation and regulatory intervention.[18]

The litigation units were reconstituted under the leadership of two deputy assistant attorneys general, one for litigation and the other for regulatory affairs. The deputy assistant attorney general for litigation was in charge of Litigation I and Litigation II, two general litigation units responsible for antitrust in the unregulated industries. The deputy assistant attorney general for regulatory affairs was placed in charge of three specialized litigating sections: the Professions and Intellectual Property Section; the Transportation, Energy and Agriculture Section; and the Communications and Finance Section. The Foreign Commerce Section, while retained, assumed a strictly advisory function; it was no longer involved in litigation but focused on the development of trade and international antitrust policies.

The most striking changes associated with the 1984 reorganization took place in the economics staff. The reorganization of the office closely paralleled the above-mentioned changes. The Economic Policy Office was reconstituted as the Economic Analysis Group. It was divided into two sections, the Economic Litigation Section and the Economic Regulation Section. The new organization promoted the greater interface of the economic and litigating units. The Economic Litigation Section is primarily involved in antitrust activities and works with Litigation I and II. The Economic Regulation Section focuses on regulatory intervention and works closely with the sections involved in regulatory affairs. The most symbolic and to many the most remarkable product of the reorganization came with the elevation of the division's chief economist. The director of the Economic Policy Office was renamed the deputy assistant attorney general for economic analysis. The ascension of the division's chief economist was formal recognition of the position that economists and economic analysis had come to occupy in the policy process. As one former division official commented: "The significance of this change could not be overstated. It sent a message to all of us that the changes were permanent."

Policy, Guidelines, and Enforcement

The Reagan appointees promoted a positive program for antitrust. Their goal was not to undermine policy in a haphazard fashion, as some critics would suggest. They sought to redefine and rationalize antitrust, to bring it into agreement with a relatively well-defined economic paradigm. The pursuit of specific priorities was combined with agency activism in enforcement. The Reagan appointees were singular in their skillful use of the division's resources and economic analytic capacities in pursuit of their goals.

The enforcement record during the 1980s reflected the new activism of the division. In some years, the number of case filings was greater than during any other period in the agency's history, an exceptional point, given the budget cuts. The composition of the caseload was in complete conformity with the demands of Chicago microeconomics and the policy proclamations of political elites. In each year, the vast majority of cases were brought against horizontal restraints (e.g., price-fixing violations) under section 1 of the Sherman Act. A small percentage of cases were brought against mergers under section 7 of the Clayton Act. Monopolization cases were infrequently filed; in many years no monopolization cases were filed at all. When the enforcement record of the Reagan era is seen in comparative perspective, it becomes clear that the composition of the caseload was but a continuation of existing trends. The enforcement agenda established during the mid-1970s only found a more striking expression in the 1980s. If the argument made in this chapter is correct, then the caseload priorities were less an expression of the policy agendas of political executives than a product of organizational evolution combined with changes in the economics profession, transmitted through the antitrust community. For comparison purposes, the caseload during the Reagan administration is presented along with that of the previous decade in figure 7-1. Although enforcement figures are suggestive, the division was quite active outside the area of strict antitrust enforcement. Relying on the economic analytic capacities developed over the prior decade, the assistant attorneys general employed a number of strategies and devices designed to articulate their goals with greater clarity and redefine antitrust policy in Chicago terms.

Administrative Guidelines

In 1982, the division released its "Merger Guidelines" to replace those composed over a decade earlier under the direction of Donald Turner; they were subsequently revised in 1984. The new guidelines were intended both to prevent violations by providing businesses with a statement of division policy and to establish standardized criteria for screening, investigations, and case selection. Unlike their predecessors, however, the new guidelines presented a sophisticated economic model for determining when a merger would be subject to division action. The 1968 guidelines were basically a codification of existing doctrine as it had developed in the division and the courts. While

Figure 7-1

Antitrust Division Case Filings, 1970–1988

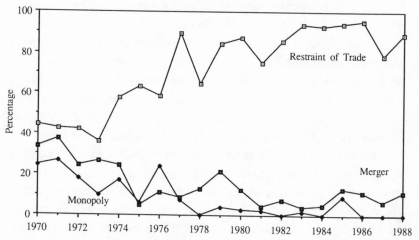

Source: Caseload data collected from appropriations hearings and Department of Justice, *Annual Report of the Attorney General*, various years.

policy was presented in economic terms complete with a set of structural decision rules, there was no central, defining, economic model. For present purposes, one of the most significant aspects of the new guidelines was the fact that they promoted—if not forced—a greater integration of the economic and legal staffs within the policy process. The theoretical sophistication of the new guidelines required that those using them possess or have access to economic expertise.[19]

The guidelines suggested a reorientation toward mergers, stressing their important and positive role in the economy. "Although they sometimes harm competition, mergers generally play an important role in a free enterprise economy. They can penalize ineffective management and facilitate the efficient flow of investment capital and the redeployment of existing productive assets. While challenging competitively harmful mergers, the Department seeks to avoid unnecessary interference with the larger universe of mergers that are either competitively beneficial or neutral."[20] In earlier decades, section 7 enforcement was referred to as antimerger policy. This depiction was less than appropriate in the 1980s. Mergers were presented as efficiency promoting, clearly in agreement with the tenets of Chicago school industrial organization.

Despite this agreement, the guidelines were reminiscent of their structuralist predecessors. The 1982–84 guidelines established concentration thresholds to direct section 7 enforcement decisions. The new guidelines employed the Herfindahl-Hirschman Index (HHI), a measure of market structure that is often considered superior because it reflects both levels of concentration and the distribution of market shares among the largest firms. The HHI is determined by summing the squares of the market shares of every firm in a market. A market with a single firm and a market share of 100 would have an HHI of 10,000; an atomistic market could have an HHI approaching 0. The guidelines stated that mergers would be challenged if they took place in a market with an HHI of 1,800 or placed the market above this threshold. Mergers in markets with an HHI of from 1,000 to 1,800 would be examined with care. A market with an HHI of 1,800 might consist of one firm with a 30 percent share, one firm with a 20 percent share, and five firms each with a market share of 10 percent. Translated into the concentration measure employed in 1968, such a market would have a four-firm concentration level of 70. When compared in this manner, the enforcement policies presented in the two guidelines appear comparable.

The differences between the two policies become clear when one considers the method of market definition presented in the new guidelines. The guidelines presented a model of a potential monopolist for defining and differentiating relevant product markets. With this model the division would consider a hypothetical situation in which a monopolist producing the product in question imposed "a small but significant and nontransitory" increase in price. If this price increase caused buyers to shift to substitutes, then this product group would be added to the market. This experiment would be repeated until product substitution was no longer possible. The division employed a similar method to identify the firms that had "productive and distributive facilities that could easily and economically be used to produce and sell the relevant product within one year" in response to a price increase. Firms which could shift into the product market (as determined in accordance with the procedure described above) were considered part of the market. A similar approach would be applied in determining the geographic market. Once again, the division considered a hypothetical situation in which a monopolist imposed a "small but significant and nontransitory" increase in price. If buyers shifted to producers in other regions, these regions would be considered part of the relevant geographic market. As before, the experiment would be continued repeatedly until a monopolist's price increase could be sustained.[21]

The approach adopted to determine the relevant market is quite important, given the composition of the Herfindahl-Hirschman Index. As the market expands in size, the market shares of individual firms decrease, thus reducing the HHI. The potential monopolist model discounts entry barriers—much in keeping with the new learning in industrial organization—thus making it possible to expand the market well beyond that which would have been identified under earlier division policy. Although the thresholds adopted in the 1968 and 1982–84 guidelines appear generally comparable, in practice the new guidelines were far more permissive than one might otherwise expect because of the expansive definition of markets.[22]

The 1968 guidelines provided pure structuralist criteria to be used when judging the legality of a merger. In contrast, the new guidelines identified a host of nonstructural factors that would prove relevant in the determination of whether to challenge a merger. For the most part, these factors would lead the division to discount the HHI when it exceeded established thresholds. These factors included foreign competition, possession of a new technology that was important to long-term competitiveness, a firm's financial difficulties, and a variety of factors such as the heterogeneity of the relevant product, differences between substitutes, and similarity and differences in products and locations of the merging firms if they affected the capacity of firms to collude. Levels of concentration would be discounted in estimating the impact on the market if firms were generally able to enter within two years, given a "small but significant and nontransitory" increase in price. Finally, the division stated that it would also consider past and present conduct in determining whether to challenge a merger.[23]

It is important to note that the 1984 guidelines, unlike those issued in 1968, explicitly stated that efficiencies would be considered in the assessment of mergers that exceeded established thresholds. "The primary benefit of mergers to the economy is their efficiency-enhancing potential, which can increase the competitiveness of firms and result in lower prices to consumers. . . . In the majority of cases, the Guidelines will allow firms to achieve available efficiencies through mergers without interference from the Department." Relevant factors included evidence that a merger held the promise of new economies of scale, the integration of productive units, plant specialization, lower transportation costs, or any of a host of enumerated efficiencies. The efficiencies defense was but another expression of the "new learning" in industrial organization and the driving concern with business efficiency.[24]

The new guidelines deemphasized vertical and conglomerate mergers. Symbolic of the new understanding, these two kinds of merger were collapsed into a single category of nonhorizontal mergers. This evidently reflected Baxter's belief that nonhorizontal mergers were of little if any competitive concern. According to Baxter: "As far as I'm concerned there is no such thing as a vertical merger. . . . Mergers are never troublesome except insofar as they give rise to horizontal problems . . . the vertical merger guidelines so far as I am concerned simply disappear."[25] According to the guidelines, vertical mergers would be challenged if the two markets would be fully integrated after the merger. Although it was acknowledged that entry at two levels could create substantial entry barriers, the guidelines quickly discounted capital barriers to two-stage entry, noting: "More capital is necessary to enter two markets than to enter one. Standing alone, however, this additional capital requirement does not constitute a barrier to entry to the primary market. If the necessary funds were available at a cost commensurate with the level of risk in the secondary market, there would be no adverse effect." This discounting of capital barriers was a pure application of the Chicago position on barriers to entry.[26]

The new guidelines presented an important departure from the policy set forth in 1968. The old guidelines were devoid of a model by which the relevant market could be defined. As a result, there was little consistency of analysis. The potential monopolist model—the core of the new guidelines—forced a much higher degree of analytic consistency. A division economist who worked with both sets of guidelines explained the critical difference in the following manner:

> The 1968 guidelines were very limited in what they said. They were just a statement of the market share numbers that Don Turner thought ought to be the standards of enforcement. There was nothing. The 1968 guidelines said nothing about market definition, except in overly general, almost useless terms. We didn't have to use the [1968] guidelines because there

was nothing to follow. The new guidelines contain a process; there is a definite, well thought out paradigm, a very specific paradigm. Two people sitting in different rooms, without communicating, could use the same facts to arrive at the same conclusion using the new guidelines. Under the old guidelines, ten people could come up with ten results—and often did.

A central problem with the 1968 guidelines was their descriptive nature. They presented a general description of policy with little concern with process. The new guidelines partially resolved this problem and allowed for a greater consistency of analysis. However, the introduction of numerous non-market-share factors allowed for greater division discretion in evaluating mergers. The guidelines' presumption that mergers were usually efficiency promoting created concern in some quarters that this discretion would be exercised to minimize enforcement.[27]

It is tempting to present the 1982–84 guidelines as an example of executive-led policy change. Baxter came to the division with a well-developed conception of merger policy; the guidelines were partially a product of his policy views. To a great extent, however, they were also the product of the organization. The guidelines' central model evolved over a span of several years. It did not simply emerge as a result of the Reagan agenda. One official presented the market-definition paradigm as the product of "an oral tradition" in the Economic Policy Office which predated the Reagan administration. Various drafts and memos circulated through the EPO for years. Indeed, one veteran economist stated that attempts to reformulate the division's merger guidelines dated back to the early years of the Economic Policy Office. In the end, the origins of the guidelines were untraceable. Baxter's influence cannot be denied. However, the ideas that were selected to provide a foundation for the new merger guidelines evolved along with the division. The origins of the guidelines can be traced to the interplay of ideas, institutions, and individuals. As a result, they appear to be a product of compromise. Concentration thresholds are combined with a discussion of factors that would otherwise render concentration insignificant.

In January 1985, the division released vertical restraint guidelines to present its policy toward nonprice restraints. The guidelines covered a number of practices, including exclusive dealing, tying, and territorial and customer

restraints. Division policy was easily summarized: "Vertical restraints generally have a procompetitive or competitively neutral effect." The division
provided a two-step test that would be applied to determine the legality of
vertical restraints. After an initial market-structure screen eliminating firms in
deconcentrated markets or with low market shares, it would conduct a structured rule-of-reason analysis. To "determine whether the restraint on balance is
anticompetitive," the division would weigh exclusionary and collusionary effects against efficiency gains. The guidelines noted: "In most cases, restraints
not 'screened out' in Step One will be found not to have an anticompetitive
effect through direct evidence of market performance. . . . In some cases,
further investigation will uncover persuasive evidence indicating that the restraint actually serves an efficient, procompetitive purpose."[28]

The vertical restraint guidelines represented a consensus both in the economics discipline and in the antitrust community with respect to the virtues of
vertical arrangements.[29] The guidelines were by no means a departure from
established division policy: the de facto policy of the 1970s became the
explicit and official policy of the 1980s. William Baxter first articulated this
policy before Congress. After noting that court doctrine in this area was
"almost totally incoherent," he stated: "There is no such thing as a harmful
vertical practice. There is no such thing as a vertical problem. . . . No one has
ever been able to explain to me with any degree of satisfaction how a vertical
arrangement by its own characteristics can give rise to an economic problem of
any kind."[30] As former assistant attorney general Thomas Kauper correctly
noted, the guidelines addressed an area of the law "in which nobody really
cares about the Division's enforcement intentions; because it is quite clear . . .
that the Justice Department does not bring these cases in any event." Kauper
could explain the guidelines only by making an analogy to "a form of simple
amicus brief" designed "to contribute to the orderly development of the law."
On the basis of the criteria put forth by the division and the stated economic
merits of most vertical arrangements, it was evident that the guidelines were
not designed for the prosecution of vertical restraints, but as an explanation of
why such prosecutions would be economically unsound. The congressional
response to the vertical restraint guidelines was less sympathetic. Members of
Congress disagreed with the guidelines on procedural and substantive
grounds. The division formulated its policy without allowing for an adequate
opportunity for public review and discussion. Moreover, the guidelines pre-

sented a policy that was in direct opposition to established court doctrine. As a result, the guidelines represented division judgments rather than the law. These objections prompted a congressional resolution demanding that the guidelines be withdrawn.[31]

The complexity of the merger guidelines forced the greater integration of the legal and economic staffs through the merger-screening process mandated by Hart-Scott-Rodino. The screening process as first established was quite similar to the general process of case selection and development. At the screening stage an economist formed a team along with one or more attorneys. Together they decided whether a proposed merger had anticompetitive effects. About 95 percent of the filings were simply discarded at this stage. When a merger appeared troublesome, the division would request additional information. If, after the analysis was completed, some grounds existed for opposing the merger, the economist and attorney(s) completed separate analyses and recommendations, which were then presented to the assistant attorney general. On the basis of the legal and economic merits, a decision was made whether to challenge a merger. If the decision was positive, the economists and attorneys were reunited to construct the case and design appropriate remedies. Since the beginning of premerger screening, only about 1 percent of the filings have found a final expression in a case; 99 percent have been screened out. This merger-screening process forced the close interaction of the professional staffs. Once the process was anchored in the relatively complex model presented by the new guidelines, a close working relationship became an absolute necessity.[32]

Toward the end of 1986, the number of premerger notifications coming into the division increased in dramatic fashion as firms sought to make acquisitions before changes in the tax code took effect. The increased demands on the division were managed by providing the economic staff with the primary role in merger screening. The process detailed above remained in place. However, the filings went directly to the Economic Analysis Group for an initial screening. The economists were granted the authority to allow early termination of the waiting period. The formal screening process was engaged and attorneys were brought into the decision-making process only when the economists believed that a competitive problem existed. It is important to stress that the revised merger-screening process was designed as a temporary measure to address an unprecedented influx of Hart-Scott-Rodino filings. According to division officials, economists, and attorneys, the new process was highly efficient. It allowed for the quick review and dismissal of filings. Since the vast majority of cases posed no competitive problem whatsoever, the benefits of an initial screening were obvious. The arrangement, nonetheless, gave rise to a number of objections on the part of the antitrust bar, former officials, and the press. There was a shared concern that Chicago school economists had taken control of the agency and would give their blessing to all mergers, thus putting an administrative end to the nation's merger policy. Although many division officials, including the assistant attorney general, suggested that the new system might be worth retaining on a permanent basis, there was a consensus that it was politically unviable.[33]

Division officials agreed that the new screening system was quite efficient and categorically rejected its political significance. A written response prepared by the division's chief economist described the origins of the revised process as "the spirit of Christmas," which led the economists to accept the "purely clerical chore of reviewing all Hart-Scott-Rodino premerger notifications." After minimizing the significance of the shift, he noted that "short of taking out the garbage, this is the least interesting job around here."[34] While the new procedure did not have a discernable impact on enforcement (it was, after all, only temporary), it was nonetheless significant. Given the conflicts and tensions of the professionalization process, it is striking that this procedural modification and the transfer of authority it entailed were possible at all. The new procedure and the lack of resistance within the division's litigating units were a testament to the enhanced position of economists in the policy process and the agency.

Given the lack of merger cases during the Reagan administration, commentators began to question whether the merger guidelines presented the division's policy as enforced. As the report of the American Bar Association's Task Force on the Antitrust Division noted:

The question remains . . . whether the 1984 Merger Guidelines accurately present the Division's enforcement policy as applied to actual cases. Guidelines should accurately advise the public of policies actually in place. Guidelines that mislead serve no advisory purpose, nor do they provide a vehicle for holding the Division accountable for its actions. The Division has brought very few cases in which the HHI levels for the postmerger industry were between 1000 and 1800, although the 1984 Guidelines indicate that in this range the Department "is likely to challenge" a merger that increases the HHI by 100 points or more, absent countervailing factors. Similarly, it appears that a significant number of mergers with HHI's in excess of 1800 and HHI increases above 100 have not been challenged, despite the 1984 Guideline's assertion that such mergers lack anticompetitive effects "only in extraordinary cases." The resulting public perception is that the Division may be pursuing an enforcement policy more lenient than the 1984 Guidelines dictate.[35]

During an interview a division official provided confirmation of the above observation, commenting: "Even the new guidelines are too damn restrictive. I think this is the consensus position here. In reality we set the Herfindahls at the 'wild blue yonder' level. In practice, this is the way it should be done."

Rewriting the Past

In addition to providing guidelines articulating division policy, agency officials needed to address the legacy of the past. A number of undesirable antitrust judgments were still on the books, some dating back to the early years of the century. Past decrees are the equivalent of administrative precedents. They are part of the public record and structure the expectations of business with respect to the division's likely response to antitrust violations. Moreover, to the extent that they restrain current economic activity and shape industrial structure, they may have a negative economic impact. As part of the attempt to rationalize antitrust policy, Baxter initiated the decree project in 1981. The project was designed to review systematically over 1,200 judgments to identify and modify or vacate those that were either simply irrelevant (e.g., the litigants were dead, the industry no longer existed) or "affirmatively undesirable," to use the words of one of Baxter's assistants. While the former were relatively benign, the latter were a cause of concern, for they often enjoined activities that were harmless, if not efficiency promoting. They frequently prohibited various forms of vertical relationships (e.g., exclusive territories and tie-ins) or forced the companies in question to give preferential treatment to particular firms.[36] Decrees that could not be justified on efficiency grounds were assigned to a litigating section and the Economic Policy Office. The economists assigned to the decree analyzed its economic impact and designed appropriate modifications, while the litigating section prepared model pleadings for the company or individuals in question. The division often pursued joint filings with the interested party seeking modification or vacation. Before the filing, division policy planners reviewed the pleadings to ensure consistency and compatibility with division policy.

The decree project, as originally conceived, was remarkably resource intensive and thus ultimately unfeasible. Only one-third of the 1,200 or more decrees under consideration were actually reviewed. Attempts were made to use resources efficiently: the most problematic decrees were commonly identified by the type of violation, under the assumption that they were the products of vertical restraint and monopolization cases. When Paul McGrath took charge of the division, the remaining decrees were allocated among the litigating sections for the final determination of whether their termination would have a positive effect. Simultaneously, the division issued a press release soliciting requests for review and modification or termination of existing judgments. While this accelerated the review process, a majority of judgments remained unaffected for obvious reasons. If judgments had become irrelevant or were not being enforced (as was often the case), firms were often unwilling to devote resources to their nullification. In other cases, companies refused to participate even when the decrees placed restrictions on their activities and they had received a guarantee of division support. In some cases, defendants feared that filings would create instability in existing relationships with distributors. Nonetheless, the decree project was a significant event in the division's history: it revealed how the agency's legal and economic-analytic capacities could be employed to bring past enforcement efforts into alignment with the new priorities.

Competition Advocacy

The Antitrust Division has been involved in regulatory intervention since the late 1960s; the importance of these activities was formally recognized in the late 1970s with the creation of the Special Regulated Industries Section. The objective was to further deregulation by placing the division's power firmly behind competition advocacy. As noted in chapter 5, the EPO played an important role in regulatory analysis and was central to the effort to limit and structure new regulatory initiatives. During the Reagan administration, competition advocacy became a division priority.[37] The division of the 1980s participated in regulatory proceedings in a number of agencies (including the Department of Transportation, the Nuclear Regulatory Commission, the Environmental Protection Agency, the Federal Energy Regulatory Administration, the Securities and Exchange Commission, the Federal Deposit Insurance Corporation, the Federal Reserve Board, the Federal Communications Commission, the Federal Home Loan Bank Board, the International Trade Commission, and the Postal Rate Commission) on more than six hundred occasions. According to the division's statement of priorities delivered as part of the appropriations process, competition advocacy was placed second, behind the goal of preventing and terminating private cartel behavior. Significantly, competition advocacy was presented well ahead of the goal of preserving a competitive market structure, a further indication of changes in antitrust enforcement.[38]

The emphasis on competition advocacy is not new. Indeed, the level of regulatory interventions is not significantly higher than that of the Carter administration. While the support for these activities was undoubtedly an expression of the widespread adherence to Chicago microeconomic norms, the emphasis has also come as a result of changes in the division's organization and caseload. The reorganization of 1984 facilitated both a greater interface between the legal and economic staffs and a higher level of specialization. The organizational separation of functions (i.e., antitrust and regulatory activities) cut across the legal and economic staffs. The creation of the economic regulation section in the Economic Analysis Group promoted the ongoing analysis of regulation. In addition, the economic staff has had greater resources to devote to regulatory analysis as the caseload has grown to include a greater proportion of criminal price-fixing cases. Economic input has always been the greatest in civil suits which address complex economic issues; criminal suits tend to be fact intensive in part because of the existence of per se rules. There is a consensus within the economic and legal staffs that price-fixing arrangements should be prosecuted as part of the division's law enforcement duties. While the division economists have been involved in using economic analysis to identify markets susceptible to price-fixing, these cases make less of a claim on the resources of the Economic Analysis Group. As the division pursued a Chicago enforcement agenda emphasizing criminal price-fixing, the agency's substantial economic analytic capacities were rechanneled into regulatory intervention.

Shaping Court Doctrine

The Reagan appointees clearly articulated a positive program for antitrust. The policy declarations of the agency leaders and the administrative guidelines left little question as to the enforcement intentions of the division. Horizontal restraints and, in extreme cases, mergers which would facilitate such restraints would be the mainstay of the division's efforts. Vertical restraints and non-horizontal mergers would be unchallenged because, it was argued, they had a positive impact on efficiencies and consumer welfare. Despite the clarity of division policy, one fact remained most troublesome: the vast majority of antitrust cases are filed by private parties and resolved in the courts. The successful reorientation of policy depended on the division's ability to influence judicial decision making. Two means were adopted toward this end: the Private Action Project and new legislation that would place restraints on judicial discretion.

Although the Antitrust Division had a history of intervening in private litigation, these activities were intensified during the 1980s. As an expression both of the division's explicit attempts to bring a greater coherence to antitrust and a recognition of the role which the courts and private antitrust suits have played in the definition of policy, Assistant Attorney General Baxter initiated the Private Action Project in 1981. This project consisted of a systematic campaign to identify pending court cases which could affect the evolution of court doctrine. Baxter explained, "We look for cases that have important potential for the shaping of doctrine, and facts that are suitable for those possibilities, good or bad: bad to be headed off; good, of course, to be encouraged."[39] When suitable cases were identified, attorneys and economists in the division drafted and filed amicus briefs, often working closely with the attorneys who were representing the accused party. By the second year of the Private Action Project, over thirty amicus briefs had been filed in federal courts. Over the span of the Reagan presidency, the division filed, on average, twelve amicus briefs per year with the Supreme Court and the Court of Appeals.[40]

The number of briefs filed was generally consistent with the level of filings during the Carter administration. However, because the goal was to reshape antitrust, the division's briefs often went well beyond the merits of individual cases and became explicit attempts to overturn well-established court doctrines. The most striking example was found in the amicus brief presented to the Supreme Court in 1983, concerning *Monsanto Co. v. Spray-Rite Service Corp.*[41] Assistant Attorney General Baxter argued the division's position, urging the Court to abandon its per se rule with respect to resale price maintenance, a precedent established in *Dr. Miles Medical Co. v. John D. Park and Sons Co.* (1911). Since the brief did not address the issues central to the case (the case was not being appealed on the basis of the per se rule), the division was unsuccessful. Nonetheless, the response to the division's attempts to alter court doctrine was quite pointed. Justice Brennan filed a concurring opinion designed solely to chastise the Justice Department for filing the brief. His decision noted that the precedent "has stood for 73 years, and Congress has certainly been aware of its existence throughout that time. Yet Congress has never enacted legislation to overrule the interpretation of the Sherman Act adopted in that case."[42] The congressional response was equally unambiguous: it placed riders on the division's 1984 and 1986 fiscal year appropriations bills, limiting its authority to devote funds to the Private Action Project.

A more explicit attempt to direct the evolution of court doctrine was made in 1986, when the administration presented Congress with a number of legislative proposals designed in large part to make the division's enforcement agenda a lasting feature of antitrust. Drafted largely by division personnel, these legislative proposals constituted a direct assault on judicial discretion and an attempt to recast much of antitrust in Chicago terms. The division recognized its vulnerability to the courts and sought to minimize it so as to maintain the integrity of the administration's policy agenda in future decades.[43] The centerpiece of the Antitrust Improvements Package was the Merger Modernization Act of 1986. The act was designed to amend section 7 of the Clayton Act to bring it into agreement with the economic theories embodied in the division's guidelines. After distinguishing between anticompetitive mergers and "procompetitive efficiency-enhancing mergers," the act mandated that when deciding on merger cases, the courts appeal to the criteria set forth by the division. The Department of Justice statement introducing the package made direct reference to the problem of judicial interpretation.

"While courts interpreting section 7 are increasingly looking to consumer welfare in their analyses of the competitive effects of mergers, the new language is a clearer expression of the goals of merger enforcement and is less likely to be misapplied. . . . The statutory requirement that these factors be considered will ensure that appropriate and complete economic analysis will guide the courts in ruling on challenges to mergers and will continue to be the basis of government enforcement efforts."[44] One agency official was more forthcoming with respect to the division's intentions. He explained: "We wanted to tie the hands of the courts. This is the way that we think mergers ought to be analyzed. Why leave it as a set of guidelines that the courts can use when and if they want."

Additional proposals included the Interlocking Directorates Act, which would have relaxed the Clayton Act section 8 prohibition of corporate interlocks between competing firms; the Foreign Trade Antitrust Improvements Act, which would have required the courts to consider a specific set of factors when deciding whether to exercise jurisdiction in private antitrust cases involving foreign firms; and the Promoting Competition in Distressed Industries Act, which would have provided the president with the authority to grant limited exemptions in the area of mergers and acquisitions for firms in industries which have been seriously injured by foreign competitors.

Correctly noting that the bulk of antitrust activity takes the form of private suits, the administration sought to limit the availability of treble damages with the proposed Antitrust Remedies Improvements Act. The act would have allowed the government and private litigants to recover treble damages for overcharges resulting from conspiracy, in broad accordance with the Chicago school concern over horizontal restraints. More important, the act would have eliminated treble damages for all other violations, allowing for the collection of an amount equal to the damages and legal fees. Reforms are needed in the area of private antitrust litigation.[45] The possibility of recovering treble damages often leads attorneys to present contractual matters as antitrust violations, thus swelling the docket with cases that have little bearing on antitrust. Nevertheless, the political goal was equally obvious. The elimination of treble damages would have reduced dramatically the number of private antitrust cases, thus limiting the courts' access to cases that have not been initiated by the Antitrust Division. By retaining treble damages in the area of horizontal arrangements, however, the majority of private cases would generally reinforce the division's enforcement agenda. Given the per se illegality of price-fixing, judicial discretion in these matters would remain relatively inconsequential.

Although there was support for some of the provisions of the administration's legislative package—particularly those sections addressing private antitrust cases—the package never emerged from committee. Indeed, many members of Congress were hostile to the administration's attempt to reform antitrust. Senator Metzenbaum, chair of the Senate Antitrust, Monopolies, and Business Rights Subcommittee, warned members of the antitrust bar who had supported some of the Reagan legislation. "I speak to you, you who are the experts who come before our Committee and suggest this exemption and that exemption, save your time, save the trip, because I'm not going to provide that exemption and you're not going to get it out of Committee."[46] The debates within the antitrust community were quite critical with respect to the Merger Modernization Act. While the economic norms which inform the division guidelines were accepted by many of the community members, there was a recognition that economic theory changes often rapidly and in a substantial manner. To codify what was in essence a set of administrative guidelines would be problematic because it would lend a certain permanence to a given understanding of the economy.

The Federal Trade Commission

The history of the FTC during the Reagan administration is remarkably similar to that of the Antitrust Division. There were common goals and similar initiatives, despite the different internal structures, external vulnerabilities, and historical legacies. The Federal Trade Commission Improvements Act of 1980 provided a vivid reminder of the limits of agency autonomy and the malleability of Congress when confronted by mobilized interests. While the act qualified agency authority, the organizational advances of the 1970s were not reversed: mechanisms for planning policy, evaluating cases, and managing resources remained in place. The economic-analytic capacities of the commission provided the foundation for the initiatives of the 1980s. The Reagan administration's agenda was imposed from above, but a similar agenda had evolved within the organization over the past decade. The coincidence of elite politics and organizational evolution made possible the policy initiatives of the Reagan administration. The structure of the commission continued to serve as an impediment to coordination and the full convergence of law and economics. However, the Reagan initiatives were largely successful because they combined with a strategy for overcoming the organizational barriers.

Reagan's FTC Transition Team analyzed the agency and its enforcement record and made a number of controversial and far-reaching recommendations with respect to structure, policy, and process. The transition team report called for an immediate 25 percent reduction in the agency's budget, suggesting that these reductions could be realized through the elimination of all ten of the regional field offices. The regional offices were presented as basically ineffectual "repositories of many of the [FTC's] misguided initiatives." In addition, it was suggested that resources could be saved through the termination of the intervenor funding program, a program which provided financial support for interested parties unable to afford the expense of appearing at commission hearings. The intervenor program had provided resources for many consumer and public interest groups supportive of the FTC's activist orientation. This constituency was no longer considered vital to the commission's activities.[47]

The transition report presented a detailed overview of policy and recommended a substantial reorientation of commission efforts. Shared-monopoly cases were condemned on the basis of their "extraordinarily weak" economic rationale. Likewise, any economic justification for merger cases was largely dismissed. There was no economic evidence that vertical mergers could harm competition. Horizontal merger cases based on concentration concerns were questioned as well. As the report noted, "Concentration, per se, is neither a necessary nor sufficient condition for adverse economic consequences." Because conglomerate mergers are either benign or efficiency promoting, "the Commission should be wary of standing in their way." Not surprisingly, activities subject to prosecution under the Robinson-Patman Act were presented as being of no concern. In keeping with the Chicago school doctrines that informed the report, the only area where increased antitrust activity was deemed appropriate was in the area of horizontal restraints. The report's recommendation was quite straightforward in this area. "Concentrate . . . resources on those horizontal collusion cases where injury is great and where the market will be slow to respond." In essence, the FTC Transition Team urged that the FTC place full emphasis on the economic merits of its cases and "terminate all cases based on 'social theories.'" To facilitate this redirection, the report recommended upgrading the status of the Bureau of Economics in the agency and requiring that all enforcement recommendations receive the joint approval of the Bureau of Economics and the appropriate litigating bureau prior to their submission to the commission.[48]

While the transition report was dismissed by many observers, its recommendations were not lost on David Stockman, director of the Office of Management and Budget. Within a month of the report's submission, Stockman proposed unprecedented reductions in the FTC's budget. Stockman's reductions would have necessitated closing the regional offices, eliminating the Bureau of Competition—and with it, the FTC's antitrust jurisdiction. Stockman justified these reductions before a House committee by noting that they were "an integral part of the Administration's efforts to redirect regulatory policy in order to reduce the burdens that misguided efforts have imposed upon the American economy."[49] The commissioners objected to the OMB budget cuts and the related reorientation of the agency. They sent Stockman a letter questioning "whether the appropriations process [was] the proper mechanism for ending over 65 years of antitrust law enforcement by the agency charged by Congress with that responsibility."[50] Subsequently, Stockman's recommendations met with the opposition of the Small Business Legislative Council, the National Federation of Independent Business, state attorneys general, consumer groups, and Congress. The budget cuts were modified: hiring freezes were imposed, and the staff was reduced in size, but the regional offices remained intact, and the Bureau of Competition retained its antitrust duties.[51]

The Political Appointees: A Revolution from Above?

The Reagan administration brought with it a number of critical appointments to the commission and each of the agency's bureaus. Most significant was the appointment of James C. Miller III to the chairmanship. Miller held a Ph.D. in economics from the University of Virginia, a school quite sympathetic to Chicago microeconomics. His economic expertise, governmental experience, and conservative pedigree were beyond question. He served on the Ford administration's Domestic Council Regulatory Review Group, the Council on Wage and Price Stability, and the staff of the Council of Economic Advisors. Since 1977, he had been a resident scholar at the American Enterprise Institute. He was the first economist ever to sit on the commission, the first nonattorney in three decades.

Miller headed the Reagan administration's FTC Transition Team and was quite sympathetic to the claims that the agency was in need of major reform. Miller would later recall: "We found that the agency had strayed far beyond the vision of Wilson and in many respects had come to embrace the interventionist, paternalistic approach that Congress had rejected in 1914. It had engaged in repeated efforts to extend the scope and reach of the nation's antitrust laws beyond any reasonable interpretations of its mandate." The FTC's failure was tied, in large part, to the status of contemporary economics in the agency. Miller noted that the agency had a "penchant for not assessing the unintended, often perverse, effects of many of its programs and policies." As he observed: "In each case the agency seemed largely out of touch with emerging trends in legal and economic research. It seemed almost incapable of comprehending the influence of such research on evolving court interpretations of the nation's laws on competition."[52] The Miller appointment was critical, given the managerial powers of the chairmanship. Miller used his authority as chairman to make a number of strategic appointments to each of the agency's bureaus, to redefine the priorities of the commission, to limit the influence of internal opposition, and to repair the agency's damaged relationship with Congress. Under his direction, the factors that had impeded the organizational integration of law and economics in agency affairs were surmounted.

Miller's appointees to the bureaus were drawn from the Chicago school and the public choice and law-and-economics movements.[53] Thomas J. Campbell was appointed director of the Bureau of Competition. He was an attorney and carried an economics Ph.D. from the University of Chicago. The Bureau of Economics was placed under the directorship of Robert Tollison, who was also named acting director of policy planning. Tollison was executive director of the Center for the Study of Public Choice at Virginia Polytechnic Institute, and a former visiting professor at the Law and Economics Center at the University of Miami. Timothy J. Muris was appointed director of the Bureau of Consumer Protection. He was a member of Reagan's Task Force on Regulatory Relief, a former professor at the University of Miami's Law and Economics

Center, and a Law and Economics Fellow at the University of Chicago Law School. He had previous experience at both of the antitrust agencies and coauthored a critical study of the FTC.[54] Economists were placed on each of their staffs as advisers. By the end of Miller's first year, each of the FTC's bureaus was under the leadership of appointees who could be characterized by their academic distinction, economic training, and adherence to free-market liberalism.

The appointees shared a common distaste for any public policies that weakened or forced a departure from market mechanisms. They argued that efficiency was in all cases the product of unfettered economic activity. The ramifications of this position could be quite astounding, especially with respect to the policies it could be used to support. As an extreme example, Robert Tollison, director of the Bureau of Economics, suggested undertaking what he referred to as "a natural experiment in the economy." He explained: "You would allow a lot of mergers to go through. You would allow a lot of people to put their money on the line, and we'll see what happens. . . . Then if there are anticompetitive problems, we can try to unscramble the eggs. . . . The idea of loosening up and letting the economy and the capital markets restructure out there, a lot, and policing ex post, is much more appealing to me."[55] While it is unclear that this "natural experiment" was anything more than an academic thought experiment, it indicated an orientation toward policy that was much different from that which had prevailed during the 1970s. Tollison and his fellows agreed with the transition report that horizontal restraints should be the primary focus of the commission's antitrust activities. Many of the business activities prohibited under existing law were seen as economically unsound, their prosecution a waste of scarce resources.[56]

In contrast with the image of the budget-maximizing bureaucrat that has animated conservative critiques of state intervention,[57] the Reagan/Miller appointees openly questioned the central mission of the FTC and challenged its existence. As one of the bureau appointees noted, "The optimum size of the Federal Trade Commission is undoubtedly much smaller than its current size; whether it's greater than zero is an open empirical question."[58] This skepticism with respect to the FTC's ultimate value was reflected in the proposed budgets for the commission. Under the Carter administration, the commission's 1981 fiscal year budget stood at $73 million, with a proposed increase to $78 for fiscal year 1982. Miller and the administration called for great reductions:

from a revised 1981 budget of $68 million, to $59 million for 1982, ending with a 1985 budget of $41 million. Once adjusted for inflation, the 1985 budget stood at approximately one-half the 1981 level. While Congress funded 1,719 workyears (i.e., full-time employees) in 1980, by the last year of the Reagan administration, this figure had declined to 986. Initially, Congress was resistant to the calls for budget reductions. However, the low levels of agency performance and the rhetoric of agency officials questioning the efficacy of the commission ultimately took its toll. By the end of the 1980s, Congress was providing less funding than requested by an already-understaffed agency.[59]

The new agency leadership agreed that a broad structuralist enforcement program would not contribute to the operation of free markets. However, the FTC could play a positive role once redirected to the areas of the economy where market power was persistent, namely, in the regulated industries and the industries in which public policy prevented the realization of efficiencies, protected competitors rather than competition, or legitimized cartel-like arrangements. As revealed by numerous indicators, the overall level of antitrust enforcement declined dramatically during the Reagan administration. The annual number of antitrust complaints declined from an average of 9.8 during the Carter years to 5.4 complaints during the Reagan administration. The commission issued but one complaint per year in 1983 and 1987. Likewise, the number of cases on the docket declined precipitously, from fifty in the last year of the Carter presidency to fifteen in the last year of the Reagan administration. The only areas that revealed greater levels of activity were competition advocacy and order modifications.[60]

A Managerial Strategy of Change

When comparing the Antitrust Division and the Federal Trade Commission over the decade of the 1970s, we may note that the movement toward a Chicago-based enforcement agenda was somewhat less pronounced in the case of the FTC. The extent of organizational change was limited both by the concentration of power in the litigating bureaus and by a policy process mandating that all filing be approved by a majority of commissioners. Miller sought to bring the caseload into complete conformity with a distinct economic paradigm. He used the extensive authority of the chairmanship in a most creative fashion to pursue a managerial strategy designed to overcome these organizational impediments.

A Reagan Revolution?

In 1982, the Federal Trade Commission was reorganized. According to Miller's own account, these activities were directed toward creating "an infrastructure to carry out a program of strong FTC enforcement . . . based on rational economic thinking." While this infrastructure was largely in place prior to the advent of the Reagan administration, the reorganization was significant for another reason. The reorganization consolidated the programs in each bureau and created a more hierarchical structure, designed to facilitate "top-down" management. In each of the litigating bureaus, separate deputy directors were placed in charge of policy and evaluation, and operations. Assistant directors were placed in charge of smaller "shops," each with between sixteen and thirty-three attorneys. The Bureau of Economics was reorganized to provide a greater interface with the litigating bureaus. The bureau had three deputy directors, one in charge of administration and research, the other two responsible for providing support for the Bureau of Competition and the Bureau of Consumer Protection. The Office of Policy Planning was eliminated, as planning functions were transferred to the Office of Executive Director and thus placed, indirectly, under the control of the chairman. Finally, the Office of Congressional Relations was moved from the Office of General Counsel to the Office of the Chairman, reflecting the need to nurture the FTC's congressional constituency.[61]

This reorganization concentrated power in the hands of the chairman and his appointees in each of the bureaus. The leadership of the bureaus could closely monitor the activities of the staff and control communications between the staffs and the commissioners. While the authority to recommend a filing remained vested in the litigating bureaus, by all accounts the bureau directors were in agreement with Miller as to the status of economic norms in antitrust analysis and the primacy of economic policy goals. This organizational reshuffling provided the basis for a managerial strategy designed to overcome the organizational barriers and vertical cleavages that had placed limits on the interplay of law and economics in the policy process. Moreover, it provided a mechanism for limiting the influence of Democratic commissioners who remained on the commission.

To pursue a coherent set of goals, Miller had to find the means of overcoming the lack of consensus on the commission and the problems this disunity could have over enforcement decisions. The evidence suggests that Miller adopted a strategy of limiting the influence of the opposition within the commission, thus enhancing his control over the agency's caseload. Commissioners Patricia Bailey and Michael Pertschuk, both Carter appointees, informed Congress that they had been officially banned from the evaluation meetings and denied access to staff reports and supporting documents. Miller justified their exclusion by arguing that the meetings were relevant only to those involved in management, namely, the chairman and his appointees. Pertschuk explained the significance of this exclusion. "Without information about which matters are mired in the evaluation process or killed outright, Commissioners other than the Chairman are nearly powerless to oversee the activities of the bureaus."[62] The universe of potential cases was now beyond the reach of the commissioners. In the end, the personal staffs and duties of Pertschuk and Bailey were reduced as well. As the agency's focus turned from antitrust to regulatory intervention, the influence of dissenting commissioners could be exercised only in the most limited of circumstances. As Commissioner Bailey explained, "The Commissioners do not select the individual targets of its intervention work—its staff selects those targets and reports its selection to the Commission by way of written notice."[63] As long as these targets were determined at the staff level under the direction of the chairman and his appointees, power was centralized in a single office.

Toward the Convergence of Law and Economics

In a progress report issued in 1982, the Miller administration stressed the commission's increasing reliance on economic expertise in each stage of the policy process. The report noted that the agency was seeking ways to "insure that cases targeted and actually brought genuinely benefit consumers and competition." The report went on to explain: "In an effort to reach that goal, the new administration successfully integrated economic analysis into all aspects of the Commission's planning, case selection, rule development, and prosecution of cases. Integration of economic analysis at all steps in the decisionmaking process not only has aided the Commission's law enforcement work . . . it has conserved resources which might otherwise have been squandered on matters which, if brought to fruition, would not make good economic sense."[64] Since the transition report was written under the direction of Miller, the goal of integrating economic analysis into the policy process could have been anticipated. However, as shown in chapter 6, this goal was less than novel: in the 1970s the economic-analytic capacities of the agency were enhanced through professionalization; economic expertise was given a greater organizational presence in all stages of the policy process. While Miller's reorganization, appointments, and managerial strategy accelerated convergence and the movement toward a conservative enforcement agenda, these efforts drew upon the results of an evolutionary process with origins in an earlier decade.

The early 1980s were a period of tight budgetary constraints. As noted above, congressional refusal to comply with the administration's budgetary requests was short lived. Competing domestic priorities, poor economic performance, and an unwillingness to support the expansion of agency resources made budget reductions a foregone conclusion. The decrease in appropriations forced the commission to reduce the size of its professional staff. While both the legal and economic staffs were reduced in size, the cuts were not equally distributed. In 1981, the Bureau of Competition staff accounted for 357 workyears. By 1984, the staff had been reduced by 15 percent to 305 workyears. In the same period, the Bureau of Economics was reduced from 156 to 151 workyears, a reduction of a mere 3 percent.[65] As a result of these changes in staffing, the economists had greater relative organizational strength than at any other time since the creation of the commission. Their strength, however, transcended their numeric presence in the agency.[66]

Under Miller's management, the directors of the Bureau of Competition and the Bureau of Economics promoted the greater integration of the attorneys and economists through in-house education conducted by staff and visiting academics. Staff attorneys were given courses in industrial organization economics; economists were given courses in antitrust law. While attendance was not mandatory, it was strongly encouraged. As a result of the closer working relationship of the two staffs and the efforts to create a general competence in antitrust law and economics, the agency's attorneys proved both capable in economic analysis and willing to consider economic criteria in their decisions to recommend cases.[67] As the head of the Bureau of Economics remarked: "Most of our attorneys are now really quite sophisticated. They are used to economic arguments. In fact, they make their own economic arguments: we have attorneys drawing economic diagrams and curves and basing their decisions on economic analysis."

The growing importance of the economists and economic analysis within the agency created pressure for change within the legal staff. Many attorneys made the necessary adjustments. Those who failed to adapt to the changing organizational environment encountered greater difficulties getting bureau leadership to act favorably on their recommendations. Many simply left the commission to find more lucrative employment in the private sector. Others unwilling to make the transition fell victim to the staff reductions. Although formal economic training never became a formal criterion when hiring new attorneys (indeed, few new attorneys were hired in the 1980s), it was viewed quite favorably. There was a consensus among the staff attorneys that one's ability to master the (correct) economic arguments underlying antitrust and willingness to grant a primacy to the economic factors had an effect on promotions within the bureau.

It would be tempting to overstate the extent of convergence. Attorneys were regularly appealing to economic analysis to support their case recommendations. However, it is difficult to determine whether this was the product of conversion or coercion. Undoubtedly, both factors were at work. As detailed in chapter 4, economic reasoning had become so central to the antitrust debates that economic competence was literally a precondition of influence. Likewise, as economists assumed a more central role in case screening and economic analysis became more important to bureau leadership and judicial decision making, a degree of economic sophistication became a precondition of successful performance. The legal and economic staffs were closely aligned by the 1980s. However, the question remains unanswered: Were the various mechanisms integrating their efforts primarily the products of a shared understanding of policy, or were they adjustments to a changing organizational environment?

An official in the Bureau of Economics suggested that the convergence of law and economics was reinforced by the new realities of the commission and the demands of the policy process. "The attorneys now understand that we bring an important dimension to antitrust. Despite our disagreements with them, we are essential to their analysis. . . . But have no illusions, we are a necessary evil and no more: they realize they really need us. If they can get through our arguments, they are usually going to get through the commission and win in court." An attorney made a similar observation when he noted: "Were trained as lawyers to build cases. That's what we do. But nobody wants to see their cases destroyed by the economists before it makes it to the commissioners. So we listen to the economists, we seek their advice. To do it any other way would be foolish."

Although we are primarily concerned with the antitrust activities of the Federal Trade Commission, it is imperative to note that similar forces were operating on the consumer protection side of the agency. During the 1970s, an evaluation committee was established to integrate law and economics in the definition of bureau policy. When Miller assumed the commission chairmanship, he gave economics a more immediate presence by assigning an economist to each rule currently under consideration. The economists were charged with determining whether the rules addressed significant economic problems and whether they could be justified on the basis of cost-benefit criteria. The Bureau of Economics continued to play a significant role in determining whether proposed rules had a sound economic basis. Those rules lacking economic justification rarely proceeded. When existing rules could not stand up to economic analysis, they were repealed. Attorneys in the Bureau of Consumer Protection were constrained by the growing role of economics in the agency, much as were their counterparts in the Bureau of Competition.[68]

Pressures from within the organization, the antitrust community, and the larger political-institutional environment interacted to enhance the role and status of economic expertise in the agency and the policy process. Even though the attorneys had more opportunities to express a position on a given enforcement recommendation, their contributions had to be justifiable in economic terms. Over the 1970s, economic analysis had become an important component of most enforcement actions as a result of the evaluation committees and the general trends in judicial decision making. During the 1980s, economic analysis became paramount, as commission officials effectively prevented case recommendations lacking in economic merits from reaching the commissioners.

Enforcement, Nonenforcement, and Competition Advocacy

James Miller came to the Federal Trade Commission with a clearly defined agenda for change. His principal goal, as stated in the transition report and before multiple audiences, was to bring the commission's policies into conformity with contemporary economic thought. The microeconomic theories which informed and reflected the administration's agenda recognized few competitive concerns anywhere outside of private cartel-like behavior and government-sanctioned restraints on trade (i.e., regulations). Vertical restraints, conglomerate and vertical mergers, and monopolization cases were eschewed by an administration convinced that economic efficiency promoted by unfettered markets and vigorous antitrust enforcement efforts were irreconcilable.

The general policy position of the FTC leadership was a pure expression of Chicago theory. Industrial concentration was rarely seen as a chief concern in merger enforcement or other areas of antitrust policy. Between 1981 and 1984, the FTC approved the nine largest mergers in the nation's history: Socal/Gulf, Texaco/Getty, Dupont/Conoco, U.S. Steel/Marathon Oil, Mobil/Superior, Southern Pacific/Santa Fe, Connecticut General/INA, Texas Gulf/Elf Aquitaine, and Cities Services/Occidental. Moreover, it approved a joint venture between the first and third largest auto manufacturers in the world. These activities would have quickly fallen victim to prosecution under the strict structural decision rules of the past. They were of little concern, however, when seen in the light of the new orthodoxy. The experimental antitrust initiatives of the past decade such as the innovative shared-monopoly investigation were allowed to expire. Support for new attempts to expand the reach of the antitrust laws would not be forthcoming. Perhaps as a final expression of the hostility toward the assumptions and predictions of economic structuralism, the commission eliminated the Line of Business program (a central source of data for the concentration studies conducted by economic structuralists) in 1984. This act was justified on the basis of cost-benefit analysis, despite the objections of other government agencies and evidence that the program yielded direct net benefits.[69]

Reflecting the lack of consensus on the commission, the FTC never articulated its goals and policies with the clarity exhibited by the Antitrust Division. In June 1982, the FTC released a statement of policy regarding horizontal mergers. The "Statement of the Federal Trade Commission concerning Horizontal Mergers" was far less detailed and specific than the Department of Justice's merger guidelines. The statement basically reaffirmed the division's policy, noting "the Department of Justice's 1982 revision to the 1968 Guidelines will be given considerable weight by the Commission and its staff in their evaluation of horizontal mergers and in the development of the Commission's overall approach to horizontal mergers." In practice, the division's guidelines have been adopted by the FTC for merger analysis, although FTC officials are skeptical regarding the guidelines' peculiar adherence to concentration thresholds. Any disagreements over the specific provisions of the guidelines are overshadowed by a consensus that two sets of guidelines issued by separate agencies analyzing the same mergers would be a source of considerable difficulties. In other areas of enforcement, the need for guidelines or policy statements has been nonexistent, since the FTC has simply failed to generate filings. The commission's failure to address policy with respect to vertical and conglomerate mergers was a genuine reflection of commission policy: it had been many years since the commission had focused attention on such cases. When the FTC has filed complaints, they have been primarily in the area of horizontal restraints, in direct accordance with the stated goals of agency leadership.[70]

The enforcement record of the 1970s was relatively unimpressive with respect to the number of cases filed. There were not the kinds of increases one might have expected, given the resources at the disposal of the revitalized commission. Nevertheless, the FTC's activities were often quite innovative. The commission made a number of attempts to extend the antitrust laws (and particularly section 5 of the FTC Act) through the filing of test cases. The caseload increasingly revealed a concern with horizontal restraints relative to vertical restraints. Continuing a trend which began during the 1970s, numerous cases were filed against professional and trade associations which were using professional "codes of ethics" (such as prohibitions on advertising) as a means of restraining competition and fixing prices. Indeed, this was one legacy of the 1970s that found consistent approval during the 1980s. If the reorientation of enforcement priorities was less distinct than that of the Antitrust Division, it undoubtedly reflected structural factors exclusive to the FTC.

The enforcement record during the Reagan administration diverges from that of the 1970s in that the number of filings per year decreased dramatically, showing little signs of recovery. However, the trend in the composition of the caseload is a continuation of changes initiated in the 1970s. A lack of Robinson-Patman cases and decreasing emphasis on vertical restraints is combined with a growing dominance of horizontal complaints. The vast majority of these cases were brought under section 5 of the Federal Trade Commission Act. A

A Reagan Revolution?

Figure 7-2

Federal Trade Commission Complaints, 1972–1988

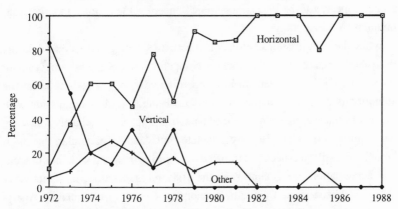

Source: Data supplied by Federal Trade Commission Bureau of Economics.

summary of caseload composition for the period 1972–88 is presented in figure 7-2.

The low number of filings and the growing presence of the conservative enforcement agenda may be closely related as products of the managerial strategy employed by Miller. All potential cases have to receive the support of a majority of commissioners. Without a consensus on the commission, this requirement could be the source of significant problems. By all indications, the Reagan appointees overcame the structural constraints and shaped the caseload by preventing economically unsound recommendations from ever reaching the commission for a vote. Apparently, vertical restraint and other cases which could not be prosecuted on efficiency grounds were simply excluded from consideration, assuming that such cases were generated in the first place. As noted above, under the Miller regime, commissioners were barred from the evaluation committee meetings—the critical institutional loci for assessing the merits of potential cases. Through this exclusionary strategy the policy expressed by the caseload could be manipulated at the bureau level, but only at the price of an overall reduction in the level of agency performance. The only part of the caseload that revealed a greater level of activism on the part of the commission was that of order modifications. The Bureau of Economics regularly suggested modification when the existing order failed to promote efficiency. By the end of the period in question, the commission's primary antitrust responsibilities were limited to deciding on horizontal restraint cases and modifying existing orders brought against activities that no longer appeared to be of any economic concern. Often, order modifications outnumbered case filings.

While the commission's enforcement activities were greatly reduced during the 1980s, regulatory intervention or competition advocacy became a major focus. The FTC's involvement in competition advocacy is nothing new. The authority is presented in section 6 of the Federal Trade Commission Act; regulatory intervention can be traced back to the years immediately following the creation of the FTC. However, the late 1970s and, in particular, the 1980s brought an explosion in competition advocacy to correspond with the competitive deregulation movement. With the 1982 reorganization, these activities were centralized in the Bureau of Economics' Division of Regulatory Analysis. In addition to filing statements before seventeen regulatory agencies and executive branch departments on a regular basis, the FTC testified at a number of congressional hearings. Moreover, it filed statements and briefs amici curiae or testified before legislatures in nineteen different states.[71] From a low of 13 interventions in 1981, the total number of interventions increased steadily, reaching a high of 102 in 1987.

Although the FTC is expected to serve as a force promoting competition in the economy, many consumer advocates and agency critics felt that the regulatory interventions of the 1980s exceeded the limits of the agency's economic expertise and legislative mandate. Pertschuk noted: "The Miller FTC seemed to want to create a deregulatory intervention program for the entire government, duplicating in some ways the oversight of the regulatory agencies by OMB. In attempting to extend the FTC's interventions to such a broad range of policy areas, the comments were often ideological in tone and analytically shallow and simply restated what the economists within the agency receiving the comments were already saying."[72] Whether Pertschuk's critique is well founded is a matter of interpretation. A recent study provides evidence suggesting that the substantive content of the commission's interventions were of critical importance, especially at the state and local levels. A survey of state and local officials who received commission comments on regulatory matters revealed that in 75 percent of the cases, the FTC provided new information or explained the significance of existing evidence that was unappreciated by the decision makers. In 39 percent of the cases, the decisions were based largely or in part on the recommendations of the FTC.[73] In contrast to Pertschuk's critique, the evidence suggests that the FTC's interventions were seldom redundant and often quite influential in shaping state and local politics.

Given the modest direct costs of competition advocacy ($2–$5 million per year) and the evidence of significant consumer savings in the hundreds of millions of dollars, there would appear to be adequate justification for the program.[74] However, one is forced to question whether a body charged with enforcing the antitrust laws can take much comfort in this limited victory. It remains a matter of fact that in some years the record number of regulatory interventions was combined with a historically low number of competition complaints. When considering the caseload and regulatory interventions in combination, it would appear that the FTC of the 1980s was best conceived as a *deregulatory* agency designed to minimize the instances in which an active expression of public authority would be tolerated. Whether this is a noble mission is open to question; whether it is the FTC's mandate is not. Regulatory intervention is neither the sole nor the primary mission of the Federal Trade Commission. When the prevailing body of economic expertise provides little justification for an agency's mission, the relevance of its legislative mandate is minimized.

Miller left the commission in 1985 to assume the directorship of the Office of Management and Budget. Daniel Oliver, a former editor of *National Review*, was appointed chairman. While Oliver's conservatism and belief in free markets brought a certain continuity to the chairmanship, his managerial style was much different from that of his predecessor. Apparently in an attempt to preserve the changes of the past several years, Oliver attempted to place a new policy office within the office of the chairman and to dominate the Office of General Counsel, thus creating intensive conflicts within the agency. While these organizational initiatives failed, they were in many ways unnecessary. Miller's innovations built upon, and were logical extensions of, the organizational changes of the 1970s. They were easily reconciled with, and supported by, the evolution of antitrust law and economics.[75]

The 1970s were a decade of capacity building at the antitrust agencies. Over the course of the previous decades, economics had been given an organizational presence in each of the two agencies, integrated into policy planning, case selection, and evaluation. These organizational innovations, when combined with a shift in economic doctrines, created a bias in the two agencies supporting a Chicago school enforcement agenda. When the Reagan executives called for a policy based in Chicago microeconomics, they were not forced to create new capacities. With the partial exception of the FTC, they were not forced to wage war against an intransigent bureaucracy or mediate conflicts between competing professional staffs. Elite politics and organizational evolution were reinforcing, supportive of a common vision of antitrust, public authority, and corporate accountability.

The changes in policy that occurred during the decade of the 1970s were largely unacknowledged by Congress and a series of presidents. Although it was dramatic, the movement toward a new enforcement agenda went largely unnoticed. The 1980s, in contrast, was a decade in which rhetoric outpaced change. As a result, resistance quickly mounted to an agenda which was already well in place. A policy that had been protected by a strong bipartisan consensus became politicized. In 1988, the American Bar Association established task forces to study the Antitrust Division and the Federal Trade Commission, in hopes of recommending changes in enforcement and management to guide the agencies as they entered the 1990s. The reports noted the low levels of performance and attributed much of it to the lack of resources at the two agencies. The ABA report on the Antitrust Division noted the well-established consensus regarding the importance of efficiency considerations in guiding antitrust activities. It went on to note the Reagan administration's anti-antitrust rhetoric and its role in limiting the support for the agencies. "The Division's statements about its vigorous anti-price fixing program are an important part of an effective enforcement program. The perception exists, however, that the Division is more concerned with its non-enforcement agenda—the studied avoidance of 'bad' cases that might hurt consumers coupled with legislative modifications that would limit the antitrust laws. . . . By primarily emphasizing the dangers of over-enforcement, the Division has contributed to a reduction in popular, political and budgetary support for the affirmative antitrust enforcement agenda that the Division must pursue if it is effectively to carry out its policy mandate."[76] The rhetoric of the Reagan administration was not without consequences. The cynicism of the political executives with respect to the efficacy and necessity of antitrust took a toll on political support for the antitrust agencies. While the initial requests for a reduced antitrust budget generated a congressional outcry, Congress quickly grew pessimistic regarding the administration's enforcement efforts and thus accepted a reduction of appropriations that made impossible anything more than a minimal enforcement agenda.

By all indications, the Bush administration has attempted to return to a more traditional antitrust enforcement effort. The appointments of James Rill as assistant attorney general for antitrust and Janet Steiger as chair of the FTC are highly suggestive. Both of these appointees claim skepticism with respect to the adequacy of efficiency explanations and have called for a reorientation of enforcement priorities, particularly in the area of mergers.[77] These and future political appointees will generally face dual administrative and political obstacles. First, they will discover a staff that is willing and able to pursue their own agenda regardless of the policy goals of political appointees. As one of the division's head economists predicted: "If a new assistant attorney general wanted us to prosecute an old fashioned structuralist case, the recommendations would come back 'Do not prosecute' from the economists and 'Do not prosecute' from the lawyers. If he wanted to go ahead with it, he would have to go it alone." Second, partially as a result of the rhetoric of the 1980s, partially as a result of the "new learning" in economics, Congress no longer views antitrust enforcement as a mainstay of American economic governance. The performance of the antitrust agencies during the Reagan administration, when combined with the claims that antitrust was largely unnecessary from an economic standpoint, may prove to have a long-term effect. Politics and economics may prove reinforcing in the sense that the economically questionable has become politically vulnerable as a result of the Reagan administration's posture in the antitrust debates. And thus, as the Sherman Act celebrates its centennial, we may have come full circle. After one hundred years of antitrust enforcement, a policy in search of a purpose may have found a mission that is, at best, a trivialization of its original goals.

CHAPTER EIGHT

The Triumph of Economics:
Institutions, Expertise, and Policy Change

In 1890, Congress passed the Sherman Antitrust Act to regulate an expanding industrial order and to restrain the power of corporate enterprises. The framers shared a liberal apprehension with respect to the growing concentration of economic power and its potential effects on local economies and individual autonomy. While they were cognizant of classic economic relations and suspicious of any business arrangement that might result in a reduction of output and an elevation of prices and profits, it would be difficult to depict Congress as having been concerned primarily with the economic ramifications of the trust movement or the economic impact of policy.[1] Antitrust was, in essence, a policy that addressed industrial organization and behavior in hopes of realizing a host of social, economic, and political goals. Purely economic objectives existed, but they did not subordinate competing objectives.

Discussing the goals of antitrust is itself problematic. Congress did not speak with a unified voice. The legislative debates surrounding the passage of the Sherman Act presented a loosely linked scattering of political, social, and economic goals. While legislators sought to prohibit unreasonable restraints of trade, the legislation failed to specify the kinds of restraints they found objectionable. The ambiguity of the legislation stands as a testament to the lack of consensus beyond the question of whether the trusts should be the object of public policy. Moreover, there was no prioritization of goals that would facilitate the interpretation of this remarkably vague piece of legislation. The task of weighing competing values and giving substantive content to the Sherman Act was delegated to those charged with enforcement: the attorney general and the courts.

While subsequent legislation brought greater precision to antitrust with respect to the forms of business conduct judged illegal, the political values that informed public policy remained largely unspecified. The goals and content of antitrust were ultimately defined through the interplay of the antitrust agencies and the courts. However, even court doctrine failed to provide a coherent and internally consistent statement of policy. Because cases were selected and framed on the basis of judicial precedent, the incoherence of court doctrine found an expression in policy. Moreover, because the antitrust agencies were underdeveloped as organizations, agency officials lacked the capacity to articulate a positive antitrust agenda or even determine whether the practices they attacked were unequivocally harmful to competition. Antitrust could be an expression of market liberalism, an instrument of economic populism, or a symbolic policy with little economic impact whatsoever. The final determination would depend on the goals one sought to emphasize and the strands of court doctrine one judged most prevalent. Antitrust was a policy in search of clarity and purpose.

It was in this context that economics was introduced into the policy process. Economics could contribute an organizing paradigm for judicial decision making. In agency management, it could allow for a weighing of competing enforcement agendas and an evaluation of past actions, thus promoting a more efficient use of agency resources. It could furnish simple decision rules for selecting cases and suggest which data were most appropriate to reveal the effects of a given restraint. As noted in chapter 4, the dominant structure-conduct-performance framework was well suited to antitrust analysis because its behavioral postulates and predictions were compatible with the collection of social, political, and economic policy goals and linked them in an intelligible fashion to industrial structure. Moreover, it provided relatively simple decision rules that could be employed without extensive, detailed analysis. Economic structuralism quickly found an expression in agency activities and court decisions.

One of the chief concerns of this book has been the dynamic and indeterminate relationship between bureaucratic organizations, expertise, and public policy. Agencies may be professionalized as a result of the initiatives of political executives or upper-level bureaucrats. The potential managerial benefits of basing planning and implementation on some objective criteria may be justified on the basis of technical merits. Alternatively, in our system of separate institutions and shared powers, professionalization may emerge as a product of politics. Oftentimes, significant changes in policy and administration will reflect broader political institutional conflicts.[2] Whether or not such initiatives are the direct result of political initiatives, they often reflect a consensus within the larger policy community that a given form of expertise is essential to the definition of public policy.

As I have argued throughout, providing expertise with a defining role in the policy process may yield significant benefits insofar as it promotes an expansion of administrative capacity. An agency may replace dependency on other institutions or clientele relationships with a degree of autonomy. Officials may possess the ability to define long-term objectives. However, this expansion of capacity remains fraught with ambiguity. As noted in chapter 1, the problematic nature of professionalization is derived, in part, from the subsequent impact of professional norms on agency affairs and the potential for new conflicts with existing staffs and bureaucratic officials.[3] However, there is a much more significant consequence, particularly in policy areas characterized by high levels of technical complexity. In such areas, the organizational inclusion of technical expertise is accompanied by a greater vulnerability to changes within the selected body of knowledge. Once professionalization has taken place, political and bureaucratic officials are forced to grant professionals a measure of autonomy to administer policy in accordance with the imperatives of their special expertise. There is no guarantee that the prevailing orthodoxy or future shifts in academic consensus will correctly address the key phenomena or reinforce the policies in question. To exert ongoing and detailed political control over deliberation by experts would be detrimental if not impossible. Even if elected officials and their political appointees possessed the technical competence to assess policy-relevant knowledge, political control would undermine professionalization by eliminating the integrity of expertise.

In the case of antitrust, the authority of economics in the policy debates and the enforcement process was expanding; at the same time significant changes were taking place within the body of economic thought. The intellectual dominance of economic structuralism was successfully challenged by the Chicago school. A body of expertise that supported the multiple goals of policy and an activist enforcement agenda was replaced by a school of thought that questioned the logic of state intervention in general and the mission of antitrust in particular. As the economic staffs at the two agencies adopted Chicago-based enforcement criteria and as court doctrine embodied the new consensus, agency caseloads evolved to reflect Chicago school priorities. The irony of this situation is striking. Economic professionalization was pursued, in large part, because it would enhance administrative capacities and invest antitrust with a new rationality. And yet, it was the reliance on economics— albeit, following an unanticipated shift in the economic consensus—that weakened the justification for enforcing most of the antitrust prohibitions. In the end, administrative capacity fed on itself, devouring the will to intervene.

While the Reagan administration claimed credit for the reorientation of antitrust, the changes were well in place before the elections of 1980. The conservative shift in antitrust was the product neither of executive-level politics nor of the business-based coalition that gained greater influence in the policy debates of the 1980s. In the end, the triumph of economics in the antitrust debates and enforcement created the conditions necessary for the growing influence of the Chicago school in the definition of policy. The triumph of conservatism was an expression of shifts in economic expertise within professionalized agencies that were beyond the control of political actors.

The Argument Extended

Lessons derived from case studies are, by their very nature, of limited applicability. In the case of antitrust, the influence of economic expertise was enhanced by features particular to the policy—the ambiguity of the legislative mandate, the incoherence of court doctrine, and the clear correspondence of economic structuralism with the original goals of policy and the practical demands of administration. However, the appeal to specialized knowledge that was essential to the changes in antitrust is not particular to this policy. Indeed, it has become increasingly common for elected officials to address complex social and economic problems that require a reliance on scientific or social scientific knowledge and a delegation of authority to expert administrators. To the extent that the administration of policy is vulnerable to shifts in the chosen expertise, the lessons drawn from the case of antitrust can be generalized.

The implications of this study go beyond the question of delegation to address the role of ideas in institutional development and policy change. A number of recent works suggest that ideas have a greater relative impact in nations with state structures that facilitate expert consultation as part of the ongoing examination of policy and administration. Advisory systems allow for the integration of intellectual advances and experiences from other nations to generate and assess innovative policy alternatives. Building on Hugh Heclo's comparative study of welfare policy initiation in Britain and Sweden,[4] researchers have examined innovations in macroeconomic management, social welfare initiation, and agricultural policy.[5] In general, the studies have found that the influence of economic or social theories in policy design and administration is dependent on the structure of state institutions. When seen in comparative perspective, intellectual advances will have a much greater impact on policy design in states with established mechanisms to provide policymakers with continual access to expert advice and the administrative capacities necessary to implement the new policies.

Ideas are a force in the definition of public policy. However, they are not free-floating entities that exercise influence independently. Rather, they interact with institutions and shape policy after having gained an organizational presence within the policy process. As revealed by recent studies of the role of Keynesian theory in designing responses to the Great Depression, these cases may be quite dramatic insofar as intellectual innovations are linked with pressing societal problems and the demands of various social groups.[6] However, ideas need not be integrated into the policy process through advisory structures, nor must they be linked with immediate crises to play a critical role in the design of policy. As the case of antitrust reveals, the interplay of ideas and institutions may be far more subtle, particularly when issue complexity is combined with relatively low levels of salience. Policy-relevant ideas may be integrated directly into bureaucratic organizations, forcing policy change at the process level.

In American political studies, the role of ideas in policy change is most often presented within the dynamics of pluralist politics. Particular ideas, though generated in highly specialized debates within policy communities, are popularized and employed, in part, because of their capacity to link the demands of otherwise diverse constituencies. Political entrepreneurs use ideas as instruments of coalition building, a necessity in a system in which the policy process bridges multiple institutions and political parties fail to lessen horizontal fragmentation.[7] At times, the mechanisms of transmission are presented as much more complex, and ideas are granted a far greater degree of independence. For example, in their influential study of deregulation, Martha

Derthick and Paul Quirk argue that the ideas surrounding the procompetitive deregulation movement influenced elected officials, who imposed demands upon the regulatory commissions via the institutional sanctions used to preserve the principal-agent relationship (e.g., appointments, oversight, budget hearings). However, political executives were not simply responding to political pressures when promoting policy change. Rather, some commission officials promoted deregulation because they were convinced that the economic costs of many regulations were exorbitant. In short, they were independently seeking deregulation even as reinforcing pressures were being placed on their agencies by other institutional actors and the economic arguments supporting deregulation were being advocated by a large and diverse interest coalition.[8]

There can be little question that the influence of policy-relevant ideas in the definition of policy is often driven by pluralist politics. Ideas can link the interests of otherwise diverse groups, serving as an instrument of coalition building. There is much to suggest that this process is the norm in the United States. However, the case of antitrust demonstrates that vigorous interest-group activity is not a necessary condition. While the decision to professionalize was politically forced—particularly in the case of the Federal Trade Commission—the same cannot be said with respect to the changes in policy that were to follow. Indeed, at the time in which the changes in policy were taking place, elected officials conceptualized antitrust in the terms suggested by economic structuralism. Congress was considering deconcentration legislation and strengthening the antitrust laws; presidents were presenting structuralist enforcement as a necessary component of competitive deregulation. If any relationship can be identified between the changes in policy and political debate, it is precisely the opposite of what one adopting a pluralist perspective might expect. There was little direct correspondence between politics and policy change. Only several years after the changes were initiated and a "new" antitrust agenda was proclaimed by the Reagan administration did the debates regarding the virtues of the Chicago school of antitrust analysis spill over into the sphere of politics. Politics, in essence, lagged behind policy. By that time, any discussion regarding the merits of a Chicago-based enforcement agenda was immaterial, for the changes in policy and administration were well in place and unlikely to prove responsive to the demands of political officials. Ideas gained a certain independence from politics, once they were integrated into institutions.

The case of antitrust provides further evidence that policy analysts must seriously consider the active role of institutions in defining the terms of policy change. Most analyses of antitrust conveniently assigned responsibility for the shifts in enforcement policy to the vociferous Reagan appointees. Why did analysts and political officials attribute policy change to the administration? In part, because the antitrust politics of the 1980s were animated by a rhetoric that had not been witnessed since the time of Thurman Arnold. The changes in policy only became apparent once they were proclaimed by the new administration. This however, is only a partial explanation. It is also necessary to attribute the common explanation of policy change to the dominance of methodological individualism—the tendency to view political phenomena as reducible to individual interests and individual behavior. Individual interests may find an expression in the activities of political elites or interest organizations representing the demands of their members. The dominance of methodological individualism is apparent in the independent variables that call out for immediate attention when analysts seek to identify the sources of policy change. The political agendas or vested interests of elected officials and interest groups, shifts in public opinion, and electoral contests are often easily linked with policy changes to construct an explanation. In the case of antitrust, the changes could not be attributed to any of these factors, despite the apparent correspondence of political proclamations and policy. Indeed, the actual sources of change are apparent only when the analytic focus shifts from individual political actors to institutions.

Scholars are only beginning to assess the nature and magnitude of the policy changes associated with the "Reagan Revolution." It is entirely possible that many of the policy changes associated with the Reagan administration and past presidencies—particularly in issue areas characterized by high levels of complexity and low levels of salience—are at least partially attributable to earlier institutional change and the critical role of policy expertise in defining policy. While it may be convenient to attribute causality to individuals in positions of influence, the case of antitrust calls attention to an observation that is as old as the study of politics, namely, that institutions matter. The organization of public authority may, in the end, prove as important as the goals of those who exercise political power.

The Future of Antitrust

The Sherman Act has recently celebrated its centennial. It is only appropriate that this study end with a consideration, however brief, of current enforcement priorities and the future of antitrust—should one exist. It is critical to emphasize at the onset that the status of economic goals remains an open question. Members of the policy community commonly portray antitrust as an economic policy with the mission of promoting business efficiency. But outside of the inner circles, the dispute has not been settled. The legislative debates and history of court decisions are ambiguous with respect to the ordering of competing political values. Active participants in the policy debates have opined as to the appropriate goals of policy; a consensus has emerged which has shaped public policy and institutional development. However, there is no clear evidence that antitrust as an economic policy must take priority over the political and social dimensions of policy. Nonetheless, the discourse surrounding antitrust has been manifestly economic, a fact that must remain paramount when considering current enforcement priorities.

As currently enforced, antitrust constitutes little more than a curb on naked price-fixing and related forms of white-collar crime. Vertical restraints go largely untouched. Mergers are seldom challenged, although they generate greater concern than vertical restraints. The bulk of the antitrust provisions remain unenforced; they stand as little more than remnants from a distant populist past. If antitrust is understood as an economic policy—and solely as an economic policy—then its current incarnation may be more appropriate than any attempt to enforce actively the complete set of antitrust prohibitions. The focus on horizontal restraints and the lack of vertical prosecutions can be justified with relative ease. The prosecution of price-fixing conspiracies is not a source of difficulty when taken by itself. There is a general consensus that cartel-like arrangements promote inefficiencies by restricting production and elevating the price of necessary inputs. Since price-fixing has always been an important object of enforcement policy, the new understanding of policy has been benign in this respect. The redefinition of policy with respect to vertical restraints can be seen as being manifestly positive. The decision not to prosecute a variety of vertical arrangements is supported by all but the most ardent structuralists. Vertical restraints may be used as part of a strategy to monopolize. However, more often then not they serve important economic functions.

The Triumph of Economics

Following transaction-cost economists such as Oliver Williamson, vertical restraints are commonly employed when markets fail to allow for the efficient supply of inputs and distribution of outputs. Nonmarket contracting arrangements are used not to eliminate competition and create monopoly power but to overcome the financial costs and uncertainties that accompany certain types of market transactions.[9] If these enforcement decisions can be readily defended on economic grounds, the same cannot be said for merger policy. One must place merger policy within a broader consideration of antitrust's role in the contemporary economy.

Antitrust is often defended as a necessary means of preserving competition in an economy in which dominant firms seek to administer prices and production to control an entire industry. This vision of the economy is anachronistic, given the monumental economic transformation of the postwar period. The growing international economic pluralism has brought an end to the sheltered domestic economy that antitrust was designed to regulate. A majority of markets are open to international trade and vulnerable to competitive challenges from foreign-based firms. Attempts to monopolize would stimulate the rapid influx of goods produced abroad. In an economy open to international competition, the strategies adopted by the monopolists of the past are no longer sufficient to gain and maintain market power. Since U.S. firms are competing in an international economy, domestic market-share data reveal little. The relevant market for finished steel is no longer the eastern United States; it is global. As a result, proponents of industrial policy and opponents of government regulation of business are united in their conviction that antitrust must be redesigned or eliminated altogether.[10]

Any attempts to assess antitrust as an economic policy must be cognizant of the growing presence of the international political economy. However, antitrust must not be redefined within the false and constrained universe of alternatives that has structured policy discourse in recent decades. To acknowledge the changing nature of economic activity and the inadequacy of the traditional vision of the corporate economy is not, simultaneously, to affirm the Chicago school vision of economic activity or the extreme position that matters of corporate organization and conduct are best resolved by the market. The Chicago school, as a variant of neoclassicism, rests on a vision of the market as a natural, self-equilibrating, network of exchange. Market activity is efficient, and market activity tends toward a Pareto optimum. Given this characterization of the market, hostility to state intervention is easily understood. The myth of separate spheres (the market and the state) conditioned the design and scope of public policy in the United States. State "intervention" is justified when markets fail, for one reason or another, to fulfill their essential functions. Nonetheless, the vision of separate spheres is highly suspect. As systems of property exchange, markets rest on the public policies that define property rights and structure transactions and on norms of behavior that have evolved over time. The market, in essence, is an artifact of public authority. Most arguments regarding antitrust reform (and deregulation in general) rest on a false distinction between a naturally efficient and responsive market and an inefficient and inflexible bureaucratic state. Whether markets function efficiently is not determined by whether or not they are free from state intervention, since this "intervention" provides the very foundation for market transactions. The effect of leaving corporate decisions to the market cannot be determined a priori. The suitability of market governance and its impact on corporate behavior is, at all times, an open empirical question.[11]

Despite the elegance of neoclassical models, reality is seldom captured by intersecting supply-and-demand curves. The corporation cannot be adequately understood as a production function adjusting rapidly and efficiently to changing objective circumstances. Corporations are organizations evolving within a specific institutional context; they are as much cultural-historical artifacts as the state institutions that have been at the heart of this study. While the behavior of corporate managers is undoubtedly conditioned by the ever-present goal of profit maximization, the strategies available for this pursuit are suggested by contextual factors. Public policy excludes certain strategies from consideration, while directing corporations to select among a more limited universe of alternatives. Likewise, corporate structures and routines will predispose firms to certain forms of behavior.

By and large, American corporations evolved to engage in standardized mass production. Large hierarchically organized firms produced standardized products for mass-consumer markets, profiting from longer production runs and a variety of scalar economies. This form of production was largely an American innovation and was the key to economic success in domestic and international markets. However, by the 1960s it was becoming increasingly apparent that standardized mass production could not provide the basis for continued economic dominance. As the technology associated with this form of production became widely available to nations with low labor costs and access to raw materials, the United States lost its comparative advantage in manufacturing. Moreover, in the uncertain environment of the international economy, the rigidities of mass standardized production created problems of adjustment, contributing to massive economic dislocations during downturns in the business cycle.[12]

In the American context, there is a managerial bias toward short-term profitability, reflecting profit horizons that are relatively short when seen in comparative perspective. Managerial performance is assessed on an annual— if not a quarterly—basis. There is little to impede large institutional investors from rapidly adjusting their portfolios in response to a decline in profitability. Maintaining a respectable short-term return on investment is a managerial imperative, a condition of survival. This is a difficult task under normal circumstances. With the pressures imposed by low productivity gains and high capital costs, it has become all but impossible in many lines of business.

The interplay of managerial incentives and industrial decline has promoted what Robert Reich refers to as paper entrepreneurialism: the attempt to produce accounting profits through the manipulation of symbols and the reshuffling of assets.[13] The need to realize profits in the short term militates against the pursuit of innovative strategies that may demand high initial investments and yield profits only after a period of up to a decade. Accordingly, an increasingly common means of promoting short-term profitability is acquiring undervalued assets through merger, only to divide and sell them at a later date. The high levels of indebtedness associated with this strategy can bear benefits with respect to taxation. Such acquisitions result in immediate accounting profits and thus promote the short-term interests of corporate managers. They are, however, far from inconsequential. While paper entrepreneurialism redistributes wealth, it does not produce wealth. Resources are redistributed among a decreasing number of firms without contributing to economic growth. Indeed, such redistribution detracts from the creation of value by diverting attention and resources from true, productive entrepreneurial activities. The laxity of section 7 merger enforcement has contributed to the attractiveness of this strategy and has fueled the wave of corporate consolidation.

The current merger wave can be best understood as the aggregate expression of paper entrepreneurial strategies rather than part of some economywide drive toward ever-greater efficiencies inspired by rational calculations of economic benefits. For a number of reasons, it appears that when the economic impacts have not been benign, they have been negative. First, because growth has taken place through conglomeration, there are few direct economic benefits: efficiency gains are particularly limited when firms are producing in unrelated lines of business. Second and more important, corporate resources are finite. When they are devoted to planning and executing acquisitions and preventing hostile takeovers, they are unavailable for research and development and the restructuring of the production process. Third, as Reich and others have shown, the changing focus of corporate officials away from productive innovations and toward creative accounting has had a direct impact on the composition of corporate management. The value of scientists and engineers has decreased relative to accountants, attorneys, and financiers. Scientists and engineers are of little importance when profits are generated through acquisition and financial manipulation. Finally, because many of the large corporate takeovers have been leveraged with high-interest bond issues, the capital available for research and development is limited. Moreover, the demands of debt repayment create new sources of corporate instability, the extent of which may become evident only during the next major downturn in the business cycle, when declining revenues make interest repayments an impossibility. Given the consequences of a failure to meet repayment schedules, the imperative of maintaining short-term profitability has become more acute, further straining the capacity of corporations to initiate meaningful, wealth-producing innovations.[14]

The structuralists and Chicago school economists have revealed a concern with the size of corporations and the extent of market concentration. Structuralists claim that large corporate enterprises in concentrated markets possess the capacity to undermine competition and engage collusive strategies to maximize profits. Chicago school critics argue that size is purely a reflection of performance and the technical demands of producing in a given industry. Indeed, many have gone on to argue that antitrust and the well-established bias against large corporations is limiting the capacity of U.S. firms to compete in international markets. The assumption that economic success is a function of corporate size is simply that: an assumption. There is mounting evidence that it is also a wrong assumption.

Increasingly, size appears to be irrelevant. In part, this is because economies of scale can be exploited at low levels of production; in part, size loses its importance once the linkages between structure, conduct, and performance are severed. However, size becomes a significant impediment if it necessitates modes of corporate governance that increase organizational rigidity. A number of studies suggest that the most successful firms in a rapidly changing international economy are not large enterprises engaged in standardized mass production but those that have the ability to specialize while remaining flexible and innovative. Companies characterized by flexible specialization are capable of identifying and exploiting specific market niches and reacting rapidly to changing demand. The nonhierarchical modes of internal governance employed by such firms promote ongoing research and development and rapid innovation.[15] Insofar as the large conglomerates that have emerged from the merger wave simply combine multiple firms operating according to standardized mass production, little has changed. Insofar as the new scale of activity engenders greater managerial rigidity and creates distortions in capital allocations, they may actually hasten the decline of American industry. Any assessment of merger policy, as it now exists, must be framed within the broader debate regarding the negative ramifications of corporate consolidation.[16]

For a number of reasons, decisions regarding the future of antitrust as an economic policy must not be left to the discretion of those charged with enforcement. First, while political executives may state they have no intention of enforcing specific antitrust provisions, investment strategies depend on long-term considerations that extend beyond the range of a single presidential administration. Such a declaration may ease short-term concerns but have little effect on overall uncertainty. If the goal of policymakers is to provide a stable investment environment designed to promote the competitiveness of U.S. firms in an international economy, the portions of the Sherman and Clayton acts deemed irrelevant must be eliminated. Piecemeal reforms of the antitrust laws such as those suggested by the Reagan administration are, at most, a second-best solution because they fail to eliminate questionable legislative prohibitions while retaining a considerable arena of agency discretion. Second, as suggested above, any reformation of antitrust would be most correctly placed within a more comprehensive revision of the public policies shaping corporate organization and behavior. In the absence of antitrust, tax, technology, and trade policy would continue to shape corporate behavior and performance. In many ways, the experience of the past two decades combined with the changes in antitrust enforcement suggest that the total revocation of antitrust, when taken by itself, would not be sufficient. Indeed, any significant efforts to enhance corporate efficiency and economic performance cannot be based on the assumption that efficiency-promoting markets will prevail, once free of public policy. The market—the aggregate expression of public policies, historical experience, and transactional norms—must be adjusted to enhance its responsiveness to the demands of producing in a new international economic order.

It is important, in this context, to reemphasize the idea that antitrust reform need not take place within the constrained universe of alternatives that has delimited recent debates. Given the difficulties associated with creating new administrative capacity, the notion of adapting existing policy tools to new purposes should be given serious consideration. Antitrust—if reformulated in a creative fashion—could potentially promote industrial productivity and the kinds of industrial-structural changes deemed most effective to enhance U.S. competitiveness. For example, the merger-screening program, if implemented on a sectoral basis, could promote a concentration of resources in the high-wage, high-technology industries deemed most critical for success in international competition. Following the example of the National Cooperative Research Act of 1984, antitrust prohibitions could be selectively relaxed to promote joint research and development. Making antitrust a centerpiece of a market-oriented industrial policy could transform the policy into a tool of economic governance suited for the competitive realities of a global economy.

To be certain, antitrust could be reformulated to realize a new set of economic objectives. This is, in my estimation, preferable to the present program of selective nonenforcement. However, the Sherman and Clayton acts could be enforced vigorously in hope of pursuing the established social and political goals. Without question, a concern with the concentration of corporate power and decision making, the lack of local ownership, or the distribution of wealth—even if balanced with efficiency considerations—would carry economic costs. But such trade-offs are commonplace in public policy-making. Aspects of social welfare and environmental policies exist, in part, because policymakers attribute secondary importance to efficiency and find the noneconomic benefits to outweigh the economic costs. As Deborah Stone notes: "Efficiency is . . . not a goal in itself. It is not something we want for its own sake but because it helps us attain more of the things we value."[17] The ultimate determination of political values—of what the ends of public authority should be—must be made through open political discourse and choices within the context of representative institutions. The decision is not one to be delegated to expert administrators, the disciplines they represent, or a broader policy community. While the latter course may be expedient, given the ongoing problems of information complexity and electoral uncertainty, it is nonetheless problematic, for the results of delegation are always indeterminate.

NOTES

Chapter One

1. The conflicts surrounding the passage of the antitrust laws were tied to regional economic conflicts. The representatives from the states in the economic periphery supported the legislation, seeking protection from the core economic interests. Once the legislation was in place, the conflicts moved to the national government. The courts resisted the redefinition of the state-economy relationship entailed by the Sherman and Clayton acts. See Sanders, "Industrial Concentration, Sectional Competition, and Antitrust Politics," and Solo, *The Political Authority and the Market System*. See the discussion of policy origination in chap. 2.

2. Hofstadter, "What Happened to the Antitrust Movement?" p. 114.

3. Shonfield, *Modern Capitalism*, p. 329.

4. See Neale and Goyder, *The Antitrust Laws of the U.S.A.*, pp. 439–74.

5. Adams, "Public Policy in a Free Enterprise Economy," p. 487.

6. Fox, "The Modernization of Antitrust," p. 1147.

7. Metzenbaum, "Address," p. 387.

8. See Mueller, "A New Attack on Antitrust."

9. See Cohodas, "Reagan Seeks Relaxation of Antitrust Laws"; Wines, "Reagan's Antitrust Line"; and Solomon, "Administration Hopes to Extend the Reagan Revolution to Antitrust."

10. Neustadt, *Presidential Power*, p. 26.

11. See Burnham, "The Appearance and Disappearance of the American Voter."

12. See Edelman, *The Symbolic Uses of Politics*.

13. See Mitnick, *The Political Economy of Regulation*, and Fiorina, "Flagellating the Federal Bureaucracy."

14. See the discussion of congressional resource constraints in Kelman, *Making Public Policy*, pp. 53–54.

15. See Mayhew, *Congress*.

16. The term "profession" is not used to describe any occupational grouping that considers itself to be a profession. As used in this book, "profession" can be understood as synonymous with what are usually referred to as the learned professions. Professionalization entails bringing experts into an agency or providing existing professional staffs with a greater role in the definition of agency affairs.

17. See Rourke, *Bureaucracy, Politics, and Public Policy*, for a discussion of expertise as a foundation of bureaucratic power. This section on the bureaucracy and professionalization reflects, in part, discussions with Russell D. Murphy.

18. Ibid., p. 94.

19. See Moe, "The Politics of Structural Choice." This section draws on Moe's discussion of professionalization.

20. Moe, "Interests, Institutions, and Positive Theory," p. 292.

21. See Scott, "Professionals in Bureaucracies"; Aberbach and Rockman, "Clashing Beliefs within the Executive Branch"; and Richard Hall, "Some Organizational Considerations in the Professional-Organizational Relationship."

22. Bell, "Professional Values and Organizational Decisionmaking," pp. 21–22.

23. Ibid., p. 23.

24. See the contributions in James Q. Wilson, *The Politics of Regulation*.

25. See Dingwall and Lewis, *The Sociology of the Professions*.

26. See Lambright and Teich, "Scientists and Government."

27. See Wollan, "Lawyers in Government," and Abel, "The Transformation of the American Legal Profession."

28. See Rueschemeyer, "Professional Autonomy and the Social Control of Expertise."

29. See MacRae, *The Social Function of Social Science*, p. 13.

30. Whitley, *The Intellectual and Social Organization of the Sciences*, p. 25.

31. Whitley, "The Structure and Conduct of Economics as a Scientific Field," p. 2.

32. Two of the best case studies on the antitrust agencies are Weaver, *Decision to Prosecute*, and Katzmann, *Regulatory Bureaucracy*.

Chapter Two

1. See the discussion of the original and amended Clayton Act, sec. 7, in Neale and Goyder, *The Antitrust Laws of the U.S.A.*, pp. 181–86.

2. Arnold, *The Folklore of Capitalism*, p. 372.

3. This discussion draws heavily on Weaver, *Decision to Prosecute*; Department of Justice, *Antitrust Division Manual*; Neale and Goyder, *The Antitrust Laws of the U.S.A.*; and Andewelt, "Organization and Operation of the Antitrust Division."

4. See Sullivan, "The Antitrust Division as a Regulatory Agency."

5. This section draws primarily on Katzmann, *Regulatory Bureaucracy*; Clarkson and Muris, *The Federal Trade Commission since 1970*; Federal Trade Commission, *Operating Manual of the Federal Trade Commission*; Welborn, *The Governance of*

Federal Regulatory Agencies; and Winslow, "Organization and Operation of the Federal Trade Commission."

6. See Katzmann, *Regulatory Bureaucracy*, on the changing relationship between law and economics in the Federal Trade Commission. The convergence of law and economics is addressed in some detail in chap. 6 below.

7. See American Bar Association, *Report of the Antitrust Law Special Committee to Study the Role of the Federal Trade Commission*, pp. 19–22.

8. Ibid., pp. 17–19.

9. See the discussion of the competing economic doctrines and their policy implications in chap. 4 below.

10. Commons, *The Legal Foundations of Capitalism*, p. 7.

11. See ibid.; Kanel, "Property and Economic Power as Issues in Institutional Economics"; and Calabresi and Melamed, "Property Rules and Inalienability."

12. See Hurst, *Law and Markets in U.S. History*.

13. Solo, *The Positive State*, pp. 38, 37.

14. Ibid., p. 80. Also see Solo, *The Political Authority and the Market System*.

15. One or more political parties have had an antitrust plank in their platforms in all but four presidential elections in the past century. In the vast majority of cases, the parties have supported antitrust and called for increased enforcement efforts without simultaneously calling for a redirection of priorities. See Johnson, *National Party Platforms*, and Hofstadter, "What Happened to the Antitrust Movement?"

16. See Sanders, "Industrial Concentration, Sectional Competition, and Antitrust Politics in America."

17. See James Q. Wilson, *Political Organizations*.

18. The question of U.S. competitiveness and antitrust is addressed in greater detail in chap. 8 below. See the discussion of antitrust and competition in Porter, *The Competitive Advantage of Nations*.

19. See Green, Moore, and Wasserstein, *The Closed Enterprise System*.

20. See Welborn, *The Governance of Federal Regulatory Agencies*.

21. Federal Trade Commission Act, sec. 1.

22. This account follows the discussion of the relationship between the executive and relevant agencies in Katzmann, *Regulatory Bureaucracy*, and Weaver, *Decision to Prosecute*.

23. See Ogul, *Congress Oversees the Bureaucracy*, and Fiorina, *Congress*.

24. See Kovacic, "The Federal Trade Commission and Congressional Oversight of Antitrust Enforcement."

25. See Pertschuk, *Revolt against Regulation*, and Weingast and Moran, "Bureaucratic Discretion or Congressional Control."

Chapter Three

1. See Pitofsky, "The Political Content of Antitrust"; Adams, "Public Policy in a Free Enterprise Economy"; and Hurst, *Law and Markets in U.S. History*.

2. See Chandler, *Strategy and Structure*, chap. 1, and Lee and Passell, *A New Economic View of American History*.

3. *Congressional Record*, 51st Cong., 1st sess., February 27, 1889, 21:1768, reprinted in Kintner, *The Legislative History of the Federal Antitrust Laws and Related Statutes*, 1:100.

4. *Congressional Record*, 51st Cong., 1st sess., February 4, 1889, 20:1458, reprinted in Kintner, *The Legislative History of the Federal Antitrust Laws and Related Statutes*, 1:77.

5. *Congressional Record*, 51st Cong., 1st sess., March 21, 1890, 21:2457, reprinted in Kintner, *The Legislative History of the Federal Antitrust Laws and Related Statutes*, 1:117.

6. "Fourth Annual Message of President Grover Cleveland, 3 December 1888," reprinted in Kintner, *The Legislative History of the Federal Antitrust Laws and Related Statutes*, 1:58.

7. For a detailed discussion of the common-law foundations of antitrust, see Thorelli, *The Federal Antitrust Policy*, pp. 9–53. See Skowronek, *Building a New American State*, on the broad efforts to expand the administrative capacities of the state during this period.

8. This discussion draws on Letwin, *Law and Economic Policy in America*, especially pp. 103–5.

9. Ibid. and Arnold, "Antitrust Law Enforcement: Past and Future."

10. See Hamilton and Till, *Antitrust in Action*, pp. 135–43.

11. See ibid.; Posner, *Antitrust Law*; and Weaver, *Decision to Prosecute*, p. 24.

12. *United States v. E. C. Knight Co.*, 156 U.S. 379 (1895).

13. See *United States v. Trans-Missouri Freight Association*, 166 U.S. 290 (1897); *United States v. Joint Traffic Association*, 171 U.S. 505 (1898); and *United States v. Addyston Pipe and Steel Co.*, 85 F. 271 (6th Cir. 1898) affd. 175 U.S. 211 (1899). For a discussion of early antitrust cases, see Thorelli, *The Federal Antitrust Policy*, pp. 432–99.

14. *United States v. Addyston Pipe and Steel Co.*, 175 U.S. 211 (1899), and *United States v. Trenton Potteries Co.*, 273 U.S. 392 (1927).

15. *United States v. Trenton Potteries Co.*, 273 U.S. 392, 397 (1927).

16. *American Column and Lumber Co. v. United States*, 257 U.S. 377 (1921).

17. *Maple Flooring Manufacturers' Association v. United States*, 268 U.S. 563 (1925).

18. *Northern Securities Co. v. United States*, 193 U.S. 197 (1904).

19. *Standard Oil Co. of New Jersey v. United States*, 221 U.S. 1 (1911), and *United States v. American Tobacco Co.*, 211 U.S. 106 (1911).

20. *United States v. United States Steel Corp.*, 251 U.S. 417, 451 (1920).

21. Bork, *The Antitrust Paradox*, p. 37. See Bork's discussion of the rule of reason, pp. 33–41.

22. See Neale and Goyder, *The Antitrust Laws of the U.S.A.*, pp. 23–32, 95–98.

23. This section draws on the distinctions made in Solo, *The Political Authority and the Market System*, pp. 95–129.

24. Sanders, "Industrial Concentration, Sectional Competition, and Antitrust Politics in America."

25. See Nelson, *Merger Movements in American History*, and McCraw, "Mercantilism and the Market."

26. Keller, "The Pluralist State," pp. 73–74.

27. Theodore Roosevelt, quoted in Blum, *The Republican Roosevelt*, pp. 116–17. Also see "Theodore Roosevelt on the Great Corporations, December 3, 1901," in Hofstadter, *The Progressive Movement, 1900–1905*.

28. Woodrow Wilson, *The New Freedom*, p. 109.

29. Ibid., p. 123. See Diamond, *The Economic Thought of Woodrow Wilson*, pp. 87–130.

30. The Federal Trade Commission has the distinction of being among the most-studied agencies in the American political system. Many fine works on the FTC have informed this chapter, including Blaisdell, *The Federal Trade Commission*; Green, Moore, and Wasserstein, *The Closed Enterprise System*; Henderson, *The Federal Trade Commission*; Herring, *Public Administration and the Public Interest*; Holt, *The Federal Trade Commission*; Katzmann, *Regulatory Bureaucracy*; Alan Stone, *Economic Regulation in the Public Interest*; and Wagner, *The Federal Trade Commission*. While none of these books directly addresses the central concern of this chapter, they have provided necessary background material.

31. On the passage of the Clayton Act and the creation of the FTC, see the legislative debates as reprinted in Kintner, *The Legislative History of the Federal Antitrust Laws and Related Statutes*, vol. 2, and Blaisdell, *The Federal Trade Commission*, chap. 1.

32. See Dulles and Dubofsky, *Labor in America*, chap. 11, and Kolko, *The Triumph of Conservatism*.

33. See the discussion of the Bureau of Corporations in Holt, *The Federal Trade*

Commission, and Letwin, *Law and Economic Policy in America.*

34. See Henderson, *The Federal Trade Commission*, and Kovacic, "The Federal Trade Commission and Congressional Oversight of Antitrust Enforcement."

35. Henderson, *The Federal Trade Commission*, p. 332.

36. Ibid., p. 337.

37. See Federal Trade Commission, *Food Investigation*; Blaisdell, *The Federal Trade Commission*, pp. 186–87; Holt, *The Federal Trade Commission*, pp. 28–29; and Boyle, "Economic Reports and the Federal Trade Commission."

38. See Blaisdell, *The Federal Trade Commission*, pp. 186–87, and Holt, *The Federal Trade Commission*, pp. 28–29.

39. See Solo, *The Political Authority and the Market System.*

40. *Federal Trade Commission v. Gratz*, 253 U.S. 421, 427–28 (1920). The Court would later restrict the scope of sec. 5 of the Federal Trade Commission Act so that it could be used only in antitrust matters. As a result, the FTC could issue a complaint against deceptive practices only if the practices could be portrayed as "unfair methods of competition." See *Federal Trade Commission v. Raladam Co.*, 282 U.S. 829 (1931).

41. *Federal Trade Commission v. Western Meat Co.*, 272 U.S. 554 (1926), and *Federal Trade Commission v. Eastman Kodak Co.*, 274 U.S. 619 (1927).

42. *Claire Furnace Co. v. Federal Trade Commission*, 285 F. 936 (D.C. Cir. 1923); *Federal Trade Commission v. American Tobacco Co.*, 264 U.S. 298 (1924); and Blaisdell, *The Federal Trade Commission*, pp. 37–74.

43. Blaisdell, *The Federal Trade Commission*, pp. 310–11.

44. See Hawley, "Three Facets of Hooverian Associationalism." Also see Hawley, "Herbert Hoover, the Commerce Secretariat, and the Vision of an 'Associative State.'"

45. Montague, "Antitrust Laws and the Federal Trade Commission."

46. See Green, Moore, and Wasserstein, *The Closed Enterprise System*, p. 324, and Kovacic, "The Federal Trade Commission and Congressional Oversight of Antitrust Enforcement."

47. *American Column and Lumber Co. v. United States*, 257 U.S. 377 (1921), and *United States v. Trenton Potteries Co.*, 273 U.S. 392 (1927). See Hawley, *The New Deal and the Problem of Monopoly*, p. 39.

48. Fainsod, Gordon, and Palamountain, *Government and the American Economy*, p. 516.

49. *Humphrey's Executor v. United States*, 295 U.S. 602 (1935). For a discussion of the Humphrey affair, see MacIntyre and Dixon, "The Federal Trade Commission after Fifty Years." For a comprehensive discussion of the NRA and its ties to the FTC's trade practice conferences, see Himmelberg, *The Origins of the National Recovery Administration.*

50. Hawley, *The New Deal and the Problem of Monopoly*, p. 82.

51. *Schechter Poultry Corp. v. United States*, 295 U.S. 495 (1935).

52. Hawley, *The New Deal and the Problem of Monopoly*, pp. 159–61, 400.

53. Figures were provided by the Federal Trade Commission, Bureau of Economics.

54. Wagner, *The Federal Trade Commission*, pp. 154–56.

55. See the discussion of this period in Green, Moore, and Wasserstein, *The Closed Enterprise System*.

56. See Edwards, *The Price Discrimination Law*.

57. *In re Cement Institute*, 37 F.T.C. 87 (1943).

58. *Federal Trade Commission v. Cement Institute*, 333 U.S. 683 (1948). See Latham, *The Group Basis of Politics*, on the basing-point controversy.

59. See Federal Trade Commission, *Report on the Present Trend of Corporate Merger and Acquisition*.

60. *Federal Trade Commission v. Morton Salt Co.*, 338 U.S. 642–43 (1950).

61. As quoted in Markham, "The Federal Trade Commission's Use of Economics," p. 413.

62. The FTC's activities focused primarily on violations of the Robinson-Patman Act between the passage of the act and the 1960s. From 1936 to 1961, a total of 588 cease-and-desist orders were issued in response to Robinson-Patman violations. In most years, the Robinson-Patman cases composed more than one-half of the antitrust caseload. Most of these cases dealt with discriminatory pricing, promotional allowances, and services. See Wagner, *The Federal Trade Commission*, pp. 126–41.

63. Commission on Organization of the Executive Branch of the Government, *Task Force Report on Regulatory Commissions*.

64. Ibid., p. 123.

65. Ibid.

66. Congress, House, Select Committee on Small Business, *Antitrust Enforcement by the Federal Trade Commission and the Antitrust Division*, p. 17.

67. See Wagner, *The Federal Trade Commission*, pp. 39–44, and Katzmann, *Regulatory Bureaucracy*, p. 87.

68. Heller, *The Federal Trade Commission Management Survey Report*, p. 38.

69. See Executive Office of the President, Bureau of the Budget, *Federal Trade Commission Study*.

70. See Auerbach, "The Federal Trade Commission." Also see Landis, *Report on the Regulatory Agencies to the President-Elect*.

71. Bureau of the Budget, *Federal Trade Commission Study*, p. 12.

72. Ibid.

73. Ibid., p. 20.

74. Figures were provided by the Federal Trade Commission, Bureau of Economics.

75. Bureau of the Budget, *Federal Trade Commission Study*, p. 30.

76. See Wagner, *The Federal Trade Commission*, pp. 39–44.

77. American Bar Association, *Report of the Commission to Study the Federal Trade Commission*, pp. 12–13.

78. See Solo, *The Political Authority and the Market System*. Solo argues that the Court's conception of the relationship between the state and market went through a redefinition as a result of the Great Depression. Also see Hawley, *The New Deal and the Problem of Monopoly*.

79. See Hawley, *The New Deal and the Problem of Monopoly*, pp. 373–76.

80. Arnold, *The Folklore of Capitalism*, pp. 215, 217.

81. Ibid., p. 211.

82. Ibid., pp. 228, 212.

83. Arnold, "Antitrust Law Enforcement," p. 9.

84. Arnold, *The Folklore of Capitalism*, pp. 161–62; Arnold, *The Bottlenecks of Business*, pp. 92–96.

85. Arnold, "Antitrust Law Enforcement," p. 9.

86. Department of Justice, *Annual Report of the Attorney General of the United States* (1938), p. 56.

87. Arnold, *The Bottlenecks of Business*, p. 92.

88. Department of Justice, *Annual Report of the Attorney General of the United States* (1938), p. 57.

89. Edwards, "Thurman Arnold and the Antitrust Laws."

90. Arnold, *The Bottlenecks of Business*, p. 125.

91. Department of Justice, *Annual Report of the Attorney General of the United States* (1941), p. 60.

92. Ibid. (1939), p. 38.

93. Hamilton and Till, *Antitrust in Action*, p. 34.

94. Ibid., p. 33.

95. See Hodges, "Complaints of Antitrust Violations and Their Investigation."

96. Department of Justice, *Annual Report of the Attorney General of the United States* (1938), p. 60; Arnold, *The Bottlenecks of Business*, p. 125.

97. Department of Justice, *Annual Report of the Attorney General of the United States* (1939), p. 40.

98. Kovaleff, *Business and Government during the Eisenhower Administration*, p. 54.

99. Department of Justice, *Annual Report of the Attorney General of the United*

States (1938), p. 66; Hawley, *The New Deal and the Problem of Monopoly*, pp. 439, 550.

100. This point is stressed in Weaver, *Decision to Prosecute*, pp. 31–35.

101. See Green, Moore, and Wasserstein, *The Closed Enterprise System*, pp. 66–68; Hawley, *The New Deal and the Problem of Monopoly*, p. 442.

102. *United States v. Aluminum Co. of America*, 148 F. 2d 416 (2 Cir. 1945). Judge Learned Hand's decision that a 90 percent market share "is enough to constitute a monopoly; it is doubtful whether 60 or 64% would be enough; and certainly 33% is not" was adopted by attorneys as an informal guide to whether a firm could be prosecuted under sec. 2 of the Sherman Act, although these figures were based on the specific facts of a single case.

103. Quoted in Neale and Goyder, *The Antitrust Laws of the U.S.A.*, pp. 108–9.

104. *American Tobacco Co. v. United States*, 328 U.S. 781 (1946); *United States v. United Shoe Machinery Corp.*, 110 F. Supp 295 (D. Mass., 1953); *United States v. United Shoe Machinery Corp.*, 374 U.S. 521 (1954).

105. *International Salt Co. v. United States*, 332 U.S. 392 (1947); *Standard Oil Co. of California v. United States*, 337 U.S. 293 (1949).

106. See *United States v. Celanese Corp. of America*, 91 F. Supp 14 (S.D.N.Y., 1950).

107. See the discussion in Neale and Goyder, *The Antitrust Laws of the U.S.A.*, pp. 183–86. Also see *United States v. Columbia Steel Co.*, 334 U.S. 495 (1948).

108. Department of Justice, *Annual Report of the Attorney General of the United States* (1955), and Kovaleff, *Business and Government during the Eisenhower Administration*.

109. See Weaver, *Decision to Prosecute*, pp. 37–38, and Kovaleff, *Business and Government during the Eisenhower Administration*.

110. See Department of Justice, *Annual Report of the Attorney General of the United States* (1965), p. 101.

111. Department of Justice, *Report of the Attorney General's National Committee to Study the Antitrust Laws* (1955), p. 359.

112. Ibid.

113. See Department of Justice, *Annual Report of the Attorney General of the United States* (1960); Kovaleff, *Business and Government during the Eisenhower Administration*; and Green, Moore, and Wasserstein, *The Closed Enterprise System*, pp. 68–72.

Chapter Four

1. See Rowe, "The Decline of Antitrust and the Delusion of Models," and Hawley, *The New Deal and the Problem of Monopoly*.

2. The labels "Chicago school" and "structure conduct performance" have been used somewhat loosely. Some economists not affiliated with the Chicago school but working within the general tradition have been labeled Chicago school. Joe Bain was responsible for the explicit connection of structure, conduct, and performance. Other economists preceding Bain addressed the same concerns in a similar manner and have been included in the SCP category. The structure-conduct-performance school is sometimes referred to as the Harvard school.

3. See Heclo, "Issue Networks and the Executive Establishment"; Gormley, "Regulatory Issue Networks in a Federal System"; Kingdon, *Agendas, Alternatives, and Public Policies*.

4. See Sabatier, "Knowledge, Policy-Oriented Learning, and Policy Change."

5. Kingdon, *Agendas, Alternatives, and Public Policies*, p. 122.

6. Heclo, "Issue Networks and the Executive Establishment," pp. 103–4.

7. Kingdon, *Agendas, Alternatives, and Public Policies*, pp. 130–31.

8. See Campbell, *Collapse of an Industry*, and Woolley, *Monetary Politics*. Other examples of policy areas that fall within this category include taxation policy (see Witte, *The Politics and Development of the Federal Income Tax*) and cancer policy (see Rushefsky, *Making Cancer Policy*). William Gormley ("Regulatory Issue Networks in a Federal System") has noted that the prevalence of regulatory issue networks will be closely tied to questions of complexity and salience. I differentiate between community formation and influence. Communities of expertise will tend to form around complex policy areas, and yet their influence remains problematic unless the technical complexity is so great that other actors are simply excluded from access, or unless the policy is not politicized due to the inherent combination of costs and benefits.

9. This section draws heavily on Whitley, *The Intellectual and Social Organization of the Sciences*.

10. See Woolley, *Monetary Politics*, chap. 5, for an important discussion of how ideas can become embedded in institutions. In the case of the Federal Reserve System, competing schools of economic thought have assumed an organizational presence in branches of the Federal Reserve. Woolley describes the Federal Reserve Bank of St. Louis as "a government-funded organizational center for monetarist economists" (p. 99).

11. See Wittrock, Wagner, and Wollman, "Social Science and the Modern State."

12. See Anderson's discussion of the antitrust community in "The Reagan Administration, Antitrust Action, and Policy Change."

13. See Zamagni, *Microeconomic Theory*, chaps. 8–10, and Latsis, "A Research Program in Economics."

14. Bain, *Industrial Organization*, p. 120. Also see Weiss, "The Concentration-Profits Relationship and Antitrust," and Weiss, "The Structure-Conduct-Performance Paradigm and Antitrust." A number of empirical studies have identified critical levels of concentration, thresholds beyond which the probability of collusion increases and price-cost margins expand. Threshold was set at an eight-firm concentration ratio of 70 in Bain, "The Profit Rate as a Measure of Monopoly Power." Bain's study was updated and reaffirmed in Mann, "Seller Concentration, Barriers to Entry, and Rates of Return in Thirty Industries." For a more recent contribution to the debate, see Bradburd and Over, "Organizational Costs, 'Sticky Equilibria,' and Critical Levels of Concentration."

15. Scherer, "Economies of Scale and Industrial Concentration," pp. 51–52, and Bain, *Industrial Organization*, p. 182.

16. Mann, "Advertising, Concentration, and Profitability," p. 138. For a detailed analysis of the competitive consequences of product differentiation, see Chamberlin, *The Theory of Monopolistic Competition*.

17. Bain, "Chamberlin's Impact on Microeconomic Theory," in Bain, *Essays on Price Theory and Industrial Organization*.

18. See Bain, *Barriers to New Competition*. According to many structuralists, the effectiveness of limit pricing rests on an assumption regarding the behavior of potential entrants. One economist presents this assumption in the form of a postulate. "Potential entrants behave as though they expected existing firms to adopt the policy most unfavorable to them, namely, the policy of maintaining output while reducing the price (or accepting reductions) to the extent required to enforce such an output policy" (Modigliani, "New Developments on the Oligopoly Front," p. 217).

19. The relationship between concentration and inflation has led many to argue that an effective antitrust policy should be added to the existing arsenal of macroeconomic policy tools. It is believed that a successful deconcentration program could shift the Phillips curve to the left. Willard Mueller explains the potential value of this combination of policies in the following manner: "The presence of unrestrained market power creates an inflationary bias in contemporary America. And, significantly, such power creates inflationary pressures even in the absence of strong demand-pull forces. Perhaps the most vexing problem is that efforts to control seller- or cost-push inflation with monetary and fiscal policies, alone, end up with unacceptably high levels of unemploy-

ment or both unemployment and inflation. Hence, to achieve the twin goals of full employment and reasonable price stability requires that restraint be placed on the use of discretionary economic power" ("Industrial Concentration," p. 302). Also see Greer, *Industrial Organization and Public Policy*, pp. 467–72.

20. See Leibenstein, "Competition and X-Efficiency," and Harberger, "Monopoly and Resource Allocation."

21. Scherer, *Innovation and Growth*, p. 247.

22. For an estimate of the distributional effects of industrial concentration, see Comanor and Smiley, "Monopoly and the Distribution of Wealth." On the assumption that excess profits account for 2 to 3 percent of the GNP and that this portion of the GNP is distributed proportionate to stock ownership, Comanor and Smiley estimate the redistributive effects of deconcentration. At present, the top 2.4 percent of the population controls 40 percent of the total wealth. The elimination of monopoly power in the American economy would reduce this segment's share of the national wealth to between 16.6 percent and 32 percent, depending on the estimate of excess profits.

23. Posner, "The Chicago School of Antitrust Analysis," p. 932.

24. Reder, "Chicago Economics," p. 11.

25. Posner, "The Chicago School of Antitrust Analysis," p. 931.

26. Reder, "Chicago Economics," pp. 13, 21.

27. McGee, "Efficiency and Economies of Size," p. 94.

28. Stigler, *The Organization of Industry*, pp. 72–74.

29. Demsetz, *The Market Concentration Doctrine*, p. 22. Also see Peltzman, "The Gains and Losses from Industrial Concentration."

30. Bork, *The Antitrust Paradox*, p. 178.

31. Stigler, *The Organization of Industry*, p. 67.

32. Posner, *Antitrust Law*, pp. 92–93, and Stigler, *The Organization of Industry*, p. 70.

33. Posner, "The Chicago School of Antitrust Analysis," p. 947.

34. Landes, "Harm to Competition," pp. 73–74.

35. See Posner, *Antitrust Law*, pp. 39–77, and Brozen, *Is Government the Source of Monopoly?* p. 53.

36. Posner, *Antitrust Law*, pp. 196–200, and Stigler, *The Organization of Industry*, p. 303.

37. Stigler and Friedland, "The Pattern of Citation in Economics," p. 173.

38. Whitley, *The Intellectual and Social Organization of the Sciences*, pp. 27–28.

39. Baxter is quoted in Brozen, "No . . . the Concentration-Collusion Doctrine," p. 92.

40. Weiss, "The Structure-Conduct-Performance Paradigm and Antitrust," p. 1119.

41. Posner, "The Chicago School of Antitrust Analysis," p. 944.

42. Eichner, "Why Economics Is Not Yet a Science."

43. Baker and Blumenthal, "Ideological Cycles and Unstable Antitrust Rules," p. 330.

44. Rowe, "The Decline of Antitrust and the Delusion of Models," p. 1561. See Bok, "Section 7 of the Clayton Act and the Merging of Law and Economics."

45. "Judicial Precedent and the New Economics," p. 9.

46. See ibid. for a discussion of the sources of judicial economics.

47. See Solo, *The Political Authority and the Market System*, and Hurst, *The Legitimacy of the Business Corporation in the Law of the United States*.

48. See *United States v. Aluminum Co. of America*, 148 F. 2d 416 (2 Cir. 1945), and *United States v. Columbia Steel Co.*, 334 U.S. 495 (1948). Also see the discussion in Neale and Goyder, *The Antitrust Laws of the U.S.A.*, pp. 104–10, 140–43.

49. See *United States v. Philadelphia National Bank*, 374 U.S. 321 (1963); *Brown Shoe Co. v. United States*, 370 U.S. 294 (1962); and *United States v. Von's Grocery Co.*, 384 U.S. 270 (1966).

50. Throughout the latter half of the 1960s, members of the antitrust community considered using antitrust to force the deconcentration of the American economy. While this debate had earlier origins, it found its most authoritative expression in the 1969 White House Task Force Report on Antitrust Policy. The task force recommended legislation to force major firms in concentrated industries to divest themselves of various holdings until the industries fell below a certain threshold of concentration. The deconcentration would have been facilitated by suspending any need to prove the anticompetitive effect of existing levels of concentration. A similar program would have been established under the "Industrial Reorganization Act" submitted for consideration by Senator Hart in 1973. In each case, deconcentration was justified by structuralist assumptions. Because firms in concentrated markets tended to engage in tacit forms of price-fixing, deconcentration would promote greater price stability while unleashing market forces. Although the deconcentration proposals failed to receive sufficient support, they were given serious consideration. That policymakers even contemplated such a complex task as reorganizing the economy suggests the influence of the SCP framework in the policy debates. See Kaysen and Turner, *Antitrust Policy*.

51. See Stigler, "The Theory of Economic Regulation."

52. Brozen, *Is Government the Source of Monopoly?* p. 53.

53. For example, see Weiss, "The Structure-Conduct-Performance Paradigm and Antitrust," where he concedes that the structuralist enforcement programs of the past

have been too extreme, based on the new findings regarding efficiency. As noted above, Weiss was one of the key structuralists cited in the policy debates. Similar concessions have been made by other structuralists.

Chapter Five

1. Much of this chapter is based on interviews conducted in January and August 1988 with attorneys and economists from the Antitrust Division. Their experiences dated back over two decades. Quotations not accompanied by a note were derived from this source.

2. Department of Justice, *Annual Report of the Attorney General of the United States* (1962), p. 103.

3. *United States v. Bethlehem Steel Corp.*, 168 F. Supp 576 (S.D.N.Y., 1958) 186.

4. *Brown Shoe Co. v. United States*, 370 U.S. 294 (1962).

5. *Brown Shoe Co. v. United States*, 370 U.S. 294, 344 (1962). See Bork, *The Antitrust Paradox*, pp. 198–216.

6. As quoted in Neale and Goyder, *The Antitrust Laws of the U.S.A.*, p. 186.

7. *United States v. Philadelphia National Bank*, 374 U.S. 321 (1963).

8. *United States v. Philadelphia National Bank*, 374 U.S. 321, 363 (1963). See Rowe, "The Decline of Antitrust and the Delusion of Models," p. 1524.

9. *United States v. Aluminum Co. of America*, 377 U.S. 271, 279 (1964). See the discussion in Neale and Goyder, *The Antitrust Laws of the U.S.A.*, p. 191.

10. Green, Moore, and Wasserstein, *The Closed Enterprise System*, pp. 73–78.

11. "Enforcement Policies and Procedures," p. 19.

12. Department of Justice, *Annual Report of the Attorney General of the United States* (1963), p. 103.

13. See Kaysen and Turner, *Antitrust Policy*, and Turner, "The Scope of Antitrust and Other Regulatory Policies."

14. See chap. 4 for a discussion of the competing economic frameworks and their implications for policy.

15. "Interview with the Honorable Donald F. Turner" (1967), p. 126.

16. See Weaver, *Decision to Prosecute*, pp. 120–29.

17. Department of Justice, "Merger Guidelines," 1968.

18. Ibid., sec. 12.

19. Ibid., secs. 14(a), 16.

20. Ibid., secs. 18–20.

21. "Interview with the Honorable Donald F. Turner" (1967), p. 136.

22. Department of Justice, "Merger Guidelines," 1968, sec. 10.

23. See Weaver, *Decision to Prosecute*, pp. 132–36.

24. See McLaren, "Recent Cases, Current Enforcement Views, and Possible New Antitrust Enforcement."

25. For a discussion of McLaren's final days in the Nixon administration, see Mueller, "A New Attack on Antitrust."

26. Kauper, "The Warren Court and the Antitrust Laws," p. 330.

27. Kauper, "The Role of Economic Analysis in the Antitrust Division," pp. 119–20. See "Former AAG Kauper Looks Back at the Antitrust Division."

28. Kauper, "The Role of Economic Analysis in the Antitrust Division," pp. 119–20.

29. Correspondence of George Hay with the author, April 1, 1988.

30. This discussion closely follows the accounts of Thomas Kauper, George Hay, and a number of interviewees who worked at the Antitrust Division during the 1970s.

31. Department of Justice, *Annual Report of the Attorney General of the United States* (1976), p. 55.

32. Ibid. (1978), p. 117.

33. Department of Justice, *Antitrust Division Manual*, pp. VI-4, 5.

34. Bork, *The Antitrust Paradox*, p. 287.

35. *United States v. Von's Grocery Co.*, 384 U.S. 270 (1966).

36. *United States v. General Dynamics Corp.*, 415 U.S. 486 (1974).

37. *United States v. Marine Bancorporation*, 418 U.S. 602 (1974).

38. See Neale and Goyder, *The Antitrust Laws of the U.S.A.*, pp. 204–5.

39. *Continental T.V. Inc. v. GTE Sylvania Inc.*, 433 U.S. 36 (1977).

40. *United States v. Arnold Schwinn & Co.*, 388 U.S. 365 (1967).

41. *Continental T.V. Inc. v. GTE Sylvania Inc.*, 433 U.S. 36, 54 (1977).

42. *Continental T.V. Inc. v. GTE Sylvania Inc.*, 433 U.S. 36, 56 (1977).

43. See Bork, *The Antitrust Paradox*, pp. 285–88.

44. *Continental T.V. Inc. v. GTE Sylvania Inc.*, 433 U.S. 36, 56–57 (1977).

45. On the new orientation at the division, see Sullivan, "The Antitrust Division as a Regulatory Agency." On the requirements associated with Hart-Scott-Rodino, see Brunner et al., *Mergers in the New Antitrust Era*.

46. See Derthick and Quirk, *The Politics of Deregulation*.

47. Department of Justice, *Antitrust Division Manual*, pp. V-2, I-26, 27, and American Bar Association, *Report of the Antitrust Law Task Force on the Antitrust Division of the U.S. Department of Justice*, p. 23.

48. Department of Justice, *Annual Report of the Attorney General of the United States* (1978), p. 117.

49. Kauper, "The Role of Economic Analysis in the Antitrust Division," p. 124.

50. Ford, "The President's Remarks," p. 349.

51. See Shenefield, *A Conversation with John H. Shenefield*.

52. See Litvack, "Report from the Antitrust Division."

Chapter Six

1. This chapter draws on information derived from interviews with individuals working at the Federal Trade Commission, both in the Bureau of Economics and in the Bureau of Competition. Interviews were conducted with upper-level bureaucrats, staff attorneys, and economists. Quotations not accompanied by a note are from these interviews.

2. For example, see Executive Office of the President, Bureau of the Budget, *Federal Trade Commission Study*, p. 32. Also see chap. 4 above for a review of earlier critiques.

3. *Federal Trade Commission v. Proctor & Gamble Co.*, 386 U.S. 568 (1967). This case originated in a complaint in 1957 and evolved over a ten-year period. The commission's approach to the case was greatly affected as the Court adopted economic structural decision rules. See Wagner, *The Federal Trade Commission*, pp. 109–25.

4. Quoted in Auerbach, "The Federal Trade Commission," pp. 401–2.

5. Markham, "The Federal Trade Commission's Use of Economics," pp. 410–11.

6. Cox, Fellmeth, and Schulz, *The Nader Report on the Federal Trade Commission*; Task Force on Productivity and Competition, *Report*; American Bar Association, *Report of the Commission to Study the Federal Trade Commission*; Green, Moore, and Wasserstein, *The Closed Enterprise System*; and Executive Office of the President, Bureau of the Budget, *Management Review of the Federal Trade Commission*. Also see "Current Antitrust Enforcement and Its Critics."

7. American Bar Association, *Report of the Commission to Study the Federal Trade Commission*, pp. 15, 1, 26–27; Green, Moore, and Wasserstein, *The Closed Enterprise System*, pp. 334–67.

8. American Bar Association, *Report of the Commission to Study the Federal Trade Commission*, p. 13.

9. Ibid., pp. 32–33; Cox, Fellmeth, and Schulz, *The Nader Report on the Federal Trade Commission*, p. 151.

10. Cox, Fellmeth, and Schulz, *The Nader Report on the Federal Trade Commission*, pp. 152, 153.

11. American Bar Association, *Report of the Commission to Study the Federal Trade Commission*, pp. 15, 29–31.

12. Ibid., pp. 74, 75; Green, Moore, and Wasserstein, *The Closed Enterprise System*, pp. 171–73. See Smith, "Policy Planning and Economic Training at the Antitrust Agencies."

13. American Bar Association, *Report of the Commission to Study the Federal Trade Commission*, pp. 13, 70, 78; Green, Moore, and Wasserstein, *The Closed Enterprise System*, p. 371.

14. American Bar Association, *Report of the Commission to Study the Federal Trade Commission*, pp. 78, 79.

15. Cox, Fellmeth, and Schulz, *The Nader Report on the Federal Trade Commission*, pp. 170–71; American Bar Association, *Report of the Commission to Study the Federal Trade Commission*, p. 35.

16. Cox, Fellmeth, and Schulz, *The Nader Report on the Federal Trade Commission*, p. 172; American Bar Association, *Report of the Commission to Study the Federal Trade Commission*, pp. 32–33.

17. American Bar Association, *Report of the Commission to Study the Federal Trade Commission*, pp. 2, 65; Task Force on Productivity and Competition, *Report*, p. 7.

18. American Bar Association, *Report of the Commission to Study the Federal Trade Commission*, p. 3.

19. "Statement of Chairman Paul Rand Dixon," reprinted in Cox, Fellmeth, and Schulz, *The Nader Report on the Federal Trade Commission*, p. 180. Also see the flawed but suggestive Ash Council Report: The President's Advisory Council on Executive Organization, *A New Regulatory Framework*; Ash, "Ash Report on the FTC"; and American Bar Association, "Report of the Section of Antitrust Law on the Ash Council Report."

20. See White House Task Force on Antitrust Policy, *Report*.

21. See Weinberger, "The Federal Trade Commission of the 1970s"; Welford, "How Ralph Nader, Tricia Nixon, the ABA, and Jamie Whitten Helped Turn the FTC Around"; Congress, Senate, Committee on Commerce, *Nomination of Miles W. Kirkpatrick to Be Chairman of the Federal Trade Commission*; and Halverson, "Whatever Happened to the Little Old Lady of Pennsylvania Avenue?"

22. Congress, Senate, Committee on the Judiciary, *Federal Trade Commission Procedures* 1:110.

23. Congress, Senate, Committee on Appropriations, *Agriculture, Environmental and Consumer Protection Appropriations for Fiscal Year 1972*, p. 267.

24. Congress, Senate, Committee on Commerce, *Nomination of Lewis A. Engman*

to Be a Commissioner of the Federal Trade Commission, pp. 4–5.

25. Budget figures were provided by the Federal Trade Commission, Bureau of Economics.

26. See the discussion of new legislation and agency powers in Clarkson and Muris, *The Federal Trade Commission since 1970.*

27. See Ellis, "Legislative Powers: FTC Rule Making," for a discussion of the procedural requirements associated with the Federal Trade Commission Improvement Act.

28. *Federal Trade Commission v. Motion Picture Advertising Service Co.*, 344 U.S. 392, 394–95 (1953).

29. *Federal Trade Commission v. Sperry and Hutchinson & Co.*, 405 U.S. 233, 244 (1972).

30. On the limits of reorganizations as a strategy of change, see March and Olsen, *Rediscovering Institutions*, chap. 5.

31. See the discussion of agency reorganization in Wagner, *The Federal Trade Commission*, pp. 35–48.

32. Katzmann, *Regulatory Bureaucracy*, p. 114. Katzmann provides an interesting interpretation of the internal dynamics of the FTC which emphasizes the interplay of attorneys and economists, their professional orientations, and the demands of managing the policy process.

33. See Clarkson and Muris, *The Federal Trade Commission since 1970*, chaps. 1 and 5, and Katzmann, *Regulatory Bureaucracy*, pp. 112–33.

34. See Clarkson and Muris, *The Federal Trade Commission since 1970*, and Katzmann, *Regulatory Bureaucracy.*

35. Green, Moore, and Wasserstein, *The Closed Enterprise System*, p. 371.

36. Figures were provided by the Federal Trade Commission, Bureau of Economics. See Stigler, "The Economist and the Problem of Monopoly," and Katzmann, *Regulatory Bureaucracy*, pp. 36–42.

37. Congress, House, Committee on Appropriations, *Agriculture, Environmental and Consumer Protection, Appropriations for Fiscal Year 1972*, p. 94. See Liebeler, "Bureau of Competition."

38. See Liebeler, "Bureau of Competition."

39. See Gardner, "Consumer Report."

40. Federal Trade Commission, Office of Policy Planning and Evaluation, "1976 Budget Overview."

41. See "Policy Director Questions FTC Priorities," A-10.

42. Federal Trade Commission, Office of Policy Planning and Evaluation, "1976 Budget Overview," p. 4.

43. Ibid., p. 13.

44. Singer, "Consumer Report."

45. "FTC Adopts Policy Protocols to Help Evaluate Cost-Benefit Ratio of Proposed Commission Actions," and Clarkson and Muris, *The Federal Trade Commission since 1970*, pp. 294–98.

46. See Singer, "Consumer Report."

47. Federal Trade Commission, "Review of Accomplishments by the Federal Trade Commission during the Calendar Year 1977," p. 1.

48. Ibid.

49. Federal Trade Commission, *Annual Report* (1973), p. 2.

50. Ibid., p. 19.

51. See discussion of Line of Business problems in *Antitrust and Trade Regulation Report* 744 (December 23, 1974): AA-1; 677 (August 20, 1974): A-2.

52. *Antitrust and Trade Regulation Report* 679 (September 10, 1974): A-4.

53. "FTC Adopts Resolution Sharply Limiting Use of Line-of-Business Reports and Data."

54. Breit and Elzinga, "Information for Antitrust and Business Activity," pp. 112–13.

55. See Brunner et al., *Mergers in the New Antitrust Era*.

56. Congress, Senate, Committee on the Judiciary, *Oversight of Antitrust Enforcement*, p. 23.

57. See Meier, *Regulation*, pp. 108–9, and Pertschuk, *Revolt against Regulation*.

58. See Pertschuk, *Revolt against Regulation*, and Liebeler, "Bureau of Competition."

59. Senators Abourezk, Clark, Hart, Hartke, Haskell, Humphrey, McGee, McIntyre, Mansfield, Metcalf, Moss, Pastore, and Tunney left the Senate during this period. See Kovacic, "The Federal Trade Commission and Congressional Oversight of Antitrust Enforcement"; Weingast and Moran, "The Myth of the Runaway Bureaucracy"; and Weingast and Moran, "Bureaucratic Discretion or Congressional Control?" Weingast and Moran argue that the shifts in FTC policy can be directly attributed to the changing ideological predisposition of the members of the relevant congressional committees. The practical and methodological problems of this thesis are many. See Moe, "An Assessment of the Positive Theory of Congressional Dominance."

60. Quoted in Pertschuk, *Revolt against Regulation*, p. 73.

61. *Congressional Record*, 96th Cong., 1st sess., November 14, 1979, vol. 125, pt. 10, p. 32457.

62. Ibid., pp. 32465–79. See Katzmann, "Capitol Hill's Current Attack against the FTC," p. 26, and "The Federal Trade Commission under Attack."

63. See Gellhorn, "The Wages of Zealotry," and Wines, "Doctors, Dairymen Join in Effort to Clip the Talons of the FTC."

64. Pertschuk, *Revolt against Regulation*, p. 115. Given the alternatives addressed during the congressional debates, Pertschuk viewed the Federal Trade Commission Improvements Act as a victory for the FTC.

65. Most of the provisions in the Federal Trade Commission Improvements Act of 1980 addressed short-term concerns (i.e., particular cases and investigations that had been the objects of interest-group lobbying). The most potentially enduring provision of the act was the use of a two-chamber legislative veto to overturn FTC actions. The Supreme Court declared the legislative veto an unconstitutional violation of the separation of powers in *Immigration and Naturalization Service v. Chadha*, 462 U.S. 919 (1983), a decision that was directly applicable to the provisions of the Federal Trade Commission Improvements Act. See the discussion of the act and the fate of the legislative veto in Harris and Milkis, *The Politics of Regulatory Change*.

66. See the discussion of the role of economics and efficiency concerns in Derthick and Quirk, *The Politics of Deregulation*.

67. See Miller, *The Economist as Reformer*, p. 8.

Chapter Seven

1. Office of the President, *Economic Report of the President*, pp. 27, 28. A similar argument is made in Friedman, *Capitalism and Freedom*.

2. See Mueller, "A New Attack on Antitrust"; Cohodas, "Reagan Seeks Relaxation of Antitrust Laws"; Wines, "Reagan's Antitrust Line"; Bickel, "The Antitrust Division's Adoption of a Chicago School Economic Policy Calls for Some Reorganization"; Kramer, "Antitrust Today"; Fox, "The Modernization of Antitrust"; Solomon, "Administration Hopes to Extend the Reagan Revolution to Antitrust Laws"; and Anderson, "The Reagan Administration, Antitrust Action, and Policy Change."

3. See Quick, "Business."

4. Fox, "The 1982 Guidelines," p. 151.

5. See *Arizona v. Maricopa County Medical Society*, 457 U.S. 332 (1982). Also see *Aspen Skiing Co. v. Aspen Highlands Skiing Corp.*, 472 U.S. 585 (1985), for a strict interpretation of sec. 2 of the Sherman Act in a case in which a business strategy was used explicitly to injure a competitor.

6. *Broadcast Music Inc. v. Columbia Broadcasting System Inc.*, 441 U.S. 1 (1979).

7. *National Collegiate Athletic Association v. Board of Regents of the University of Oklahoma*, 468 U.S. 85 (1984).

8. *National Collegiate Athletic Association v. Board of Regents of the University of Oklahoma*, 468 U.S. 85, 100–101 (1984).

9. See "Baxter Offers Enforcement Position on Price Fixing, Corporate Acquisitions," AA1–3.

10. See "Justice Settles AT&T Case; Bell System Agrees to Divest Local Operating Companies," *Antitrust and Trade Regulation Report* 1047 (January 14, 1982): 82–87, and "Antitrust Division Dismisses IBM Case; Baxter Questions Facts," ibid., 88–89.

11. Baxter, "Responding to the Reaction," p. 308.

12. Ibid.

13. Baxter, "Separation of Powers, Prosecutorial Discretion, and the 'Common Law' Nature of Antitrust Law," p. 693.

14. Figures were provided by Frederick Warren-Boulton, deputy assistant attorney general for economic analysis, Antitrust Division.

15. See the transaction-cost analysis of vertical restraints in Williamson, *The Economic Institutions of Capitalism*.

16. See Department of Justice, *Annual Report of the Attorney General of the United States* (1982).

17. After Baxter's resignation was announced in the division, some attorneys believed that the agency would return to its traditional focus. A staff attorney reportedly warned an official in the EPO that the lawyers would "run through the Economic Policy Office with long knives" in Baxter's absence. Many soon realized that the status of economics in agency affairs was not dependent on the objectives of a single assistant attorney general.

18. See Gorinson, "Antitrust Division Reorganized."

19. See Fox, "The 1982 Guidelines," and Brunner et al., *Mergers in the New Antitrust Era*.

20. Department of Justice, "Merger Guidelines," 1984, sec. 1.

21. Ibid., secs. 2.2–2.4.

22. On the HHI and its role in creating an expansive definition of the market, see Harris and Jorde, "Market Definition in the Merger Guidelines."

23. Department of Justice, "Merger Guidelines," 1984, secs. 3.21–3.23, 3.41–3.45.

24. Ibid., sec. 3.5.

25. Baxter quoted in "Justice Department's New Merger Guidelines May Be Ready by Winter, Baxter Indicates," *Antitrust and Trade Regulation Report* 1027 (August 13, 1981): A4–6.

26. Department of Justice, "Merger Guidelines," 1984, sec. 4.212.

27. See American Bar Association, *Report of the Antitrust Law Task Force on the Antitrust Division of the U.S. Department of Justice*, p. S-10.

28. Department of Justice, "Statement concerning Vertical Restraints," secs. 16–30.

29. See Posner, *Antitrust Law*.

30. Congress, House, Committee on the Judiciary, *Antitrust Division of the Department of Justice* (1981), p. 7.

31. Ibid. (1985), p. 5. The joint resolution (sec. 605, P.L. 99–180, 99 Stat. 1169) stated that the vertical restraint guidelines did not have the force of law and should be recalled by the attorney general. In the same month, the National Association of Attorneys General adopted alternative guidelines because they did not feel that the Department of Justice statement was a correct expression of the law. See American Bar Association, *Report of the Antitrust Law Task Force on the Antitrust Division of the U.S. Department of Justice*.

32. See Warren-Boulton, "Merger Policy and Enforcement at the Antitrust Division," and Andewelt, "Organization and Operation of the Antitrust Division."

33. See Owen, "Economists as Trustbusters?" and *FTC Watch!* 246 (December 19, 1986): 8.

34. Frederick Warren-Boulton, deputy assistant attorney general for economic analysis, in an unpublished written response to critical coverage of merger screening, dated January 1987.

35. American Bar Association, *Report of the Antitrust Law Task Force on the Antitrust Division of the U.S. Department of Justice*, p. S-10.

36. See "Antitrust Division Begins Review of Old Discredited Consent Decrees," *Antitrust and Trade Regulation Report* 1032 (September 12, 1981): A16–17, and Baxter, "Separation of Powers, Prosecutorial Discretion, and the 'Common Law' Nature of Antitrust Law."

37. See Sullivan, "The Antitrust Division as a Regulatory Agency."

38. This information is taken from Senate appropriations hearings, 1981–85.

39. Baxter, "Responding to the Reaction," p. 141.

40. See American Bar Association, *Report of the Antitrust Law Task Force on the Antitrust Division of the U.S. Department of Justice*, p. S-22.

41. *Monsanto Co. v. Spray-Rite Service Corp.*, 465 U.S. 752 (1984).

42. *Monsanto Co. v. Spray-Rite Service Corp.*, 465 U.S. 752, 769 (1984).

43. The proposed legislation and Justice Department "Fact Sheet" are reprinted in *Antitrust Law and Economics Review*, 17, 4 (1986): 38–44. See Boyle and Piette, "How Economists View Reagan's Five Proposed Antitrust Changes." For an indication of the congressional response, see Senate, Committee on the Judiciary, *The Antitrust Remedies Improvement Act and the Intellectual Property Reform Act of 1987*.

44. Department of Justice, "Statement by Attorney General Edwin Meese III, February 19, 1986."

45. See White, *Private Antitrust Litigation*, for a discussion of the Georgetown Study, the most comprehensive examination of private antitrust litigation ever conducted. Many were surprised that the study failed to yield unambiguous evidence that treble-damages cases carry high economic costs.

46. Metzenbaum, "Address," p. 393.

47. See "FTC Transition Team Report Urges One-Quarter Cutback in Agency Size." On the intervenor funding program, see Harris and Milkis, *The Politics of Regulatory Change*, pp. 173–77.

48. "Conclusions and Recommendations: Federal Trade Commission Transition Team Report."

49. Congress, House, Committee on Government Operations, *Impact of OMB-Proposed Budget Cuts for the Federal Trade Commission*, p. 162.

50. "Letter to David Stockman, Director of Office of Management and Budget, February 14, 1981," reprinted in *Antitrust and Trade Regulation Report* 1002 (February 19, 1981): F1–3.

51. See "FTC Commissioners Foresee Budget Cuts as Instant Doom for Competition Programs," *Antitrust and Trade Regulation Report* 1002 (February 19, 1981): A1–2, and "Budget Cuts Won't Scrap FTC's Competition Mission," ibid., 1004 (March 5, 1981): A4–5.

52. Miller, *The Economist as Reformer*, pp. 2, 8, 43.

53. The law-and-economics movement is driven by the belief that judicial decision making can be improved if guided by economic reasoning. The members of this movement tend to be trained in law and economics. In recent years, law-and-economics centers have been established at the University of Miami and George Mason University to train law professors in economics and economics professors in law. More important, these centers have provided programs to train federal judges and administrative law judges. By the mid-1980s, it was estimated that up to one-half the federal judiciary had attended programs at the law-and-economics centers. While there is some anecdotal evidence that the law-and-economics training has affected the decision making of some judges, no comprehensive studies exist. See "Antitrust Law and Economics at the University of Miami." For provocative discussion of the broad applicability of economics in legal reasoning, see Posner, *The Economics of Justice*.

54. See Clarkson and Muris, *The Federal Trade Commission since 1970*.

55. "Interview with Robert Tollison, FTC's Chief Economist," p. 612.

56. See Miller, "The Role of Economic Research at the Federal Trade Commission," and Cambell, "Antitrust Enforcement at the FTC."

57. See Niskanen, *Bureaucracy and Representative Government*.

58. See Ferguson, "Where Did Joe Bain Go Wrong?"

59. Pertschuk, *The Performance of the Federal Trade Commission*, pp. II, 10–14. Figures on workyears cited from American Bar Association, *Report of the Antitrust Law Special Committee to Study the Role of the Federal Trade Commission*, p. S-28.

60. See Pertschuk, *The Performance of the Federal Trade Commission*, p. II, 17; "In the Matter of Regional Offices, in re: Personnel and Consolidation Issues," reprinted in *Antitrust and Trade Regulation Report* 1067 (June 3, 1982): 1115; and "FTC Suspends Its Proposal to Close Four Regional Offices," reprinted in ibid., 1155. Performance figures are drawn from American Bar Association, *Report of the Antitrust Law Special Committee to Study the Role of the Federal Trade Commission*, appendix.

61. See Federal Trade Commission, *First Year of the New Administration*; "Miller Reorganizes Commission, Consolidates Bureau's Programs," *Antitrust and Trade Regulation Report* 1047 (January 14, 1982): 76–77; "FTC Commissioners, Staff, Are Antagonized by New Chairman's Management Style, Not Ideas," ibid., 1049 (January 28, 1982): 213–17; "FTC Holds Policy Session, Instructs Staff to Consult Closely with Commissioners," ibid., 1069 (June 17, 1982): 1265–66; and "Interview with James C. Miller III" (1982).

62. Pertschuk, *The Performance of the Federal Trade Commission*, p. VII, 4.

63. Congress, House, Committee on Government Operations, *Oversight of the Federal Trade Commission*, pp. 338–40.

64. Federal Trade Commission, *First Year of the New Administration*, pp. 5–6.

65. The *Quarterly Financial Report* was moved to the Commerce Department, taking with it the portion of the economics staff that had been involved in its compilation. The staffing figures have been adjusted to exclude this staff in both periods.

66. Pertschuk, *The Performance of the Federal Trade Commission*, pp. II, 13–14. Toward the end of the Reagan administration, the cuts were distributed more evenly. See American Bar Association, *Report of the Antitrust Law Special Committee to Study the Role of the Federal Trade Commission*.

67. See Federal Trade Commission, *Annual Report*, 1982.

68. For a discussion of the FTC's consumer protection activities during the 1980s, see Harris and Milkis, *The Politics of Regulatory Change*.

69. See Pertschuk, *The Performance of the Federal Trade Commission*, pp. III, 2–4.

70. Federal Trade Commission, "Statement concerning Horizontal Mergers," June 1982. See Congress Watch, "Antitrust Enforcement at the Federal Trade Commission." Also see Miller's discussion of the FTC's merger policy in *The Economist as Reformer*, pp. 50–53.

71. Figures were compiled from the FTC's annual reports, for the years 1981–86.

72. Pertschuk, *The Performance of the Federal Trade Commission*, p. II, 26.

73. Celnicker, "The Federal Trade Commission's Competition and Consumer Advo-

cacy Program," *St. Louis Law Journal* (forthcoming), discussed in American Bar Association, *Report of the Antitrust Law Special Committee to Study the Role of the Federal Trade Commission*, p. S-23.

74. See American Bar Association, *Report of the Antitrust Law Special Committee to Study the Role of the Federal Trade Commission*, pp. S-23, 34, for a discussion of the benefits of the Competition and Consumer Advocacy Program.

75. See Harris and Milkis, *The Politics of Regulatory Change*, pp. 222–24.

76. American Bar Association, *Report of the Antitrust Law Special Committee to Study the Role of the Federal Trade Commission*, p. S-5.

77. Dweyer, "Putting the 'Anti' Back in the Antitrust Division," and Barrett, "FTC Promises Greater Vigilance on Merger Plans."

Chapter Eight

1. Compare the emphasis placed on the economic content of the policy debates in Bork, "Legislative Intent and the Policy of the Sherman Act," and Letwin, *Law and Economic Policy in America*.

2. See Skowronek, *Building a New American State*; Moe, "Interests, Institutions, and Positive Theory"; and Knott and Miller, *Reforming Bureaucracy*.

3. See James Q. Wilson, *The Politics of Regulation*.

4. See Heclo, *Modern Social Politics in Britain and Sweden*. Heclo introduces the concept of institutions of social learning to describe the Swedish investigatory commissions, where political demands, intellectual innovations, and cross-national experiences were integrated in the ongoing examination of policy problems. In many ways, the community of expertise presented in chap. 4 can be understood as serving similar functions, albeit outside the confines of state institutions. The inability of policymakers to control the results of expert deliberation and thus actively select knowledge that will conform with existing public policies may be a result of situating debates outside of the state.

5. See Weir and Skocpol, "State Structures and Possibilities for 'Keynesian' Responses to the Great Depression in Sweden, Britain, and the United States"; Skocpol and Finegold, "State Capacity and Economic Intervention in the Early New Deal"; Amenta et al., "The Political Origins of Unemployment Insurance in Five American States"; Peter Hall, *The Political Power of Economic Ideas*; and Peter Hall, *Governing the Economy*.

6. See Peter Hall, *The Political Power of Economic Ideas*, for a number of essays addressing the influence of Keynesian theory in policy innovation.

7. See Sabatier, "Knowledge, Policy-Oriented Learning, and Policy Change," and Kingdon, *Agendas, Alternatives, and Public Policies*.

8. See Derthick and Quirk, *The Politics of Deregulation*.

9. See Williamson, *Markets and Hierarchies* and *The Economic Institutions of Capitalism*. Even the structuralists have conceded that vertical restraints promote efficiency and thus must not be attacked indiscriminately. See Scherer, *Industrial Market Structure and Economic Performance*, and Rhoads, *The Economist's View of the World*, chap. 5.

10. Compare the policy alternatives proposed by Armentano, *Antitrust and Monopoly*, and Thurow, *The Zero-Sum Society*.

11. See the discussion of markets in Reich, *Tales of a New America*.

12. See Chandler, *The Visible Hand*.

13. See Reich, *The Next American Frontier*.

14. Ibid., pp. 140–72.

15. See Piorie and Sable, *The Second Industrial Divide*; Ouchi, *The M-Form Society*; and Nelson and Winter, *An Evolutionary Theory of Economic Change*.

16. Reich discusses the implications of paper entrepreneurialism for corporate management and structure in *The Next American Frontier*. See Adams and Brock, *The Bigness Complex*.

17. Deborah A. Stone, *Policy Paradox and Political Reason*, p. 49.

BIBLIOGRAPHY

Primary Sources

Court Cases

American Column and Lumber Co. v. United States, 257 U.S. 377 (1921).

American Tobacco Co. v. United States, 328 U.S. 781 (1946).

Appalachian Coals v. United States, 288 U.S. 344 (1933).

Arizona v. Maricopa County Medical Society, 457 U.S. 332 (1982).

Aspen Skiing Co. v. Aspen Highlands Skiing Corp., 472 U.S. 585 (1985).

Broadcast Music Inc. v. Columbia Broadcasting System Inc., 441 U.S. 1 (1979).

Brown Shoe Co. v. United States, 370 U.S. 294 (1962).

Claire Furnace Co. v. Federal Trade Commission, 285 F. 936 (D.C. Cir. 1923).

Continental T.V. Inc. v. GTE Sylvania Inc., 433 U.S. 36 (1977).

Federal Trade Commission v. American Tobacco Co., 264 U.S. 298 (1924).

Federal Trade Commission v. Cement Institute, 333 U.S. 683 (1948).

Federal Trade Commission v. Eastman Kodak Co., 274 U.S. 619 (1927).

Federal Trade Commission v. Gratz, 253 U.S. 421 (1920).

Federal Trade Commission v. Morton Salt Co., 334 U.S. 37 (1948).

Federal Trade Commission v. Motion Picture Advertising Service Co., 344 U.S. 392 (1953).

Federal Trade Commission v. Proctor & Gamble Co., 386 U.S. 568 (1967).

Federal Trade Commission v. Raladam Co., 282 U.S. 829 (1931).

Federal Trade Commission v. Sperry and Hutchinson & Co., 405 U.S. 233 (1972).

Federal Trade Commission v. Western Meat Co., 272 U.S. 554 (1926).

Humprey's Executor v. United States, 295 U.S. 602 (1935).

Illinois Brick Co. v. State of Illinois, 431 U.S. 720 (1977).

Immigration and Naturalization Service v. Chadha, 462 U.S. 919 (1983).

In re Cement Institute, 37 F.T.C. 87 (1943).

International Salt Co. v. United States, 332 U.S. 392 (1947).

Maple Flooring Manufacturers' Association v. United States, 268 U.S. 563 (1925).

Monsanto Co. v. Spray-Rite Service Corp., 465 U.S. 752 (1984).

National Collegiate Athletic Association v. Board of Regents of the University of Oklahoma, 468 U.S. 85 (1984).

Northern Securities Co. v. United States, 193 U.S. 197 (1904).

Schechter Poultry Corp. v. United States, 295 U.S. 495 (1935).

Standard Oil Co. v. Federal Trade Commission, 340 U.S. 231 (1951).

Standard Oil Co. v. United States, 283 U.S. 163 (1931).

Standard Oil Co. of California v. United States, 337 U.S. 293 (1949).

Standard Oil Co. of New Jersey v. United States, 221 U.S. 1 (1911).

Sugar Institute Inc. v. United States, 297 U.S. 553 (1936).

United States v. Addyston Pipe and Steel Co., 85 F. 271 (6 Cir. 1898).

United States v. Aluminum Co. of America, 148 F. 2d 416 (2 Cir. 1945).

United States v. Aluminum Co. of America, 377 U.S. 271 (1964).

United States v. American Tobacco Co., 221 U.S. 106 (1911).

United States v. Bethlehem Steel Corp., 168 F. Supp 576 (S.D.N.Y., 1958).

United States v. Celanese Corp. of America, 91 F. Supp 14 (S.D.N.Y., 1950).

United States v. Columbia Steel Co., 334 U.S. 495 (1948).

United States v. General Dynamics Corp., 415 U.S. 486 (1974).

United States v. Joint Traffic Association, 171 U.S. 505 (1898).

United States v. E. C. Knight Co., 39 U.S. 301 (1895).

United States v. Marine Bancorporation, 418 U.S. 602 (1974).

United States v. Philadelphia National Bank, 374 U.S. 321 (1963).

United States v. Arnold Schwinn & Co., 388 U.S. 365 (1967).

United States v. Socony-Vacuum Oil Co. Inc., 310 U.S. 150 (1940).

United States v. Trans-Missouri Freight Association, 166 U.S. 290 (1897).

United States v. Trenton Potteries Co., 273 U.S. 392 (1927).

United States v. United Shoe Machinery Corp., 110 F. Supp 295 (D. Mass., 1953).

United States v. United Shoe Machinery Corp., 374 U.S. 521 (1954).

United States v. United States Steel Corp., 251 U.S. 417 (1920).

United States v. Von's Grocery Co., 384 U.S. 270 (1966).

Government Publications and Documents

Commission on Organization of the Executive Branch of the Government. *Task Force Report on Regulatory Commissions*. Washington, D.C.: Government Printing Office, 1949.

"Conclusions and Recommendations: Federal Trade Commission Transition Team Report, Submitted to the Reagan Administration." Reprinted in *Antitrust and Trade Regulation Report* 999 (January 29, 1981): G1–3.

Congress. House. Committee on Appropriations. *Agriculture, Environmental and Consumer Protection, Appropriations for Fiscal Year 1972. Hearings before a*

Bibliography

Subcommittee of the House Committee on Appropriations. 92d Cong., 1st sess., 1972.

Congress. House. Committee on Government Operations. *Impact of OMB-Proposed Budget Cuts for the Federal Trade Commission. Hearings before a Subcommittee of the Committee on Government Operations, House of Representatives.* 97th Cong., 1st sess., 1981.

_____. *Oversight of the Federal Trade Commission: Fiscal Years 1982 and 1983. Hearings before a Subcommittee of the Committee on Government Operations, House of Representatives.* 98th Cong., 1st sess., 1983.

Congress. House. Committee on the Judiciary. *Antitrust Division of the Department of Justice. Oversight Hearings before the Subcommittee on Monopolies and Commercial Law of the Committee on the Judiciary, House of Representatives.* 97th Cong., 1st and 2d sess., 1981.

_____. *Antitrust Division of the Department of Justice. Oversight Hearings before the Subcommittee on Monopolies and Commercial Law of the Committee on the Judiciary, House of Representatives.* 99th Cong., 1st sess., 1985.

_____. *Investigation of Conglomerate Corporations. Hearings before the Antitrust Subcommittee of the House Committee on the Judiciary.* 91st Cong., 2d sess., 1970.

Congress. House. Select Committee on Small Business. *Antitrust Enforcement by the Federal Trade Commission and the Antitrust Division, Department of Justice—a Preliminary Report.* Washington, D.C.: Government Printing Office, 1951.

Congress. Senate. Committee on Appropriations. *Agriculture, Environmental and Consumer Protection Appropriations for Fiscal Year 1972. Hearings before a Subcommittee of the Senate Committee on Appropriations.* 92d Cong., 1st sess., 1971.

Congress. Senate. Committee on Commerce. *Nomination of Caspar W. Weinberger to Be Chairman of the Federal Trade Commission. Hearings before the Senate Committee on Commerce.* 91st Cong., 1st sess., 1970.

_____. *Nomination of Lewis A. Engman to Be a Commissioner of the Federal Trade Commission. Hearings before the Senate Committee on Commerce.* 93d Cong., 1st sess., 1973.

_____. *Nomination of Miles W. Kirkpatrick to Be Chairman of the Federal Trade Commission. Hearings before the Senate Committee on Commerce.* 91st Cong., 2d sess., 1970.

Congress. Senate. Committee on the Judiciary. *The Antitrust Remedies Improvement Act and the Intellectual Property Reform Act of 1987. Hearings before the Subcommittee on Antitrust, Monopolies, and Business Rights of the Committee on the Judiciary.* 100th Cong., 2d sess., 1987–88.

Bibliography

_____. *Federal Trade Commission Procedures. Hearings before a Subcommittee on Administrative Practices and Procedures of the Senate Committee on the Judiciary.* 91st Cong., 1st sess., 1969.

_____. *Oversight of Antitrust Enforcement. Hearings before the Subcommittee on Antitrust and Monopoly of the Committee on the Judiciary, United States Senate.* 95th Cong., 1st sess., 1977.

_____. *To Amend the Sherman Act regarding Retail Competition. Hearing before the Committee on the Judiciary, United States Senate.* 101st Cong., 1st sess., 1990.

_____. *To Amend the Sherman and Clayton Acts. Hearing before the Committee on the Judiciary, United States Senate.* 101st Cong., 1st sess., 1990.

Department of Justice. *Annual Report of the Attorney General of the United States.* Washington, D.C.: Government Printing Office, various years.

_____. *Antitrust Division Manual.* Washington, D.C.: Government Printing Office, 1979.

_____. "Department of Justice Merger Guidelines," 1968.

_____. "Department of Justice Merger Guidelines," 1982.

_____. "Department of Justice Merger Guidelines," 1984.

_____. "Department of Justice Statement concerning Vertical Restraints," 1985.

_____. *Report of the Attorney General's National Committee to Study the Antitrust Laws.* Washington, D.C.: Government Printing Office, 1955.

_____. "Statement by Attorney General Edwin Meese III, February 19, 1986."

Executive Office of the President. Bureau of the Budget. *Federal Trade Commission Study,* 4, 1960.

_____. *Management Review of the Federal Trade Commission,* January 1970.

Federal Trade Commission. *Annual Report.* Washington, D.C.: Government Printing Office, various years.

_____. "First Year of the New Administration: A Progress Report." October 20, 1982. Mimeo.

_____. *Food Investigation: Report of the Federal Trade Commission on the Meatpacking Industry.* Washington, D.C.: Government Printing Office, 1919.

_____. *Operating Manual of the Federal Trade Commission.* Washington, D.C.: Government Printing Office, 1975.

_____. *Organization, Procedures, Rules of Practice, and Standards of Conduct.* Washington, D.C.: Government Printing Office, 1979.

_____. *Report on the Present Trend of Corporate Merger and Acquisition.* Washington, D.C.: Government Printing Office, 1947.

_____. "Review of Accomplishments by the Federal Trade Commission during the

Bibliography

Calendar Year 1977." Reprinted in *Antitrust and Trade Regulation Report* 845 (January 5, 1978): G-1.

———. "Statement of the Federal Trade Commission concerning Mergers," 1984.

Federal Trade Commission. Office of Policy Planning and Evaluation. "1976 Budget Overview." Reprinted in *Antitrust and Trade Regulation Report* 692 (December 10, 1974).

Federal Trade Commission Transition Team. "Conclusion and Recommendations: Federal Trade Commission Team Report, Submitted to the Reagan Administration." Reprinted in *Antitrust and Trade Regulation Report* 999 (January 29, 1981): G-1.

Ford, Gerald. "The President's Remarks and a Question and Answer Session at Bradley University's Everett McKinley Dirksen Forum, March 5, 1976." *Presidential Documents: Gerald R. Ford* 12, 11 (1976).

Hamilton, Walton, and Irene Till. *Antitrust in Action.* Temporary National Economic Committee Monograph no. 19. Washington, D.C.: U.S. Government Printing Office, 1941.

Heller, Robert, and Associates. *The Federal Trade Commission Management Survey Report*, February 1, 1954.

Landis, James M. *Report on the Regulatory Agencies to the President Elect.* Senate Committee on the Judiciary, 86th Cong., 2d sess., 1960.

Office of the President. *Economic Report of the President.* Washington, D.C.: Government Printing Office, 1982.

Pertschuk, Michael. "The Performance of the Federal Trade Commission, 1977–1984." Report to the Subcommittee on Oversight and Investigations, House Committee on Energy and Commerce, September 1984. Mimeo.

President's Advisory Council on Executive Organization. *A New Regulatory Framework: Report on Selected Regulatory Agencies.* Washington, D.C.: Government Printing Office, 1971.

Task Force on Productivity and Competition. *Report of the Task Force on Productivity and Competition*, February 18, 1969.

White House Task Force on Antitrust Policy. *Report of the White House Task Force on Antitrust Policy.* Reprinted in *Antitrust and Trade Regulation Report* 415 (May 26, 1969).

Secondary Sources

Abel, Richard L. "The Transformation of the American Legal Profession." *Law and Society Review* 20 (1986): 7–17.

Bibliography

Aberbach, Joel D., and Bert A. Rockman. "Clashing Beliefs within the Executive Branch: The Nixon Administration Bureaucracy." *American Political Science Review* 70 (June 1976): 456–68.

Adams, Walter. "Economic Power and the Constitution." *Challenge*, July/August 1987, pp. 17–25.

———. "Public Policy in a Free Enterprise Economy." In *The Structure of Industry*, 6th ed., edited by Walter Adams. New York: Macmillan, 1982.

Adams, Walter, and James W. Brock. *The Bigness Complex: Industry, Labor, and Government in the American Economy*. New York: Pantheon Books, 1986.

———. "Mr. Reagan and Antitrust." In *Public Policy toward Corporations*, edited by Arnold A. Heggestad. Gainesville: University of Florida Press, 1988.

Amenta, Edwin, Elisabeth S. Clemens, Jefren Olsen, Sunita Parikh, and Theda Skocpol. "The Political Origins of Unemployment Insurance in Five American States." In *Studies in American Political Development*, vol. 2, edited by Karen Orren and Stephen Skowronek. New Haven, Conn.: Yale University Press, 1987.

American Bar Association. *Report of the ABA Commission to Study the Federal Trade Commission, September 15, 1969*. Chicago: American Bar Association, 1969.

———. *Report of the American Bar Association Section of Antitrust Law Special Committee to Study the Role of the Federal Trade Commission*, April 7, 1989. Reprinted in *Antitrust and Trade Regulation Report* 56, 1410, April 6, 1989.

———. *Report of the American Bar Association Section of Antitrust Law Task Force on the Antitrust Division of the U.S. Department of Justice, July 19, 1989*. Reprinted in *Antitrust and Trade Regulation Report* 57, 1425, July 20, 1989.

———. "Report of the Section of Antitrust Law on the Ash Council Report." *Antitrust Law Journal* 40 (1971): 220–22.

"Anatomy of a Policy Revolution." *Antitrust Law and Economics Review* 14, 4 (1982): 1–7.

Anderson, James E. "The Reagan Administration, Antitrust Action, and Policy Change." Paper presented at annual meeting of the Midwest Political Science Association, Chicago, April 1986.

Andewelt, Roger B. "Organization and Operation of the Antitrust Division." *Antitrust Law Journal* 54 (1985): 71–83.

"Antitrust Law and Economics at the University of Miami." *Antitrust Law and Economics Review* 14, 2 (1982): 1–8.

Armentano, Dominick T. *Antitrust and Monopoly: Anatomy of a Policy Failure*. New York: John T. Wiley & Sons, 1982.

Arnold, Thurman W. "Antitrust Law Enforcement: Past and Future." *Law and Contemporary Problems* 7 (Winter 1940): 5–23.

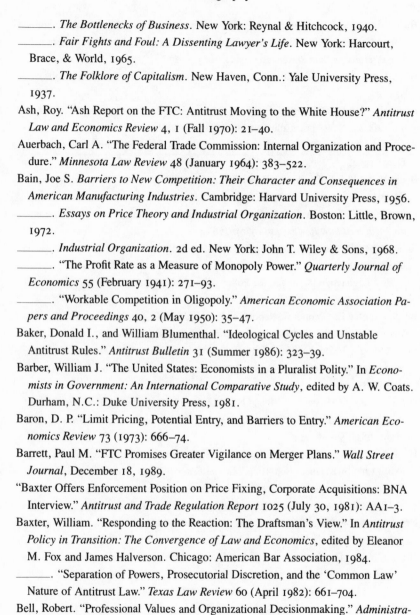

Bibliography

————. *The Bottlenecks of Business.* New York: Reynal & Hitchcock, 1940.

————. *Fair Fights and Foul: A Dissenting Lawyer's Life.* New York: Harcourt, Brace, & World, 1965.

————. *The Folklore of Capitalism.* New Haven, Conn.: Yale University Press, 1937.

Ash, Roy. "Ash Report on the FTC: Antitrust Moving to the White House?" *Antitrust Law and Economics Review* 4, 1 (Fall 1970): 21–40.

Auerbach, Carl A. "The Federal Trade Commission: Internal Organization and Procedure." *Minnesota Law Review* 48 (January 1964): 383–522.

Bain, Joe S. *Barriers to New Competition: Their Character and Consequences in American Manufacturing Industries.* Cambridge: Harvard University Press, 1956.

————. *Essays on Price Theory and Industrial Organization.* Boston: Little, Brown, 1972.

————. *Industrial Organization.* 2d ed. New York: John T. Wiley & Sons, 1968.

————. "The Profit Rate as a Measure of Monopoly Power." *Quarterly Journal of Economics* 55 (February 1941): 271–93.

————. "Workable Competition in Oligopoly." *American Economic Association Papers and Proceedings* 40, 2 (May 1950): 35–47.

Baker, Donald I., and William Blumenthal. "Ideological Cycles and Unstable Antitrust Rules." *Antitrust Bulletin* 31 (Summer 1986): 323–39.

Barber, William J. "The United States: Economists in a Pluralist Polity." In *Economists in Government: An International Comparative Study,* edited by A. W. Coats. Durham, N.C.: Duke University Press, 1981.

Baron, D. P. "Limit Pricing, Potential Entry, and Barriers to Entry." *American Economics Review* 73 (1973): 666–74.

Barrett, Paul M. "FTC Promises Greater Vigilance on Merger Plans." *Wall Street Journal,* December 18, 1989.

"Baxter Offers Enforcement Position on Price Fixing, Corporate Acquisitions: BNA Interview." *Antitrust and Trade Regulation Report* 1025 (July 30, 1981): AA1–3.

Baxter, William. "Responding to the Reaction: The Draftsman's View." In *Antitrust Policy in Transition: The Convergence of Law and Economics,* edited by Eleanor M. Fox and James Halverson. Chicago: American Bar Association, 1984.

————. "Separation of Powers, Prosecutorial Discretion, and the 'Common Law' Nature of Antitrust Law." *Texas Law Review* 60 (April 1982): 661–704.

Bell, Robert. "Professional Values and Organizational Decisionmaking." *Administration and Society* 17 (May 1985): 21–60.

Bernstein, Marver H. *Regulating Business by Independent Commission.* Princeton, N.J.: Princeton University Press, 1955.

Bickel, David R. "The Antitrust Division's Adoption of a Chicago School Economic Policy Calls for Some Reorganization: But Is the Division's New Policy Here to Stay?" *Houston Law Review* 20 (1982): 1083–1127.

Blair, John. "Planning for Competition." *Columbia Law Review* 64 (March 1964): 524–42.

Blaisdell, Thomas C. *The Federal Trade Commission: An Experiment in the Control of Business.* New York: Columbia University Press, 1932.

Blum, John Morton. *The Republican Roosevelt.* Cambridge: Harvard University Press, 1954.

Bock, Betty. "Line of Business Reporting: A Quest for a Snark?" *Conference Board Record* 12 (November 1975): 18–22.

Bok, Derek C. "Section 7 of the Clayton Act and the Merging of Law and Economics." *Harvard Law Review* 74 (1960): 226–47.

Bork, Robert H. *The Antitrust Paradox: A Policy at War with Itself.* New York: Basic Books, 1978.

———. "Legislative Intent and the Policy of the Sherman Act." *Journal of Law and Economics* 9 (October 1966): 7–48.

Boyle, Stanley E. "Economic Reports and the Federal Trade Commission: Fifty Years' Experience." *Federal Bar Journal* 24 (Fall 1964): 489–509.

Boyle, Stanley E., and Michael J. Piette. "How Economists View Reagan's Five Proposed Antitrust Changes: A Survey." *Antitrust Law and Economics Review* 18, 2 (1986): 85–92.

Bradburd, Ralph M., and A. Mead Over. "Organizational Costs, 'Sticky Equilibria,' and Critical Levels of Concentration." *Review of Economics and Statistics* 64 (February 1982): 50–58.

Breit, William, and Kenneth G. Elzinga. "Information for Antitrust and Business Activity: Line-of-Business Reporting." In *The Federal Trade Commission since 1970: Economic Regulation and Bureaucratic Behavior,* edited by Kenneth W. Clarkson and Timothy J. Muris. Cambridge: Cambridge University Press, 1981.

Brock, James W. "Bigness Is the Problem, Not the Solution." *Challenge,* July/August 1987, pp. 11–16.

Brozen, Yale. "The Antitrust Task Force Deconcentration Recommendation." *Journal of Law and Economics* 13 (October 1970): 279–92.

———. "Bain's Concentration and Rates of Return Revisited." *Journal of Law and Economics* 14 (October 1971): 351–69.

———. *Is Government the Source of Monopoly? and Other Essays.* San Francisco: Cato Institute, 1980.

———. "No . . . the Concentration-Collusion Doctrine." In *Industrial Concentration and the Market System: Legal, Economic, Social, and Political Consequences*, edited by Eleanor M. Fox and James T. Halverson. Chicago: American Bar Association Press, 1979.

Brunner, Thomas W., Thomas G. Krattenmaker, Robert A. Skitol, and Ann Adams Webster. *Mergers in the New Antitrust Era*. Washington, D.C.: Bureau of National Affairs, 1985.

Bullock, Charles S., and Joseph Stewart. "New Programs in Old Agencies: Lessons in Organizational Change from the Office of Civil Rights." *Administration and Society* 15 (February 1984): 387–412.

Burnham, Walter Dean. "The Appearance and Disappearance of the American Voter." In *The Political Economy*, edited by Thomas Ferguson and Joel Rogers. Armonk, N.Y.: M. E. Sharpe, 1984.

Calabresi, Guido, and A. Douglas Melamed. "Property Rules and Inalienability: One View of the Cathedral." *Harvard Law Review* 85 (April 1972): 1089–1128.

Cambell, Thomas J. "Antitrust Enforcement at the FTC." *Antitrust Law and Economics Review* 14, 4 (1982): 91–110.

Campbell, John L. *Collapse of an Industry: Nuclear Power and the Contradictions of U.S. Policy*. Ithaca, N.Y.: Cornell University Press, 1988.

Canterbery, E. Ray, and Robert J. Burkhardt. "What Do We Mean by Asking Whether Economics Is a Science?" In *Why Economics Is Not Yet a Science*, edited by Alfred Eichner. Armonk, N.Y.: M. E. Sharpe, 1983.

Caves, Richard E. "Industrial Organization, Corporate Strategy, and Structure." *Journal of Economic Literature* 18 (1980): 64–92.

Chamberlin, Edward H. *The Theory of Monopolistic Competition: A Re-Orientation of the Theory of Value*. 8th ed. Cambridge: Harvard University Press, 1962.

Chandler, Alfred D., Jr. *Strategy and Structure: Chapters in the History of American Industrial Enterprise*. Cambridge: MIT Press, 1962.

———. "The United States: Seedbed of Managerial Capitalism." In *Managerial Hierarchies: Comparative Perspectives on the Rise of the Modern Business Enterprise*, edited by Alfred D. Chandler and Herman Daems. Cambridge: Harvard University Press, 1980.

———. *The Visible Hand: The Managerial Revolution in American Business*. Cambridge: Harvard University Press, 1977.

Clarkson, Kenneth W., and Timothy J. Muris, eds. *The Federal Trade Commission since 1970: Economic Regulation and Bureaucratic Behavior*. Cambridge: Cambridge University Press, 1981.

Cohodas, Nadine. "Reagan Seeks Relaxation of Antitrust Laws." *Congressional Quarterly Weekly Report* 44, 3 (February 1, 1986): 187–92.

Bibliography

Comanor, William S., and Robert H. Smiley. "Monopoly and the Distribution of Wealth." *Quarterly Journal of Economics* 87 (May 1975): 179–94.

Commons, John R. *The Legal Foundations of Capitalism*. Madison: University of Wisconsin Press, 1954.

Congress Watch. "Antitrust Enforcement at the Federal Trade Commission: The Reagan-Miller FTC, the Carter-Pertschuk FTC, and the Last Twenty Years." Mimeo, 1984.

Cox, Edward F., Robert C. Fellmeth, and John E. Schulz. *The Nader Report on the Federal Trade Commission*. New York: Richard W. Baron, 1969.

"Current Antitrust Enforcement and Its Critics: Recent Proposals for Reform and Restructure in the Antitrust Division, the FTC, and the Courts." *Antitrust Law Journal* 40 (1971): 341–87.

Davis, G. Collum. "The Transformation of the Federal Trade Commission, 1914–1929." *Mississippi Valley Historical Review* 49 (December 1962): 437–55.

Demsetz, Harold. *Economic, Legal, and Political Dimensions of Competition*. Amsterdam: North-Holland Publishing, 1982.

———. "Industry Structure, Market Rivalry, and Public Policy." *Journal of Law and Economics* 16 (April 1973): 1–9.

———. *The Market Concentration Doctrine: An Examination of Evidence and a Discussion of Policy*. Washington, D.C.: American Enterprise Institute for Policy Research, 1973.

———. "Two Systems of Belief about Monopoly." In *Industrial Concentration: The New Learning*, edited by Harvey J. Goldschmid, H. Michael Mann, and J. Fred Weston. Boston: Little, Brown, 1974.

Derthick, Martha, and Paul J. Quirk. *The Politics of Deregulation*. Washington, D.C.: Brookings Institute, 1985.

Diamond, William. *The Economic Thought of Woodrow Wilson*. Baltimore: Johns Hopkins University Press, 1943.

DiMaggio, Paul. "Interest and Agency in Institutional Theory." In *Institutional Patterns and Organizations: Culture and Environment*, edited by Lynne G. Zucker. Cambridge, Mass.: Ballinger Publishing, 1988.

———. "State Expansion and Organizational Fields." In *Organizational Theory and Public Policy*, edited by Richard H. Hall and Robert E. Quinn. Beverly Hills, Calif.: Sage Publications, 1983.

Dingwall, Robert, and Philip Lewis, eds. *The Sociology of the Professions: Lawyers, Doctors, and Others*. New York: St. Martin's Press, 1983.

Dulles, Foster Rhea, and Melvyn Dubofsky. *Labor in America*. 4th ed. Arlington Heights, Ill.: Harlan Davidson, 1984.

Bibliography

Dweyer, Paula. "Putting the 'Anti' Back in the Antitrust Division." *Business Week*, June 19, 1989.

Dyson, Kenneth. "The Cultural, Ideological, and Structural Context." In *Industrial Crisis*, edited by Kenneth Dyson and Stephen Wilks. Oxford: Martin Robertson, 1983.

Edelman, Murray. *The Symbolic Uses of Politics*. Urbana: University of Illinois Press, 1964.

Edwards, Corwin D. *The Price Discrimination Law*. Washington, D.C.: Brookings Institution, 1959.

————. "Thurman Arnold and the Antitrust Laws." *Political Science Quarterly* 58 (September 1943): 338–55.

Eichner, Alfred. "Why Economics Is Not Yet a Science." In *Why Economics Is Not Yet a Science*, edited by Alfred Eichner. Armonk, N.Y.: M. E. Sharpe, 1983.

Eisner, Marc Allen, and Kenneth J. Meier. "Presidential Control versus Bureaucratic Power: Explaining the Reagan Revolution in Antitrust." *American Journal of Political Science* 34, 1 (February 1990): 269–87.

Ellis, Dorsey D., Jr. "Legislative Powers: FTC Rule Making." In *The Federal Trade Commission since 1970: Economic Regulation and Bureaucratic Behavior*, edited by Kenneth W. Clarkson and Timothy J. Muris. Cambridge: Cambridge University Press, 1981.

Elzinga, Kenneth G. "The Antimerger Law: Pyrrhic Victories?" *Journal of Law and Economics* 12 (1969): 43–78.

"Enforcement Policies and Procedures—the Past as Prologue: A Panel Discussion." *Antitrust Law Journal* 42 (1973): 1–45.

Engel, Gloria V. "Professional Autonomy and Bureaucratic Organization." *Administrative Science Quarterly* 15 (March 1970): 12–21.

Fainsod, Merle, Lincoln Gordon, and Joseph C. Palamountain, Jr. *Government and the American Economy*. New York: W. W. Norton, 1955.

"The Federal Trade Commission under Attack: Should the Commission's Role Be Changed?" *Antitrust Law Journal* 49 (1982): 1481–97.

Ferguson, James M. "Where Did Joe Bain Go Wrong? In Entering Economics." *Antitrust Law and Economics Review* 15, 4 (1983): 19–48.

Fiorina, Morris P. *Congress: Keystone of the Washington Establishment*. New Haven, Conn.: Yale University Press, 1977.

————. "Flagellating the Federal Bureaucracy." *Society* 20, 3 (1983): 66–74.

————. "Legislative Choice or Regulatory Forms: Legal Process or Administrative Process?" *Public Choice* 39 (1982): 33–66.

Fischer, Frank. "Policy Expertise and the 'New Class': A Critique of the

Neoconservative Thesis." In *Confronting Values in Policy Analysis: The Politics of Criteria*, edited by Frank Fischer and John Forester. Beverly Hills, Calif.: Sage Publications, 1987.

"Former AAG Kauper Looks Back at the Antitrust Division: An Interview." *Antitrust* I (Fall 1986): 4–10.

Fox, Eleanor M. "The Modernization of Antitrust: A New Equilibrium?" *Cornell Law Review* 66 (June 1981): 1140–92.

———. "The 1982 Guidelines: When Economists Are Kings?" In *Antitrust Policy in Transition: The Convergence of Law and Economics*, edited by Eleanor M. Fox and James Halverson. Chicago: American Bar Association, 1984.

Friedman, Milton. *Capitalism and Freedom*. Chicago: University of Chicago Press, 1962.

"FTC Adopts Policy Protocols to Help Evaluate Cost-Benefit Ratio of Proposed Commission Actions." *Antitrust and Trade Regulation Report* 953 (March 2, 1976): A19.

"FTC Adopts Resolution Sharply Limiting Use of Line-of-Business Reports and Data." *Antitrust and Trade Regulation Report* 730 (September 16, 1975): A2.

"FTC Transition Team Report Urges One-Quarter Cutback in Agency Size." *Antitrust and Trade Regulation Report* 999 (January 29, 1981): A8.

Galbraith, John Kenneth. *The New Industrial State*. New York: Mentor, 1967.

Gardner, Judy. "Consumer Report: FTC Seeks Wider Impact in Antitrust Work. Puts New Emphasis on Planning." *National Journal* 4 (July 15, 1972): 1151–59.

Geithman, Frederick E. "Mergers: Does Empirical Evidence Support a Change in Public Policy?" In *Issues after a Century of Federal Competition Policy*, edited by Robert C. Wills, Julie A. Caswell, and John D. Culbertson. Lexington, Mass.: D. C. Heath, 1987.

Gellhorn, Ernest. "Regulatory Reform and the Federal Trade Commission's Antitrust Jurisdiction." *Tennessee Law Review* 49 (1982): 471–510.

———. "Two's a Crowd: The FTC's Redundant Antitrust Powers." *Regulation* 5, 6 (November 1981): 32–42.

———. "The Wages of Zealotry: The FTC Under Siege." *Regulation* 4, 1 (January 1980): 33–40.

Glassman, Michael L. "The Role of Economists in Developing Antitrust Remedies." In *The Antitrust Dilemma*, edited by James A. Dalton and Stanford L. Levine. Lexington, Mass.: Lexington Books, 1974.

Goldman, Eric F. *Rendezvous with Destiny: A History of Modern American Reform*. New York: Alfred A. Knopf, 1952.

Gorinson, Stanley M. "Antitrust Division Reorganized." *Antitrust* 7 (October 1985): 18–19.

Gormley, William T. "Regulatory Issue Networks in a Federal System." *Polity* 18 (June 1986): 595–620.

Green, Mark J. "Nader Group Report on Antitrust Enforcement: A Summary." *Antitrust Law and Economics Review* 4, 1 (Fall 1970): 7–20.

Green, Mark J., Beverly C. Moore, and Bruce Wasserstein. *The Closed Enterprise System: Ralph Nader's Study Group Report on Antitrust Enforcement*. New York: Grossman Publishers, 1972.

Greer, Douglas F. *Industrial Organization and Public Policy*. New York: Macmillan, 1980.

Hall, Peter. *Governing the Economy: The Politics of State Intervention in Britain and France*. New York: Oxford University Press, 1986.

———, ed. *The Political Power of Economic Ideas: Keynesianism across Nations*. Princeton, N.J.: Princeton University Press, 1989.

Hall, Richard. "Some Organizational Considerations in the Professional-Organizational Relationship." *Administrative Science Quarterly* 12 (December 1967): 461–78.

Halverson, James T. "Whatever Happened to the Little Old Lady of Pennsylvania Avenue?" *Antitrust and Trade Regulation Report* 634 (October 16, 1973): D1, 2.

Harberger, Arnold. "Monopoly and Resource Allocation." *American Economics Association Papers and Proceedings* 44, 2 (May 1954): 77–87.

Harris, Richard A., and Sidney M. Milkis. *The Politics of Regulatory Change: A Tale of Two Agencies*. New York: Oxford University Press, 1989.

Harris, Robert G., and Thomas M. Jorde. "Market Definition in the Merger Guidelines: Implications for Antitrust Enforcement." In *Antitrust Policy in Transition: The Convergence of Law and Economics*, edited by Eleanor M. Fox and James Halverson. Chicago: American Bar Association, 1984.

Hawley, Ellis W. "Herbert Hoover, the Commerce Secretariat, and the Vision of an 'Associative State,' 1921–1928." *Journal of American History* 61 (June 1974): 116–40.

———. *The New Deal and the Problem of Monopoly*. Princeton, N.J.: Princeton University Press, 1965.

———. "Three Facets of Hooverian Associationalism: Lumber, Aviation, and Movies, 1921–1930." In *Regulation in Perspective: Historical Essays*, edited by Thomas K. McCraw. Cambridge: Harvard University Press, 1981.

Hay, George A. "Pigeonholes in Antitrust." *Antitrust Bulletin* 29 (Spring 1984): 133–45.

Bibliography

Heclo, Hugh. "Issue Networks and the Executive Establishment." In *The New American Political System*, edited by Anthony King. Washington, D.C.: American Enterprise Institute, 1978.

―――. *Modern Social Politics in Britain and Sweden: From Relief to Income Maintenance*. New Haven, Conn.: Yale University Press, 1974.

Henderson, Gerard C. *The Federal Trade Commission: A Study in Administrative Law and Procedure*. New Haven, Conn.: Yale University Press, 1924.

Herring, Pendleton. *Public Administration and the Public Interest*. New York: McGraw-Hill, 1936.

Himmelberg, Robert F. *The Origins of the National Recovery Administration: Business, Government, and the Trade Association Issue, 1921–1933*. New York: Fordham University Press, 1976.

Hodges, Edward P. "Complaints of Antitrust Violations and Their Investigation: The Work of the Complaints Section of the Antitrust Division." *Law and Contemporary Problems* 7 (Winter 1940): 90–95.

Hofstadter, Richard. *The Age of Reform: From Bryan to F.D.R.* New York: Random House, 1955.

―――. "What Happened to the Antitrust Movement? Notes on the Evolution of an American Creed." In *The Business Establishment*, edited by Earl F. Cheit. New York: John T. Wiley & Sons, 1966.

―――, ed. *The Progressive Movement, 1910–1915*. Englewood Cliffs, N.J.: Prentice-Hall, 1963.

Holt, W. Stull. *The Federal Trade Commission: Its History, Activities, and Organization*. New York: D. Appleton, 1922.

Hurst, James Willard. *Law and Markets in U.S. History: Different Modes of Bargaining among Interests*. Madison: University of Wisconsin Press, 1982.

―――. *Law and the Conditions of Freedom in the Nineteenth Century United States*. Madison: University of Wisconsin Press, 1956.

―――. *The Legitimacy of the Business Corporation in the Law of the United States, 1780–1970*. Charlottesville: University of Virginia Press, 1970.

"Interview with the Honorable Donald F. Turner, Assistant Attorney General in Charge of the Antitrust Division." Parts 1, 2. *Antitrust Law Journal* 36 (1967): 113–37; 37 (1968): 290–308.

"Interview with James C. Miller III, Chairman, Federal Trade Commission." Parts 1, 2. *Antitrust Law Journal* 51 (1982): 3–21; 52 (1983): 3–22.

"Interview with Richard W. McLaren, Assistant Attorney General, Antitrust Division." *Antitrust Law Journal* 39 (1970): 368–84.

"Interview with Robert Tollison, FTC's Chief Economist." *Antitrust and Trade Regulation Report* 1083 (September 30, 1982): 612–14.

Johnson, Donald Bruce, ed. *National Party Platforms, 1840–1976.* 2 vols. Urbana: University of Illinois Press, 1978.

"Judicial Precedent and the New Economics." In *Antitrust Policy in Transition: The Convergence of Law and Economics*, edited by Eleanor M. Fox and James Halverson. Chicago: American Bar Association, 1984.

Kanel, Don. "Property and Economic Power as Issues in Institutional Economics." *Journal of Economic Issues* 8 (December 1974): 827–40.

Katzmann, Robert A. "The Attenuation of Antitrust." *Brookings Review*, Summer 1984, pp. 23–27.

————. "Capitol Hill's Current Attack against the FTC." *Wall Street Journal*, May 7, 1980.

————. *Regulatory Bureaucracy: The Federal Trade Commission and Antitrust Policy*. Cambridge: MIT Press, 1980.

Kaufmann, Herbert. *The Limits of Organizational Change*. University: University of Alabama Press, 1971.

Kauper, Thomas E. "New Approaches to Old Problems." *Antitrust Law Journal* 46 (1977): 235–47.

————. "The Role of Economic Analysis in the Antitrust Division before and after the Establishment of the Economic Policy Office: A Lawyer's View." *Antitrust Bulletin* 29 (Spring 1984): 111–32.

————. "The Warren Court and the Antitrust Laws: Of Economics, Populism, and Cynicism." *Michigan Law Review* 67 (1968): 310–30.

Kaysen, Carl, and Donald F. Turner. *Antitrust Policy*. Cambridge: Harvard University Press, 1959.

Keller, Morton. "The Pluralist State: American Economic Regulation in Comparative Perspective, 1900–1930." In *Regulation in Perspective: Historical Essays*, edited by Thomas K. McCraw. Cambridge: Harvard University Press, 1981.

Kelman, Steven. *Making Public Policy: A Hopeful View of American Government*. New York: Basic Books, 1987.

Kingdon, John. *Agendas, Alternatives, and Public Policies*. Boston: Little, Brown, 1984.

Kintner, Earl W., ed. *The Legislative History of the Federal Antitrust Laws and Related Statutes*. 5 vols. New York: Chelsea House Publishers, 1978.

Knott, Jack H., and Gary J. Miller. *Reforming Bureaucracy: The Politics of Structural Choice*. Englewood Cliffs, N.J.: Prentice-Hall, 1987.

Bibliography

Kolko, Gabriel. *The Triumph of Conservatism: A Reinterpretation of American History, 1900–1916.* New York: Free Press, 1963.

Kovacic, William E. "The Federal Trade Commission and Congressional Oversight of Antitrust Enforcement: A Historical Perspective." In *Public Choice and Regulation: View from Inside the Federal Trade Commission*, edited by Robert J. MacKay, James C. Miller III, and Bruce Yandle. Stanford, Calif.: Hoover Institution Press, 1987.

Kovaleff, Theodore Philip. *Business and Government during the Eisenhower Administration: A Study of the Antitrust Policy of the Antitrust Division of the Justice Department.* Athens: Ohio University Press, 1980.

Kramer, Victor H. "Antitrust Today: The Baxterization of the Sherman and Clayton Acts." *Wisconsin Law Review* 6 (1981): 1287–1302.

Krasner, Stephen. "Approaches to the State: Alternative Conceptions and Historical Dynamics." *Comparative Politics* 16 (January 1984): 223–46.

Kristol, Irving. "On Corporate Capitalism in America." In *Reflections of a Neoconservative: Looking Back, Looking Ahead.* New York: Basic Books, 1983.

Kurtz, Howard. "Justice Shifts Antitrust Responsibilities: Switching Initial Review to Economists Said to Further Weaken Merger Enforcement." *Washington Post*, December 11, 1986, p. 5.

Lambright, W. Henry, and Albert H. Teich. "Scientists and Government: A Case of Professional Ambivalence." *Public Administration Review* 38 (March/April 1978): 133–39.

Landes, William. "Harm to Competition: Cartels, Mergers, and Joint Ventures." In *Antitrust Policy in Transition: The Convergence of Law and Economics*, edited by Eleanor M. Fox and James Halverson. Chicago: American Bar Association, 1984.

Latham, Earl. *The Group Basis of Politics.* Ithaca, N.Y.: Cornell University Press, 1954.

Latsis, Spiro J. "A Research Program in Economics." In *Method and Appraisal in Economics*, edited by Spiro J. Latsis. Cambridge: Cambridge University Press, 1976.

Lee, Susan Previant, and Peter Passell. *A New Economic View of American History.* New York: W. W. Norton, 1979.

Leibenstein, Harvey. "Competition and X-Efficiency." *Journal of Political Economy* 93 (May 1973): 765–810.

Letwin, William. *Law and Economic Policy in America: The Evolution of the Sherman Antitrust Act.* New York: Random House, 1965.

Liebeler, Wesley J. "Bureau of Competition: Antitrust Enforcement Activities." In

Bibliography

The Federal Trade Commission since 1970: Economic Regulation and Bureaucratic Behavior, edited by Kenneth W. Clarkson and Timothy J. Muris. Cambridge: Cambridge University Press, 1981.

Lindberg, Leon N. "The Production and Selection of Economic Knowledge: Economic Theory, Economic Advice, and the Societal Role of Economists." Paper presented to the Wissenschaftskolleg zu Berlin, 1985.

Lindblom, Charles. "The Market as Prison." *Journal of Politics* 44 (May 1982): 324–36.

_____. *Politics and Markets: The World's Political Economic Systems*. New York: Basic Books, 1977.

Link, Arthur S. *Woodrow Wilson and the Progressive Era, 1910–1917*. New York: Harper & Row, 1954.

Litvack, Sanford M. "Report from the Antitrust Division." *Antitrust Law Journal* 49 (1981): 1073–78.

Lovett, William A. "Antitrust in the Current Economic Environment." In *Public Policy toward Corporations*, edited by Arnold A. Heggestad. Gainesville: University of Florida Press, 1988.

_____. "Theory and Practice in Antitrust." In *Issues after a Century of Federal Competition Policy*, edited by Robert L. Wills, Julie A. Caswell, and John D. Culbertson. Lexington, Mass.: D. C. Heath, 1987.

Lowi, Theodore J. *The End of Liberalism: The Second Republic of the United States*. 2d ed. New York: W. W. Norton, 1979.

Lustig, R. Jeffrey. *Corporate Liberalism: The Origins of Modern Political Theory, 1890–1920*. Berkeley: University of California Press, 1982.

McCraw, Thomas K. "Mercantilism and the Market: Antecedents of American Industrial Policy." In *The Politics of Industrial Policy*, edited by Claude E. Barfield and William A. Schambra. Washington D.C.: American Enterprise Institute, 1986.

_____. "Rethinking the Trust Question." In *Regulation in Perspective: Historical Essays*, edited by Thomas K. McCraw. Cambridge: Harvard University Press, 1981.

McGee, John S. "Efficiency and Economies of Size." In *Industrial Concentration: The New Learning*, edited by Harvey J. Goldschmid, H. Michael Mann, and J. Fred Weston. Boston: Little, Brown, 1974.

_____. *In Defense of Industrial Concentration*. New York: Praeger Publishers, 1971.

MacIntyre, A. Everette, and Paul Rand Dixon. "The Federal Trade Commission after Fifty Years." *Federal Law Journal* 24 (1964): 377–424.

McLaren, Richard W. "Recent Cases, Current Enforcement Views, and Possible New

Bibliography

Antitrust Enforcement." *Antitrust Law Journal* 38 (1969): 211–17.

MacRae, Duncan. *The Social Function of Social Science.* New Haven, Conn.: Yale University Press, 1976.

Mann, H. Michael. "Advertising, Concentration, and Profitability: The State of Knowledge and Directions for Public Policy." In *Industrial Concentration: The New Learning*, edited by Harvey J. Goldschmid, H. Michael Mann, and J. Fred Weston. Boston: Little, Brown, 1974.

———. "Seller Concentration, Barriers to Entry, and Rates of Return in Thirty Industries, 1950–1960." *Review of Economics and Statistics* 43 (August 1966): 296–307.

Mann, H. Michael, and James W. Meehan, Jr. "Policy Planning for Antitrust Activities: Present Status and Future Prospects." In *The Antitrust Dilemma*, edited by James A. Dalton and Stanford L. Levin. Lexington, Mass.: Lexington Books, 1974.

March, James O., and Johan P. Olsen. "The New Institutionalism: Organizational Factors in Political Life." *American Political Science Review* 78 (August 1984): 734–49.

———. *Rediscovering Institutions: The Organizational Basis of Politics.* New York: Free Press, 1989.

Markham, Jesse W. "The Federal Trade Commission's Use of Economics." *Columbia University Law Review* 54 (March 1964): 405–14.

Mayhew, David R. *Congress: The Electoral Connection.* New Haven, Conn.: Yale University Press, 1974.

Meier, Kenneth J. *Regulation: Politics, Bureaucracy, and Economics.* New York: St. Martin's Press, 1985.

Meier, Kenneth J., and John Plumlee. "Regulatory Administration and Organizational Rigidity." *Western Political Quarterly* 31 (1978): 80–95.

Metzenbaum, Howard M. "Address." *Antitrust Law Journal* 56 (1987): 387–93.

Miller, James C., III. *The Economist as Reformer: Revamping the FTC, 1981–1985.* Washington, D.C.: American Enterprise Institute, 1989.

———. "The Role of Economic Research at the Federal Trade Commission." Remarks before the Council for a Competitive Economy, Washington, D.C., September 14, 1983.

Mitnick, Barry M. *The Political Economy of Regulation: Creating, Designing, and Removing Regulatory Forms.* New York: Columbia University Press, 1980.

Modigliani, Franco. "New Developments on the Oligopoly Front." *Journal of Political Economy* 66 (1958): 215–32.

Bibliography

Moe, Terry. "An Assessment of the Positive Theory of Congressional Dominance."
Legislative Studies Quarterly 12 (November 1987): 475–520.
————. "Interests, Institutions, and Positive Theory: The Politics of the NLRB." In
Studies in American Political Development, vol. 2, edited by Karen Orren and Ste-
phen Skowronek. New Haven, Conn.: Yale University Press, 1987.
————. "The Politics of Structural Choice: Toward a Theory of Public Bureaucracy."
Paper delivered at the annual meeting of the American Political Science Associa-
tion, Washington, D.C., September 1988.
Montague, Gilbert H. "Antitrust Laws and the Federal Trade Commission, 1914–
1927." *Columbia Law Review* 27 (June 1927): 650–78.
Mosher, Frederick. *Democracy and the Public Service*. New York: Oxford University
Press, 1968.
————. "Professions in Public Service." *Public Administration Review* 38
(March/April 1978): 144–50.
Mueller, Willard F. "The Anti-Antitrust Movement and the Case of Lester Thurow."
Antitrust Law and Economics Review 13, 3 (1983): 59–91.
————. "Industrial Concentration: An Important Inflationary Force?" In *Industrial
Concentration: The New Learning*, edited by Harvey J. Goldschmid, H. Michael
Mann, and J. Fred Weston. Boston: Little, Brown, 1974.
————. "A New Attack on Antitrust." In *Public Policy toward Corporations*, edited
by Arnold A. Heggestad. Gainesville: University of Florida Press, 1988.
Nathan, Richard. *The Administrative Presidency*. New York: John T. Wiley & Sons,
1983.
Neale, A. D., and D. G. Goyder. *The Antitrust Laws of the U.S.A.: A Study of Com-
petition Enforced by Law*. 3d ed. Cambridge: Cambridge University Press, 1980.
Nelson, Ralph. *Merger Movements in American History, 1895–1956*. Princeton, N.J.:
Princeton University Press, 1959.
Nelson, Richard, and Sidney Winter. *An Evolutionary Theory of Economic Change*.
Cambridge: Harvard University Press, 1983.
Neustadt, Richard E. *Presidential Power: The Politics of Leadership from FDR to
Carter*. New York: John T. Wiley & Sons, 1980.
Niskanen, William. *Bureaucracy and Representative Government*. Chicago: Aldine-
Atherton, 1971.
Ogul, Morris S. *Congress Oversees the Bureaucracy*. Pittsburgh: University of Pitts-
burgh Press, 1976.
Ouchi, William G. *The M-Form Society*. Reading, Mass.: Addison-Wesley, 1984.
Owen, Bruce. "Economists as Trustbusters?" *Washington Post*, December 22, 1986.

Peltzman, Sam. "The Gains and Losses from Industrial Concentration." *Journal of Law and Economics* 20 (October 1977): 229–63.

Pertschuk, Michael. *Revolt against Regulation: The Rise and Pause of the Consumer Movement*. Berkeley: University of California Press, 1982.

Piorie, Michael J., and Charles F. Sabel. *The Second Industrial Divide: Possibilities for Prosperity*. New York: Basic Books, 1984.

Pitofsky, Robert. "The Political Content of Antitrust." *University of Pennsylvania Law Review* 127 (April 1979): 1051–75.

Plumlee, John. "Lawyers and Bureaucrats: The Impact of Legal Training on Higher Civil Service." *Public Administration Review* 41 (March/April 1981): 220–28.

"Policy Director Questions FTC Priorities: Urges Reform of Agency Policies, Programs." *Antitrust and Trade Regulation Report* 692 (December 10, 1974): A-10.

Porter, Michael E. *The Competitive Advantage of Nations*. New York: Free Press, 1990.

Posner, Richard A. *Antitrust Law: An Economic Perspective*. Chicago: University of Chicago Press, 1976.

———. "The Chicago School of Antitrust Analysis." *University of Pennsylvania Law Review* 127 (April 1979): 925–48.

———. *The Economics of Justice*. Cambridge: Harvard University Press, 1981.

———. "The Federal Trade Commission." *University of Chicago Law Review* 37 (1969): 47–89.

———. "A Statistical Study of Antitrust Law Enforcement." *Journal of Law and Economics* 13 (October 1970): 365–419.

Quick, Perry D. "Business: Reagan's Industrial Policy." In *The Reagan Record: An Assessment of America's Changing Domestic Priorities*, edited by John L. Palmer and Isabel V. Sawhill. Cambridge, Mass.: Ballinger Publishing, 1984.

Rainey, Hal G., and H. Brinton Milward. "Public Organizations: Policy Networks and Environments." In *Organizational Theory and Public Policy*, edited by Richard H. Hall and Robert E. Quinn. Beverly Hills, Calif.: Sage Publications, 1983.

Randall, Ronald. "Presidential Power versus Bureaucratic Intransigence: The Influence of the Nixon Administration in Welfare Policy." *American Political Science Review* 73 (September 1979): 795–810.

Reder, Melvin W. "Chicago Economics: Permanence and Change." *Journal of Economic Literature* 20 (March 1982): 1–38.

Reich, Robert B. "The Antitrust Industry." *Georgetown Law Review* 68 (June 1980): 1053–73.

———. *The Next American Frontier*. New York: Times Books, 1983.

———. *Tales of a New America: The Anxious Liberal's Guide to the Future.* New York: Random House, 1987.

Rhoads, Steven E. "Economists and Policy Analysis." *Public Administration Review* 38 (March/April 1978): 112–20.

———. *The Economist's View of the World: Government, Markets, and Public Policy.* Cambridge: Cambridge University Press, 1985.

Romer, Thomas, and Howard Rosenthal. "Modern Political Economy and the Study of Regulation." In *Public Regulation: New Perspectives on Institutions and Policies*, edited by Elizabeth E. Bailey. Cambridge: MIT Press, 1987.

Rourke, Francis E. *Bureaucracy, Politics, and Public Policy.* 2d ed. Boston: Little, Brown, 1987.

Rowe, Frederick M. "The Decline of Antitrust and the Delusion of Models: The Faustian Pact of Law and Economics." *Georgetown Law Review* 72 (June 1984): 1511–71.

Rubless, George S. "The Original Plan and Early History of the Federal Trade Commission." *Proceedings of the Academy of Political Science* 11 (January 1926): 666–72.

Rueschemeyer, Dietrich. "Professional Autonomy and the Social Control of Expertise." In *The Sociology of the Professions: Lawyers, Doctors, and Others*, edited by Robert Dingwall and Philip Lewis. New York: St. Martin's Press, 1983.

Rueschemeyer, Dietrich, and Peter B. Evans. "The State and Economic Transformation: Toward an Analysis of the Conditions Underlying Effective Intervention." In *Bringing the State Back In*, edited by Peter B. Evans, Dietrich Rueschemeyer, and Theda Skocpol. Cambridge: Cambridge University Press, 1985.

Rushefsky, Mark E. *Making Cancer Policy.* Albany: State University of New York Press, 1986.

Sabatier, Paul A. "Knowledge, Policy-Oriented Learning, and Policy Change: An Advocacy Coalition Framework." *Knowledge: Creation, Diffusion, Utilization* 8 (June 1987): 649–92.

Sanders, Elizabeth. "Industrial Concentration, Sectional Competition, and Antitrust Politics in America, 1880–1980." In *Studies in American Political Development*, vol. 1, edited by Karen Orren and Stephen Skowronek. New Haven, Conn.: Yale University Press, 1986.

Scheffman, David T. "Merger Policy and Enforcement at the Federal Trade Commission: The Economist's View." *Antitrust Law Journal* 54 (1985): 117–21.

Scherer, F. M. "Economies of Scale and Industrial Concentration." In *Industrial Concentration: The New Learning*, edited by Harvey J. Goldschmid, H. Michael

Mann, and J. Fred Weston. Boston: Little Brown, 1974.

————. *Industrial Market Structure and Economic Performance*. 2d ed. Boston: Houghton Mifflin, 1980.

————. *Innovation and Growth: Schumpeterian Perspectives*. Cambridge: MIT Press, 1984.

Scott, W. Richard. "Professionals in Bureaucracies—Areas of Conflict." In *Professionalization*, edited by Howard M. Vollmer and Donald L. Mills. Englewood Cliffs, N.J.: Prentice-Hall, 1966.

————. "Reaction to Supervision in a Heteronomous Professional Organization." *Administrative Sciences Quarterly* 97 (Summer 1965): 255–78.

Shapiro, Martin. "The Supreme Court's 'Return' to Economic Regulation." In *Studies in American Political Development*, vol. 1, edited by Karen Orren and Stephen Skowronek. New Haven, Conn.: Yale University Press, 1986.

Shenefield, John H. *A Conversation with John Shenefield*. Washington, D.C.: American Enterprise Institute, 1979.

Shonfield, Andrew. *Modern Capitalism: The Changing Balance of Public and Private Power*. London: Oxford University Press, 1965.

Shughart, William F., II. "Antitrust Policy in the Reagan Administration: Pyrrhic Victories?" In *Regulation and the Reagan Era: Politics, Bureaucracy, and the Public Interest*, edited by Roger E. Meiners and Bruce Yandle. New York: Holmes and Meier, 1989.

Simon, Herbert. *Administrative Behavior: A Study of the Decision-Making Process in Administrative Organizations*. 2d ed. New York: Free Press, 1957.

Singer, James. "Consumer Report: FTC Planning Office Plays Role in Decision-making." *National Journal* 7 (September 1973): 1298–1302.

————. "The Federal Trade Commission—Business's Government Enemy No. 1." *National Journal* 13 (October 13, 1979): 559–81.

Skocpol, Theda. "Bringing the State Back In: Strategies of Analysis in Current Research." In *Bringing the State Back In*, edited by Peter B. Evans, Dietrich Rueschemeyer, and Theda Skocpol. Cambridge: Cambridge University Press, 1985.

Skocpol, Theda, and Kenneth Finegold. "State Capacity and Economic Intervention in the Early New Deal." *Political Studies Quarterly* 97 (Summer 1982): 255–78.

Skowronek, Stephen. *Building a New American State: The Expansion of National Administrative Capacities, 1877–1920*. Cambridge: Cambridge University Press, 1982.

Smith, Samuel A. "Policy Planning and Economic Training at the Antitrust Agencies:

Bibliography

A Comment on the Nader Antitrust Report." *Antitrust Law and Economics Review* 4, 3 (Spring 1971): 51–62.

Solo, Robert A. *The Political Authority and the Market System*. Cincinnati, Ohio: South-Western Publishing, 1974.

———. *The Positive State*. Cincinnati, Ohio: South-Western Publishing, 1980.

Solomon, Burt. "Administration Hopes to Extend the Reagan Revolution to Antitrust Laws." *National Journal* 18 (January 1986): 144–46.

Stanfield, J. Ron. "Institutional Analysis: Toward Progress in Economic Science." In *Why Economics Is Not Yet a Science*, edited by Alfred Eichner. Armonk, N.Y.: M. E. Sharpe, 1983.

Stigler, George J. "Capitalism and Monopolistic Competition: The Theory of Oligopoly." *American Economics Association Papers and Proceedings* 40, 2 (May 1950): 23–34.

———. "The Economist and the Problem of Monopoly." *American Economic Association Papers and Proceedings* 72, 2 (May 1982): 1–11.

———. *The Organization of Industry*. Homewood, Ill.: Richard D. Irwin, 1968.

———. "The Theory of Economic Regulation." *Bell Journal of Economics and Management Science* 2 (Spring 1971): 3–21.

Stigler, George J., and Claire Friedland. "The Pattern of Citation in Economics." In *The Economist as Preacher and Other Essays*, edited by George Stigler. Chicago: University of Chicago Press, 1982.

Stone, Alan. *Economic Regulation in the Public Interest: The Federal Trade Commission in Theory and Practice*. Ithaca, N.Y.: Cornell University Press, 1977.

Stone, Deborah A. *Policy Paradox and Political Reason*. Glenview, Ill.: Scott, Foresman, 1988.

Sullivan, E. Thomas. "The Antitrust Division as a Regulatory Agency: An Enforcement Policy in Transition." *Washington University Law Quarterly* 64 (1986): 997–1055.

Thompson, Huston. "Highlights in the Evolution of the Federal Trade Commission." *George Washington University Law Review* 8 (January/February 1940): 260–75.

Thorelli, Hans. *The Federal Antitrust Policy: The Origination of an American Tradition*. Baltimore: Johns Hopkins University Press, 1954.

Thurow, Lester C. *Dangerous Currents: The State of Economics*. New York: Random House, 1983.

———. *The Zero-Sum Society: Distribution and the Possibilities for Economic Change*. New York: Basic Books, 1980.

Turner, Donald F. "The Scope of Antitrust and Other Regulatory Policies." *Harvard*

Law Review 82 (April 1969): 1207–44.

Wagner, Susan. *The Federal Trade Commission.* New York: Praeger Publishers, 1971.

Warren-Boulton, Frederick R. "Merger Policy and Enforcement at the Antitrust Division: The Economist's View." *Antitrust Law Journal* 54 (1985): 109–15.

————. "Thanks but No Thanks (or) It Must Have Been a Slow Day in the Newspaper Business." Mimeo, 1987.

Weaver, Suzanne. *Decision to Prosecute: Organization and Public Policy in the Antitrust Division.* Cambridge: MIT Press, 1977.

Weber, Max. *From Max Weber: Essays in Sociology.* Edited and translated by H. H. Gerth and C. Wright Mills. New York: Oxford University Press, 1946.

Weinberger, Casper W. "The Federal Trade Commission of the 1970s." *Antitrust Law Journal* 39 (Spring 1970): 426–44.

Weingast, Barry R., and Mark J. Moran. "Bureaucratic Discretion or Congressional Control: Regulatory Policy Making by the Federal Trade Commission." *Journal of Political Economy* 91 (October 1983): 765–800.

————. "The Myth of the Runaway Bureaucracy: The Case of the FTC." *Regulation* 6, 3 (May/June 1982): 22–28.

Weir, Margaret, and Theda Skocpol. "State Structures and Possibilities for 'Keynesian' Responses to the Great Depression in Sweden, Britain, and the United States." In *Bringing the State Back In*, edited by Peter B. Evans, Dietrich Rueschemeyer, and Theda Skocpol. Cambridge: Cambridge University Press, 1985.

Weiss, Leonard W. "The Concentration-Profits Relationship and Antitrust." In *Industrial Concentration: The New Learning*, edited by Harvey J. Goldschmid, H. Michael Mann, and J. Fred Weston. Boston: Little, Brown, 1974.

————. "The Structure-Conduct-Performance Paradigm and Antitrust." *University of Pennsylvania Law Review* 127 (April 1979): 1104–40.

Welborn, David M. *The Governance of Federal Regulatory Agencies.* Knoxville: University of Tennessee Press, 1977.

Welford, Harrison. "How Ralph Nader, Tricia Nixon, the ABA, and Jamie Whitten Helped Turn the FTC Around." *Washington Monthly* 4, 8 (October 1972): 5–13.

West, William F. "Institutionalizing Rationality in Regulatory Agencies." *Public Administration Review* 43 (July/August 1983): 236–334.

White, Lawrence J., ed. *Private Antitrust Litigation: New Evidence, New Learning.* Cambridge: MIT Press, 1988.

Whitley, Richard. *The Intellectual and Social Organization of the Sciences.* London: Oxford University Press, 1984.

————. "The Structure and Conduct of Economics as a Scientific Field." Manchester Business School, Mimeo, 1985.

Bibliography

Wiles, Peter. "Ideology, Methodology, and Neoclassical Economics." In *Why Economics Is Not Yet a Science*, edited by Alfred Eichner. Armonk, N.Y.: M. E. Sharpe, 1983.

Williamson, Oliver E. *The Economic Institutions of Capitalism*. New York: Free Press, 1986.

————. *Economic Organizations: Firms, Markets, and Policy Control*. New York: New York University Press, 1984.

————. *Markets and Hierarchies: Analysis and Antitrust Implications*. New York: Free Press, 1975.

Wilson, James Q. *Political Organizations*. New York: Basic Books, 1973.

————, ed. *The Politics of Regulation*. New York: Basic Books, 1980.

Wilson, Woodrow. *The New Freedom: A Call for the Emancipation of the Generous Energies of a People*. Englewood Cliffs, N.J.: Prentice-Hall, 1961.

Wines, Michael. "Doctors and FTC Eye Truce That Would Keep Most Antitrust Powers." *National Journal* 15 (March 23, 1983): 831, 859.

————. "Doctors, Dairymen Join in Efforts to Clip Talons of the FTC." *National Journal* 14 (September 18, 1982): 1589–94.

————. "From Doctors to Dairy Farmers, Critics Gunning for FTC." *National Journal* 15 (January 29, 1983): 221–23.

————. "FTC About-Face under Miller May Not Be Enough for Congressional Critics." *National Journal* 14 (June 2, 1982): 992–96.

————. "Legislative Veto Debate Threatens to Hogtie FTC Reauthorization Bill." *National Journal* 15 (September 10, 1983): 1830–35.

————. "Reagan's Antitrust Line—Common Sense or an Invitation to Corporate Abuse?" *National Journal* 15 (July 3, 1982): 132–40.

Winslow, Walter T. "Organization and Operation of the Federal Trade Commission." *Antitrust Law Journal* 54 (1985): 85–91.

Witte, John. *The Politics and Development of the Federal Income Tax*. Madison: University of Wisconsin Press, 1985.

Wittrock, Björn, Peter Wagner, and Helmut Wollman. "Social Science and the Modern State: Knowledge, Institutions, and Societal Transformations." Wissenschaftskolleg zu Berlin, Paper 87-3, n.d.

Wollan, Laurin A. "Lawyers in Government—'The Most Serviceable Instruments of Authority.'" *Public Administration Review* 38 (March/April 1978): 105–12.

Woolley, John T. *Monetary Politics: The Federal Reserve and the Politics of Monetary Policy*. Cambridge: Cambridge University Press, 1984.

Zamagni, Stephano. *Microeconomic Theory*. Translated by Anthony Fletcher. Oxford: Basil Blackwell, 1987.

INDEX

Adams, Walter, 2
Administrative Procedures Act, 162, 173
Aiken, George, 70
American Bar Association, 165; report
  on Federal Trade Commission (1969),
  154–59, 160, 163; report on Antitrust
  Division, 203–4, 226; report on Fed-
  eral Trade Commission (1989), 226
*American Column and Lumber Co. v.
  United States*, 52–53, 66
American Tobacco Co. v. United States,
  85
Antitrust Civil Process Act, 121, 162
Antitrust community: role of economics
  in, 34, 98–99; reputational structure,
  107–11; shifts in, 107–13. *See also*
  Community of expertise
Antitrust Division. *See* Justice
  Department
Antitrust Improvements Act of 1976,
  23–24, 28, 30–31, 40, 144, 162, 174
Antitrust policy: and liberalism, 1–2, 38,
  48–50, 78, 79, 229; goals, 1–3, 38,
  49–50, 78, 116–17, 121–22, 188–89,
  228–29, 235, 241; private litigation,
  22, 36, 207, 209–10, 265 (n. 45);
  state level, 48; future of, 227, 240–42
Antitrust Procedures and Penalties Act,
  27
Arnold, Thurman, 24, 77–83, 86, 234
*Aspen Skiing Co. v. Aspen Highlands
  Skiing Corp.*, 262 (n. 5)
Associationalism, 64–65, 67

Attorney General's National Committee
  to Study the Antitrust Laws, 87–88,
  120

Bailey, Patricia, 217
Bain, Joe, 100, 109, 252 (n. 2), 253
  (n. 14)
Baker, Donald, 112
Barriers to entry, 101, 105–6, 109–10,
  115, 199
Baxter, William, 109, 188–89, 199,
  200, 201, 204, 207
Bell, Robert, 11
Bereuter, Doug, 177
Blaisdell, Thomas, 63
Blumenthal, William, 112
Borah, William E., 67
Bork, Robert, 54, 105, 141, 143
Brandeis, Louis, 57
Brennan, William, 208
Breyer, Stephen, 113
*Broadcast Music Inc. v. Columbia
  Broadcasting System Inc.*, 186
Brownell, Herbert, 87
Brown Shoe Co. v. United States, 121–
  22, 141–42
Brozen, Yale, 116
Budget Bureau reports on the Federal
  Trade Commission, 74–75, 154
Bureaucracy, 6–15
Bureau of Corporations, 59–60

295